'A terrific book – essential reading for everyone seeking to make sense of Artificial Intelligence'
Professor Sir Adrian Smith,
Director and Chief Executive of the Alan Turing Institute

'Calm, informative and refreshingly free of hype, Wooldridge's effortlessly readable book is the perfect guide to the history and future of AI'
Tom Chivers, author of
The AI Does Not Hate You

'Takes us expertly by the hand through the labyrinth of Artificial Intelligence. A penetrating and lucid contribution to our digital understanding, which dispels many of the myths surrounding AI. Authoritative but accessible and highly readable'
Lord Clement-Jones CBE,
Chair of the House of Lords Select Committee
on Artificial Intelligence 2017–18

'Nobody understands the past, the present, the promise and the peril of this new technology better than Michael Wooldridge. He has written the definitive account of the new AI'
Lord Matt Ridley, author of
The Rational Optimist

'The buzz around AI has unearthed many questions and in *The Road to Conscious Machines* you get answers'
Tabitha Goldstaub, co-founder of CognitionX and Chair
of the UK Government's AI Council

ABOUT THE AUTHOR

Michael Wooldridge is a professor of Computer Science and Head of the Department of Computer Science at the University of Oxford, where he is a Fellow of Hertford College. He has been an AI researcher since 1989, and has published more than 400 scientific articles on the subject. From 2014 to 2016, he was President of the European Association for AI, and from 2015 to 2017 he was President of the International Joint Conference on AI (IJCAI). He lives in Oxford with his wife and two children.

MICHAEL WOOLDRIDGE

The Road to Conscious Machines
The Story of AI

A PELICAN BOOK

PELICAN
an imprint of
PENGUIN BOOKS

PELICAN BOOKS

UK | USA | Canada | Ireland | Australia
India | New Zealand | South Africa

Penguin Books is part of the Penguin Random
House group of companies whose addresses can
be found at global.penguinrandomhouse.com.

Penguin
Random House
UK

First published 2020
Published in paperback 2021

007

Text copyright © Michael Wooldridge, 2020

The moral right of the author has been asserted

Book design by Matthew Young
Set in 11/16.13 pt FreightText Pro
Typeset by Jouve (UK), Milton Keynes
Printed and bound in Great Britain by
Clays Ltd, Elcograf S.p.A.

The authorized representative in the EEA
is Penguin Random House Ireland, Morrison
Chambers, 32 Nassau Street, Dublin DO2 YH68

A CIP catalogue record for this book is available
from the British Library

ISBN: 978-0-241-33390-7

For the Principal, Fellows and Scholars of Hertford
College in the University of Oxford

Contents

Acknowledgements

I am enormously grateful to my agent Felicity Bryan and my editor Laura Stickney for their support, encouragement and advice throughout this project. And, I should add, for their (ahem) good-natured patience.

Special thanks to: Ian J. Goodfellow, Jonathon Shlens and Christian Szegedy for their permission to use the 'panda/gibbon' images that appear in Figure 17, from their paper 'Explaining and Harnessing Adversarial Examples'; Peter Millican for permission to adapt some material from a paper we wrote together; Subbarao Kambhampati for useful feedback on some of my main arguments, and pointing me towards Pascal's wager; Nigel Shadbolt for discussion, encouragement and fantastic anecdotes about the history of AI; and Reid G. Smith for his permission to adapt some of his teaching materials relating to the MYCIN system.

I am grateful to those colleagues, students and unlucky acquaintances who read drafts of the book at short notice and gave enormously valuable feedback. Thanks here to Ani Calinescu, Tim Clement-Jones, Carl Benedikt Frey, Paul Harrenstein, Andrew Hodges, Matthias Holweg, Will Hutton, Graham May, Aida Mehonic, Peter Millican, Steve New, André Nilsen, James Paulin, Emma Smith, Thomas Steeples, André

Stern, John Thornhill and Kiri Walden. Naturally, the many errors which surely remain are entirely my responsibility.

I am honoured to acknowledge the support of the European Research Council under Advanced Grant 291528, which funded me and my research group from 2012 to 2018. My work was made infinitely more productive and immensely more pleasurable by an energetic, brilliant and endlessly supportive research group led by Julian Gutierrez and Paul Harrenstein. I very much hope we will continue to collaborate far into the future.

Introduction

About halfway through writing this book, I was having lunch with a colleague.

'What are you working on?' she asked me.

This is a standard question for academics – we ask it of each other all the time. I should have been ready for it, and had an impressive answer ready to hand.

'Something a bit different. I'm writing a popular science introduction to artificial intelligence.'

She snorted. 'Does the world really need *yet another* popular science introduction to AI? What's the main idea then? What's your new angle?'

I was crestfallen. I needed a clever comeback. So I made a joke.

'It's the story of AI through failed ideas.'

She looked at me, her smile now faded. 'It's going to be a bloody long book, then.'

Artificial intelligence (AI) is my life. I fell in love with AI as a student in the mid-1980s, and I remain passionate about it today. I love AI, not because I think it will make me rich (although that would be nice), nor because I believe it will transform our world (although, as we will see in this book, I believe it *will* do so, in many important ways). I love AI because it is the most endlessly fascinating subject I know of. It draws upon and contributes to an astonishing range of disciplines, including philosophy, psychology, cognitive science, neuroscience, logic, statistics, economics and robotics. And ultimately, of course, AI appeals to fundamental questions about the human condition, and our status as *homo sapiens* – what it means to be human, and whether humans are unique.

What AI Is and Isn't

My first main goal in this book is to tell you what AI is – and, perhaps more importantly, what it is not. You might find this a little surprising, because it may seem obvious to you what AI is all about. Surely, the long-term dream of AI is to build machines that have the full range of capabilities for intelligent action that people have – to build machines that are self-aware, conscious and autonomous in the same way that people like you and me are. You will probably have encountered this version of the AI dream in science-fiction movies, TV shows and books.

This version of AI may seem intuitive and obvious, but as we will see when we try to understand what it really means, we encounter many difficulties. The truth is we don't remotely understand what it is we want to create, or the mechanisms that create it in people. Moreover, it is by no means the case that there is agreement that this really *is* the goal of AI. In fact, it is fiercely contentious – there isn't even any consensus that this kind of AI is feasible, let alone desirable.

For these reasons, this version of AI – *the grand dream* – is difficult to approach directly, and although it makes for great books, movies and video games, it isn't in the mainstream of AI research. Of course, the grand dream raises quite profound philosophical questions – and we will discuss many of these in this book. But beyond these, much of what is written

about this version of AI is really nothing more than speculation. Some of it is of the lunatic fringe variety – AI has always
attracted crackpots, charlatans and snake oil salesmen as well
as brilliant scientists.

Nevertheless, the public debate on AI, and the seemingly
never-ending press fascination with it, is largely fixated on
the grand dream, and on alarmist dystopian scenarios that
have become a weary trope when reporting on AI (AI will
take all our jobs; AI will get smarter than us, and then it will
be out of control; super-intelligent AI might go wrong and
eliminate humanity). Much of what is published about AI in
the popular press is ill-informed or irrelevant. Most of it is
garbage, from a technical point of view, however entertaining it might be.

In this book, I want to change that narrative. I want to
tell you about what AI *actually* is, what AI researchers *actually* work on and *how they go about it*. The reality of AI for
the foreseeable future is very different to the grand dream.
It is perhaps less immediately attention-grabbing, but it is,
as I will show in this book, tremendously exciting in its own
right. The mainstream of AI research today is focused around
getting machines to do specific tasks which currently require
human brains (and also, potentially, human bodies), and for
which conventional computing techniques provide no solution. This century has witnessed important advances in this
area, which is why AI is so fêted at present. Automated translation tools are one example of an AI technology that was
firmly in the realm of science fiction 20 years ago, which has
become a practical, everyday reality within the past decade.
Such tools have many limitations, but they are successfully

used by millions of people across the globe every day. Within the next decade, we will see high-quality real-time spoken-word language translation, and augmented reality tools that will change the way we perceive, understand and relate to the world we live in. Driverless cars are a realistic prospect, and AI looks set to have transformative applications in health-care, from which we will all stand to benefit: AI systems have proven to be better than people at recognizing abnormalities such as tumours on X-rays and ultrasound scans, and wear-able technology, coupled with AI, has the potential to moni-tor our health on a continual basis, giving us advance warnings of heart disease, stress and even dementia. *This* is the kind of thing that AI researchers actually work on. *This* is what ex-cites me about AI. And this is what the AI narrative should be about.

To understand what AI today is, and why AI is for the most part not concerned with the grand dream, we also need to understand why AI is hard to create. Over the past 60 years, huge amounts of effort (and research funding) have flowed into AI, and yet, sadly, robot butlers are not likely any time soon. So, why has AI proved to be so difficult? To under-stand the answer to this question, we need to understand what computers are and what computers can do, at their most fundamental level. This takes us into the realm of some of the deepest questions in mathematics, and the work of one of the greatest minds of the twentieth century: Alan Turing.

The History of AI

My second main goal in this book is to tell you the story of AI from its inception. Every story must have a plot, and we are told there are really only seven basic plots for all the stories in existence, so which of these best fits the story of AI? Many of my colleagues would dearly like it to be 'Rags to Riches', and it has certainly turned out that way for a clever (or lucky) few. For reasons that will become clear later, we could also plausibly view the AI story as 'Slaying the Beast' – the beast, in this case, being an abstract mathematical theory called computational complexity, which came to explain why so many AI problems proved fearsomely hard to solve. 'The Quest' would also work, because the story of AI is indeed rather like that of medieval knights on a quest to find the Holy Grail: full of religious fervour, hopeless optimism, false leads, dead ends and bitter disappointments. But, in the end, the plot that best fits AI is 'Fall and Rise', because, only 20 years ago, AI was a rather niche area with a somewhat questionable academic reputation – but since then it has risen to be the most vibrant and celebrated area in contemporary science. It would be more accurate, though, to say that the plot to the AI story is 'Rise and Fall and Rise and Fall and Rise'. AI has been the subject of continuous research for more than half a century, but during this time AI researchers have repeatedly claimed to have made breakthroughs that bring the dream of intelligent machines within reach, only to have their claims exposed as hopelessly over-optimistic in every case. As a consequence, AI is notorious for boom-and-bust cycles – there have been at least three such cycles in the past four decades. At several points over the past 60 years, the bust has been so severe that it seemed like AI might never recover – and yet, in each case, it did. If you imagine that science is all about orderly progress from ignorance to enlightenment, then I'm afraid you are in for a bit of a shock.

Right now, we are in boom times yet again, and excitement is at fever pitch. At such a time of fevered expectations it is, I think, essential that the troubled story of AI is told and told again. AI researchers have, more than once, thought they had discovered the magic ingredient to propel AI to its destiny – and the breathless, wide-eyed discussion of current AI has precisely the same tone. Sundar Pichai, CEO of Google, was reported to have claimed that 'AI is one of the most important things humanity is working on. It is more profound than, I dunno, electricity or fire.'[1] This followed an earlier claim by Andrew Ng, to the effect that AI was 'the new electricity'.[2] It is important to remember what came of such hubris in the past. Yes, there have been real advances, and yes, they are cause for celebration and excitement – but they do not take us to the end of the road: to conscious machines. As an AI researcher with 30 years of experience, I have learned to be obsessively cautious about the claims made for my field: I have a very well-developed sense of scepticism about claims for breakthroughs. What AI needs now, perhaps more than anything, is a very large injection of humility. I am reminded of the story from Ancient Rome of the *auriga* – a slave who would accompany a triumphant general on his victory march through the city, repeatedly whispering in the general's ear the Latin phrase *memento homo* – 'Remember, you are only human'.

The second part of this book therefore tells the story of AI, warts and all, in broadly chronological order. The story of AI begins just after the creation of the first computers following the Second World War. I will take you through each of the boom periods – starting with the Golden Age of AI, a period of unbridled optimism, when it seemed for a while that rapid progress was being made on a broad range of fronts; next through the 'knowledge era', when the big idea was to give machines all the knowledge that we have about our world; and, more recently, the behavioural period, which insisted that robots should be centre stage in AI, taking us up to the present time. In each case, we'll meet the ideas and the people that shaped AI in their time.

The Future for AI

While I believe it is important to understand the present hubbub about all things AI within the context of a long history of failed ideas (and to temper one's excitement accordingly), I also believe there is real cause for optimism about AI right now. There *have* been genuine scientific breakthroughs, and these, coupled with the availability of 'big data' and very cheap computer power, have made possible in the past decade AI systems that the founders of the field would have hailed as miraculous. So, my third main goal is to tell you what AI systems can actually do right now, and what they might be able to do soon – and to point out their limitations.

This leads me into a discussion of fears about AI. As I mentioned above, the public debate about AI is dominated by dystopian scenarios such as AI taking over the world. Recent advances in AI *do* raise issues that we should all be concerned about, such as the nature of employment in the age of AI, and how AI technologies might affect human rights – but discussions about whether robots will take over the world (or whatever) take the headlines away from these very important, very real concerns. So, once again, I want to change the narrative. I want to take you through the main areas of concern, and to signpost as clearly as I can what you *should* be afraid of, and what you should not.

Finally, I want us to have some fun. So, in the final chapter, we will return to the grand dream of AI – conscious, self-aware, autonomous machines. We will dig into that dream in more detail, and ask what it would mean to realize it, what such machines would be like – and whether they would be like us.

How to Read This Book

The remainder of this book is structured around these overarching goals: to tell you what AI is and why it is hard; to tell you the story of AI – the ideas and people that drove it through each of its boom periods; and, finally, to showcase what AI can do now, and what it can't, and to talk a little about the long-term prospects for AI – the road to conscious machines.

One of the pleasures of writing this book has been to cast off the usual important but tiresome conventions of academic writing. Thus, there are relatively few references, although I give citations for the most important points.

Not only have I avoided giving extensive references, I've also steered clear of technical details – by which I mean *mathematical* details. My hope is that, after reading this book, you will have a broad understanding of the main ideas and concepts that have driven AI throughout its history. Most of these ideas and concepts are, in truth, highly mathematical in nature. But I am acutely aware of Stephen Hawking's dictum that every equation in a book will halve its readership.

For those that feel up to the challenge, I have included some appendices that dig a little deeper into some of the technical ideas, and I also include some points for further reading.

The book is *highly* selective. I really had no choice here: AI is an enormous field, and it would be utterly impossible to do justice to all the different ideas, traditions and schools of thought that have influenced AI over the past 60 years. Instead, I have tried to single out what I see as being the main threads which make up the complex tapestry that is the story of AI.

Finally, I should caution that this is not a textbook. Reading this book will not equip you with the skills to start a new AI company, or to join the staff of Google or Facebook. What you will gain from this book is an understanding of what AI is and where it might be heading. I hope that, after reading it, you will be properly informed about the *reality* of AI – and that, after reading it, you will help me to change the narrative.

Oxford, May 2019

PART ONE

What Is AI?

Turing's Electronic Brains

> I propose to consider the question, 'Can machines think?'
> — Alan Turing (1950)

Every story needs to start somewhere, and for AI we have many possible choices, because the dream of AI, in some form or other, is an ancient one.

We could choose to begin in Classical Greece, with the story of Hephaestus, blacksmith to the gods, who had the power to bring metal creatures to life.

We could begin in the city of Prague in the 1600s, where, according to legend, the head rabbi created the Golem – a magical being fashioned from clay, intended to protect the city's Jewish population from anti-Semitic attacks.

We could begin with James Watt in eighteenth-century Scotland, designing the 'Governor', an ingenious automatic control system for the steam engines he was building, thereby laying the foundations for modern control theory.

We could begin in the early nineteenth century with the young Mary Shelley, cooped up in a Swiss villa during a spell of bad weather, creating the story of Frankenstein to entertain her husband, the poet Percy Bysshe Shelley, and their family friend, the notorious Lord Byron.

We could begin in London in the 1830s with Ada Lovelace, estranged daughter of the same Lord Byron, striking up a friendship with Charles Babbage, curmudgeonly inventor of mechanical calculating machines, and inspiring the brilliant young Ada to speculate about whether machines might ultimately be creative.

We could equally well begin with the eighteenth-century fascination with automata – cunningly designed machines that gave some illusion of life.

We have many possible choices for the beginning of AI, but for me the beginning of the AI story coincides with the beginning of the story of computing itself, for which we have a pretty clear starting point: King's College, Cambridge, in 1935, and a brilliant but unconventional young student called Alan Turing.

Cambridge, 1935

It is hard to imagine now, because he is about as famous as any mathematician could ever hope to be, but until the 1980s, the name of Alan Turing was virtually unknown outside the fields of mathematics and computer science. While students of mathematics and computing might have come across Turing's name in their studies, they would have known little about the full extent of his achievements, or his tragic, untimely death. In part this is because some of Turing's most important work was carried out in secret for the UK government during the Second World War, and the facts of this remarkable work remained classified until the 1970s.[1] But there was surely also prejudice at work here, because Turing was gay, at a time when homosexuality was a criminal offence in the United Kingdom. In 1952 he was prosecuted and convicted for what was then called 'gross indecency'. His penalty was to take a crude hormone drug that was intended to reduce his sexual desires – a form of 'chemical castration'. He died, apparently by his own hand, two years later, at the age of just 41.[2]

Nowadays, of course, we all know a little of the Turing story, although perhaps not quite as much as we should. The best-known part of the story relates to his code-breaking work at Bletchley Park in the Second World War, made famous in the popular (albeit spectacularly inaccurate) 2014 Hollywood movie *The Imitation Game*. And he certainly deserves enormous credit for that work, which played an important role in the Allied victory. But AI researchers and computer scientists revere him for quite different reasons. He was, for all practical purposes, the inventor of the computer; and shortly after that, he largely invented the field of AI.

Turing was remarkable in many ways, but one of the most remarkable things about him is that he invented computers by accident. As a mathematics student at Cambridge University in the mid-1930s, Turing set himself the precocious challenge of settling one of the leading mathematical problems of the day – a problem that went by the impressive and frankly daunting name of the *Entscheidungsproblem*. The problem had been posed by the mathematician David Hilbert in 1928. The *Entscheidungsproblem* asks whether there are mathematical questions that cannot be answered by simply following a recipe. Of course, the questions Hilbert was concerned with were not questions like 'Is there a God?' or 'What is the meaning of life?' but, rather, what mathematicians call **decision**

problems ('*Entscheidungsproblem*' is German for 'decision problem'). Decision problems are mathematical questions that have a yes/no answer. Here are some examples of decision problems:

- Is it the case that $2 + 2 = 4$?
- Is it the case that $4 \times 4 = 16$?
- Is it the case that 7919 is a prime number?

As it happens, the answer to all of these decision problems is 'yes'. I hope you will agree the first two are obvious, but unless you have an unhealthy obsession with prime numbers, you would have had to work a little to answer the last one. So, let's think about this final question for a moment.

A prime number, as you will no doubt recall, is a whole number that is only exactly divisible by itself and one. Now, with this in mind, I'm pretty sure you could, at least in principle, find the answer to the final question on your own. There is an obvious method for doing so that is very straightforward, albeit rather tedious for numbers as large as 7919: check every number that could possibly be a divisor to see whether it divides 7919 exactly. Follow this procedure carefully, and you will discover that none do: 7919 is indeed a prime number.[3]

What is important here is that there are precise and unambiguous methods for answering questions like those above. These methods don't require any *intelligence* to apply them – they are nothing more than *recipes*, which can be followed by rote. All we need to do to find the answer is to follow the recipe *precisely*.

Since we have a technique that is guaranteed to answer

the question (given sufficient time), we say that questions in the form 'Is *n* a prime number?' are **decidable**. I emphasize that all this means is that, whenever we are faced with a question in the form 'Is *n* a prime number?', we know that we can definitely find the answer if we are given sufficient time: we follow the relevant recipe, and eventually we will get the correct answer.

Now, the *Entscheidungsproblem* asks whether all mathematical decision problems like those we saw above are decidable, or whether there are problems for which there is *no* recipe for finding the answer – no matter how much time you are prepared to put in.

This is a very fundamental question – it asks whether mathematics can be reduced to merely following recipes. And answering this fundamental question was the daunting challenge that Turing set himself in 1935 – and which he triumphantly resolved, with dizzying speed.

When we think of deep mathematical problems, we imagine that any solution to them must involve complex equations and long proofs. And sometimes, this is indeed the case – when the British mathematician Andrew Wiles famously proved Fermat's Last Theorem in the early 1990s, it took years for the mathematical community to understand the hundreds of pages of his proof, and become confident that it was indeed correct. By these standards, Turing's solution to the *Entscheidungsproblem* was positively eccentric.

Apart from anything else, Turing's proof is short and comparatively accessible (once the basic framework has been established, the proof is really just a few lines long). But most importantly, to solve the *Entscheidungsproblem*, Turing

17

realized that he needed to be able to make the idea of a recipe that can be followed precisely exact. To do this, he invented a mathematical problem-solving machine – nowadays, we call these **Turing machines** in his honour. A Turing machine is a mathematical description of a recipe, like the one for checking prime numbers mentioned above. All a Turing machine does is to follow the recipe it was designed for. I should emphasize that, although Turing called them 'machines', at this point they were nothing more than an abstract mathematical idea. The idea of solving a deep mathematical problem by *inventing a machine* was unconventional, to say the least – I suspect many mathematicians of the day were mystified.

Turing machines are very powerful beasts. Any kind of mathematical recipe that you might care to think of can be encoded as a Turing machine. And, if all mathematical decision problems can be solved by following a recipe, then for any decision problem, you should be able to design a Turing machine to solve it. To settle Hilbert's problem, all you had to do was show that there was some decision problem that could not be answered by any Turing machine. And that is what Turing did.

His next trick was to show that his machines could be turned into *general-purpose* problem-solving machines. He designed a Turing machine that will follow *any* recipe that you give it. We now call these general-purpose Turing machines **Universal Turing Machines**:[4] and a computer, when stripped down to its bare essentials, is simply a Universal Turing Machine made real. The programs that a computer runs are just recipes, like the one for prime numbers that we discussed above.

Although it isn't central to our story, it is worth at least mentioning how Turing settled the *Entscheidungsproblem* using his new invention – apart from the fact that it was extraordinarily ingenious, it also has some bearing on the question of whether AI is ultimately possible.

His idea was that Turing machines could be programmed to *answer questions about other Turing machines.* He considered the following decision problem: given a Turing machine and an associated input, will it be guaranteed to eventually halt with an answer, or could it carry on doing its work forever? This is a decision problem of the type that we discussed above – albeit a much more involved one. Now, suppose there was a machine that could solve this problem. Turing saw that the existence of a Turing machine that could answer this question would create a contradiction. It followed that there could be no recipe for checking whether a Turing machine halts, and so the question 'Does a Turing machine halt?' is an **undecidable problem**. He had thus established that there are decision problems which cannot be solved by simply following a recipe. He thereby settled Hilbert's *Entscheidungsproblem*: mathematics could not be reduced to following recipes.[5]

This result was one of the greatest achievements of twentieth-century mathematics. This alone would have guaranteed him immortality amongst mathematicians. But a by-product of his proof was the invention of the Universal Turing Machine – a general-purpose problem-solving machine. Turing didn't invent his machines with the idea of actually building them, but the idea occurred to him soon enough, and many others, too. In wartime Munich, Konrad Zuse designed a computer called the Z3 for the German Air

Ministry – although it was not quite a modern computer, it introduced many of the key ingredients of one. Across the Atlantic in Pennsylvania, a team led by John Mauchly and J. Presper Eckert developed a machine called ENIAC to compute artillery tables. With some tweaks by the brilliant Hungarian mathematician John von Neumann, ENIAC established the fundamental architecture of the modern computer (the architecture of conventional computers is called the Von Neumann architecture, in his honour). Over in post-war England, Fred Williams and Tom Kilburn built the Manchester Baby, which led directly to the world's first commercial computer, the Ferranti Mark 1 – Turing himself joined the staff of Manchester University in 1948, and wrote some of the first programs to run on it.

By the 1950s, all the key ingredients of the modern computer had been developed. Machines that realized Turing's mathematical vision were a practical reality – all you needed was enough money to buy one, and a building big enough (to house the Ferranti Mark 1 required two storage bays, each 16 feet long, 8 feet high and 4 feet wide; the machine consumed 27kW of electricity – about enough to power three modern homes). Of course, they have been getting smaller and cheaper ever since.

What Electronic Brains Actually Do

Nothing pleases a newspaper editor more than a catchy headline, and when the first computers were built after the Second World War, newspapers across the world heralded the arrival of a miraculous new invention – *the electronic brain*. These fearsomely complex machines were apparently capable of dazzling feats of mathematics, for example, processing huge volumes of convoluted arithmetic problems much faster and more accurately than any human could ever dream of doing. To those unacquainted with the realities of computers, it must have seemed that machines capable of such tasks must be gifted with some kind of superior intelligence. *Electronic brain* therefore seemed like an obvious label, and it stuck. (One still came across this kind of language as late as the early 1980s, when I first became interested in computers.) In fact, it turns out that what these electronic brains were doing was something incredibly useful, and something that people find tremendously difficult, but not something that requires *intelligence*. And understanding exactly what computers are designed to do – and what they can't do – is central to understanding AI, and why it is so difficult.

Remember that Turing machines, and their physical manifestation in the form of computers, are nothing more than *machines for following instructions.* That is their sole purpose – that is all they are designed to do, and all they can do. The instructions that we give a Turing machine are what we nowadays call an algorithm, or program.[6] Most programmers are probably not even aware of the fact that they are interacting with what amounts to a Turing machine, and for good reason – programming Turing machines directly is incredibly fiddly and irksome, as generations of frustrated computer science students would confirm. Instead, we build higher-level languages on top of the Turing machines, to make it simpler to program them – programming languages like Python, Java and C. All these languages really do is hide some of the gory details of the machine from the programmer in order to make it a bit more accessible. But they are still incredibly fiddly and irksome, which is why programming is hard, why computer programs crash so often and why good programmers get paid so much.

I have no intention of trying to teach you to program, but it is useful to have some sense of what kinds of instructions computers can follow. Roughly speaking, all a computer can do is follow lists of instructions such as the following:[7]

- Add A to B
- If the result is bigger than C, then do D, otherwise, do E
- Repeatedly do F until G

Every computer program boils down to lists of instructions similar to these. Microsoft Word and PowerPoint boil down to instructions like these. Call of Duty and Minecraft boil down to instructions like these. Facebook, Google and eBay boil down to instructions like these. The apps on your smart-phone, from your web browser to Tinder, all boil down to instructions like these. *And if we are to build intelligent machines, then their intelligence must ultimately reduce to simple, explicit instructions like these.* This, in essence, is the fundamental challenge of AI. The question of whether AI is possible ultimately amounts to whether we can produce intelligent behaviour by following lists of instructions like these.

In the remainder of this chapter, I want to dig into this observation, and try to make explicit some of the implications it has for AI. Before I do this, however, in case it seems like I'm trying to convince you that computers are actually rather useless beasts, I feel obliged to point out several features that make computers rather more useful than they might at this stage appear.

The first point to make is that computers are *fast*. Very, very, very fast. Of course, you know this – but our experiences in the everyday world do not really equip us to understand quite how fast computers actually are. So, let us quantify this statement. At the time of writing, a reasonable desktop computer operating at full speed can carry out up to 100 *billion instructions of the type listed above every second.* One hundred billion is approximately the number of stars in our galaxy, but that probably doesn't help much. So let me put it this way. Suppose you wanted to emulate the computer, by manually carrying out the computer's instructions yourself. Imagine you carry out one instruction every ten seconds, and that you don't pause for breaks – you work 24 × 7 × 365 to get the job done. Then it would take you about 3,700 *years* to do what the computer does in *just one second.*

Of course, as well as being *much* slower, as a machine for following recipes, you are different from a computer in one other key respect: there is just no way that you could spend a serious amount of time following instructions in this way without making mistakes. Computers, by contrast, very rarely make mistakes. While programs frequently crash, these crashes are almost invariably the fault of the people who wrote the program, rather than a fault in the computer itself. Modern computer processors are phenomenally reliable – they are expected to operate on average for up to 50,000 hours before failing, faithfully carrying out tens of billions of instructions for every second of those hours.

One final observation. Although computers are just

machines for following instructions, this does not mean that they are incapable of making decisions. Computers certainly *can* make decisions – it is just that we have to give them precise instructions about *how* to make the decision. And a computer can subsequently adjust these instructions for itself, as long as we have instructed it how to do so. In this way, as we will see, a computer can change its behaviour over time – it can *learn*.

Why Is AI Hard?

Computers, then, can *reliably* follow *very simple* instructions *very, very quickly*; and they can *make decisions*, as long as those decisions are precisely specified. Now, some things that we might want computers to do for us are very easy to encode in this way – but others are not. To understand why AI is hard – why progress has proved so elusive over the years – it helps to look at problems that are easy to encode in this way, and problems that are not, and to see why this is the case. Figure 1 displays some tasks that we might want computers to do, and shows how difficult it has proved to get computers to achieve them.

At the top is arithmetic. It was very easy to get computers to do arithmetic, because all the basic arithmetical operations (addition, subtraction, multiplication, division) can be carried out by a very simple recipe – you were taught such recipes at school, even if you don't recall them now. These recipes can be directly translated into computer programs, and so problems involving the straightforward application of arithmetic were solved in the very earliest days of computing. (The first program Turing wrote for the Manchester Baby computer when he joined the staff of Manchester University

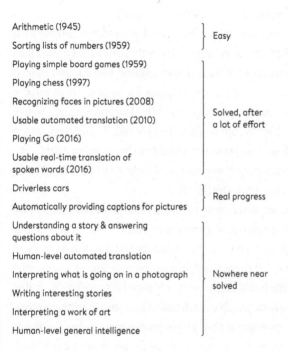

Arithmetic (1945)
Sorting lists of numbers (1959)
} Easy

Playing simple board games (1959)
Playing chess (1997)
Recognizing faces in pictures (2008)
Usable automated translation (2010)
Playing Go (2016)
Usable real-time translation of
spoken words (2016)
} Solved, after
a lot of effort

Driverless cars
Automatically providing captions for pictures
} Real progress

Understanding a story & answering
questions about it
Human-level automated translation
Interpreting what is going on in a photograph
Writing interesting stories
Interpreting a work of art
Human-level general intelligence
} Nowhere near
solved

Figure 1
Some tasks that we want computers to be able to do ranked in
order of difficulty. Years in parentheses indicate approximately
when the problem was solved. At present we have no idea about
how to get computers to do the tasks at the bottom of the list.

in 1948 was to carry out long division – it must have been an odd experience for Turing, returning to arithmetic he'd been taught at school after solving one of the deepest mathematical problems of the twentieth century.)

Next we have sorting, by which I just mean arranging a list of numbers into (say) ascending order, or a list of names into alphabetical order. This doesn't sound like AI, and indeed there are some very simple recipes for sorting. However, the most obvious recipes were painfully slow and scarcely usable: 1959 saw the invention of a technique called QuickSort, which for the first time provided a really efficient way to do this. (In the 50 years since it was invented, nobody has managed to do much better than QuickSort.)[8]

Then we move on to problems that required much more effort. Playing board games well turned out to be a major challenge, for a reason that is fundamental to the AI story. It turns out that there is in fact a very simple and elegant recipe for playing board games well; it is based on a technique called **search**, about which we will hear a lot more in the next chapter. The problem is that, although the basic recipe for game-playing by search is very easy to program, it doesn't work on all but the most trivial of games, because it requires too much time and too much computer memory – even if we could use every atom in the universe to build a computer, that computer would not be remotely powerful enough to be able to play chess or Go using naive search. To make search viable, we need something extra – and, as we will see in the next chapter, this is where AI comes in.

This situation – we know how to solve a problem in principle, but these techniques don't work in practice because they would require impossibly large amounts of computing resources – is extremely common in AI, and a huge body of research has grown up around dealing with it.

The next problems on the list, though, are very much not of this type. Recognizing faces in a picture, automated translation and usable real-time translation of spoken words are all very different kinds of problems because, unlike board games, conventional computing techniques give us no clues about how to write a recipe to solve them. We need a completely new approach. In each of these cases, though, the problem has been solved by a technique called machine learning, about which we will hear a lot more later on in this book.

Next we move on to driverless cars. This problem is fascinating because it is something that seems so straightforward for people to do. We don't associate the ability to drive a car with *intelligence*. But it turned out to be fearsomely hard to get computers to drive cars. The main problem is that a car needs to understand where it is, and what is going on around it. Imagine a driverless car at a busy road intersection in New York City. There will probably be many vehicles in continual movement, with pedestrians, cyclists, road works, traffic signs and road markings in the picture as well. It may be raining or snowing or foggy, just to complicate things further (and in New York, it may well be all three at the same time). In situations like this, the main difficulty is not *deciding what to do* (slow down, speed up, turn left, right, etc.), but rather *making sense of what is going on around you* – identifying where you are, what vehicles are present, where they are and what they are doing, where the pedestrians are and so on. If you have all that information, then deciding what you need to do is usually going to be pretty easy. (We will discuss the specific challenges of driverless cars later in the book.)

Then we move on to problems that we really have little idea how to solve. How can a computer understand a complex story and answer questions about it? How can a computer translate a rich nuanced text such as a novel? How can a computer interpret what is going on in a picture – not just identifying the people in it, but *actually interpreting what is going on*? How can a computer write an interesting story or interpret a work of art such as a painting? And the final one – the grand dream of computers with general-purpose human-level intelligence – is the greatest challenge of all.

Progress in AI, then, means progressively getting computers to do more and more of these tasks in Figure 1. Those that are difficult in Figure 1 are so for one of two reasons. The first possibility is that while we may in fact have a recipe for the problem that works *in principle*, it doesn't work *in practice* because it would require impossibly large amounts of computing time and memory. Board games like chess and Go fall into this category. The second possibility is that we just have no idea what a recipe for solving the problem might look like (e.g. recognizing faces), in which latter case we would need something completely new (e.g. machine learning). Pretty much all of contemporary AI is concerned with problems that fall into one of these two categories.

Let's now turn to the hardest problem in Figure 1 – the grand dream of general-purpose, human-level intelligence. Not surprisingly, this challenge has attracted a lot of attention, and one of the earliest and most influential thinkers on the subject was our old friend Alan Turing.

The Turing Test

The development of the first computers in the late 1940s and early 1950s prompted a flurry of public debate about the potential of these wondrous feats of modern science. One of the highest-profile contributions to the debate at the time was a book entitled *Cybernetics*, written by a Massachusetts Institute of Technology (MIT) mathematics professor called Norbert Wiener. The book made explicit parallels between machines and animal brains and nervous systems, and touched on many ideas relating to AI. It attracted huge public interest, despite the fact that it was surely incomprehensible to any but the most dedicated and mathematically adept reader. Questions such as whether machines could 'think' began to be seriously debated in the press and on radio shows (in 1951, Turing himself participated in a BBC radio show on this very subject). Although it didn't yet have a name, the idea of AI was in the air.

Prompted by the public debate, Turing began to think seriously about the possibility of artificial intelligence. He was particularly irritated with claims being made in the public debate along the lines of 'Machines will never be able to do X' (where X is, for example, think, reason or be creative). He wanted to definitively silence those who argued that 'machines cannot think'. To this end, he proposed a test, which we now call the **Turing test**. Turing's test has been hugely influential since he first described it in 1950, and is still the subject of serious research to the present day. Sadly, though, for reasons that will become clear below, it failed to silence the doubters.

Turing's inspiration was a Victorian-era parlour game called the Imitation Game. The basic idea of the Imitation Game was for someone to try to tell if another person was a man or a woman simply on the basis of the answers they gave to questions that were posed to them. Turing proposed that you could use a similar test for AI. The way the test is usually described is something like this:

> Human interrogators interact via a computer keyboard
> and screen with something that is either a person or a
> computer program – the interrogator does not know
> in advance whether it is a person or a program. The
> interaction is purely in the form of textual questions and
> answers: the interrogator types a question, and a response
> is displayed. The task of the interrogator is to determine
> whether the thing being interrogated is a person or a
> computer program.

Now, suppose that the thing being interrogated is indeed a computer program, but after some reasonable amount of time, the interrogators cannot reliably tell whether they are interacting with a program or a person. Then surely, Turing argued, you should accept that the program has some sort of human-level intelligence (or whatever you want to call it).

Turing's brilliant move here is to sidestep all the questions and debate whether a program was 'really' intelligent (or conscious or whatever). Whether or not the program is 'really' thinking (or is conscious or self-aware or whatever) is irrelevant because it is doing something that makes it *indistinguishable from the 'real thing'*. The key word here is *indistinguishable*.

The Turing test is a neat example of a standard technique in science. If you want to find out whether two things are the same or different, ask whether there is some reasonable test you can apply that would distinguish them. If there is a reasonable test that one would pass, but the other would not, then you can be confident that they are different. If you can't distinguish them by any such test, then you can't claim they are different. Turing's test is concerned with distinguishing machine intelligence from human intelligence; and the test is whether a person can distinguish the behaviour that each produces.

We need to be a bit careful here, however. A difficulty with many approaches to characterizing AI over the years is that they define it with respect to the *techniques* or *methods* that are used. For example, if your favourite AI technique is 'Temporally Recurrent Optimal Learning' (to pick some random AI buzzwords of the present day), then you might be tempted to define AI as the task of passing the Turing test using Temporally Recurrent Optimal Learning, thereby ruling out any other approach. Thus, we want a test for intelligent behaviour that is *independent* of the techniques or methods that are used to achieve it. The Turing test achieves this by clearly separating the interrogators from the thing that is being interrogated: the only evidence that the interrogators have to go on are the inputs and outputs – the questions sent by the interrogator, and the responses that the interrogator later receives. The thing on the other end is a *black box* as far as the Turing test is concerned, in the sense that we are not allowed to examine its internal structure: all that we have are the inputs and outputs.

Turing's article 'Computing Machinery and Intelligence', describing his test, was published in the prestigious international journal *Mind* in 1950.[9] Although many articles touching on AI-like ideas had been published before this, Turing approached the subject for the first time from the standpoint of the modern digital computer. As such, his article is generally recognized as the first AI publication.

Turing Test Nonsense

The Turing test is simple, elegant and easy to understand. However, it had the unfortunate side effect of establishing the test as the holy grail of AI – with unfortunate consequences that resonate to the present day.

The problem is that most attempts to tackle the Turing test tend to use cheap tricks to try to befuddle the interrogators into believing that they are dealing with a person, rather than by trying to engage with the actual issues of intelligent behaviour. The most famous example of this was a program called **ELIZA**, written by the German-American MIT computer scientist Joseph Weizenbaum in the mid-1960s. ELIZA was never intended by Weizenbaum to be a contender for the Turing test – it was a serious and influential scientific experiment in its own right – but sadly it has since become synonymous with superficial approaches to AI generally, and the Turing test in particular.

ELIZA takes the role of a psychiatrist talking to a patient, asking open-ended questions to get the interviewee to contemplate themselves. ELIZA worked by picking up on key words like 'family', 'friends', 'lonely', 'sad' and so on, and then used canned scripts associated with the relevant word to issue follow-on questions. You don't have to be very perceptive to see beyond its smoke and mirrors. Here is a dialogue with a modern version of the system (ELIZA responses are in italics):[10]

I am lonely.
Are you lonely often?

Yes. Almost every day.
Why do you say almost every day?

I think it is my family.
Tell me something about your family.

They hate me.
What makes you believe they hate you?

They are mean to me.
Earlier you said you felt lonely?

What is the meaning of life?
Maybe your life has something to do with this.

What is the purpose of existence?
Is it because of your plans that you say what is the purpose of existence?

The opening is promising enough, but even after a couple of sentences, the superficiality of the interaction becomes painfully clear – ELIZA obviously has no understanding of the dialogue (and of course Weizenbaum never claimed that it did – that was not the point of his experiment).

Weizenbaum could hardly have anticipated the impact that ELIZA would have, both within academia and beyond.

He was, apparently, startled to discover that users took his simple experiment seriously. It immediately entered the folklore of AI. I remember as a PhD student in the 1980s hearing that lonely and socially ill-adjusted graduate students would converse all night with ELIZA, as a proxy for the human relationships they were incapable of forming; there was even a story – hopefully apocryphal – about ELIZA unwittingly encouraging a depressed student to commit suicide. Apparently Weizenbaum asked his secretary to try the program out, and to his astonishment she asked him to leave the room while the dialogue was under way, despite reassurances that the interaction was essentially fake.

ELIZA's legacy lives on to this day, in the form of the annual Loebner Prize Competition. It isn't clear whether Turing imagined that anyone would ever actually try out his test for real, but, in 1990, that is precisely what American millionaire inventor Hugh Loebner decided to do. Every year, the Loebner Foundation invites the submission of computer programs to engage in the Turing test, attempting to convince a panel of judges that they are in fact people. A successful entry stands to win $100,000.

Loebner's competition was instantly controversial – famous AI scientist Marvin Minsky dismissed it as a 'meaningless publicity stunt'. The competition seems to generate at least one hopelessly misleading headline every year. The problem is that entries in the Loebner competition are, for the most part, variations on the ELIZA theme. Rather than trying to win by engaging the interrogators in a meaningful conversation that demonstrates human-level comprehension, common-sense and understanding, they use tricks to misdirect and mislead. Here is a fragment of a conversation with the 2009 winning entry, called 'Do-Much-More' – the program was written by David Levy, a well-known AI commentator and computer chess expert (Do-Much-More responses are in italics):

Hi, how is it going?
Hello. How are you doing?

Good, who are you?
Well, I am studying engineering. That ought to give you an idea about who I am.

No, not really?
I have a terrific yearning to know something more about experiments?

Where are you from?
I don't know, but don't forget I can't be in three places at once.

What city do you live in?
What city – that's rather a tricky question. The trouble is, one city seems to be much like another.

Not really. Where do you live?
In the old dairy next to the river, I believe.

Interesting, so you are a farmer then?
Well, if you ask a physiologist what I am, he won't say I'm a farmer. He'll say I consist mostly of water – enough to fill a large beer barrel – plus some iron, phosphorus and lots of other prosaic ingredients.

Weird answer to a simple question, wouldn't you say?

I certainly would. Just watch me!

Arguably more sophisticated than ELIZA, but clearly a long way from a human conversation participant.

ELIZA is the direct ancestor of a phenomenon that makes AI researchers groan whenever it is mentioned: the Internet chatbot. These are Internet-based programs that attempt to engage users in conversation, often via social media platforms such as Twitter. While the problem of developing programs that can engage in meaningful conversations is the subject of serious research, the overwhelming majority of Internet chatbots use little more than keyword-based canned scripts in the same way that ELIZA did, and as a consequence the conversations they produce are every bit as superficial and uninteresting. Chatbots of this kind are not AI.

Varieties of Artificial Intelligence

For all the nonsense it has given rise to, the Turing test is an important part of the AI story because, for the first time, it gave researchers interested in this emerging discipline a target to aim at. When someone asked you what your goal was, you could give a straightforward and precise answer: *My goal is to build a machine that can meaningfully pass the Turing test.* Today, I think very few, if any, serious AI researchers would give this answer, but it had a crucial historical role, and I believe it still has something important to tell us today.

Much of the attraction of the Turing test undoubtedly lies in its simplicity, but clear as the test appears to be, it nevertheless raises many problematic questions about AI.

Imagine that you are an interrogator in the Turing test. The answers you receive in the test convince you that you are not interacting with a chatbot: whatever is on the other end is demonstrating the kind of understanding of your questions, and producing the kinds of answers, that a human might demonstrate. It subsequently transpires that the thing on the other end is in fact a computer program. Now, as far as the Turing test is concerned, the matter is settled. The program is doing something indistinguishable from human behaviour: end of debate. But there are still at least two logically distinct possibilities:

1. The program *actually understands* the dialogue, in much the same sense that a person does.
2. The program does not have any understanding, but can *simulate* such understanding.

There is a big difference between the two claims. The first claim – that the program *really does understand* – is much stronger than the second. The second requires only that we can create programs that *appear to have* understanding.

I suspect most AI researchers – and probably most readers of this book – would have little difficulty in accepting that programs of type 2 are feasible, at least in principle, but would need a good deal more convincing before they accepted that programs of type 1 are. And indeed, it is not obvious how we could substantiate a claim that a program was of type 1 – this is not what the Turing test claims to do. (Turing, I suspect, would have been irritated by the distinction: he would have pointed out that one of the main reasons he invented the test was to put an end to arguments about such distinctions.) Aiming to build a program of type 1 is therefore a much more ambitious and controversial goal than building a program of type 2.

The goal of building programs *that really do have understanding (consciousness, etc.) in the way that people do* is called **strong AI**; the weaker goal, of building programs that demonstrate the same capability but without any claim that they *actually possess these attributes*, is called **weak** AI.

Beyond the Turing Test

There are many variations of Turing's indistinguishability test. For example, in a much stronger version of the test, we can imagine robots that attempt to pass themselves off as people in the everyday world. Here, 'indistinguishability' is interpreted in a very demanding way – it means that the machines are indistinguishable from people. (I'm assuming that you aren't allowed to dissect them, so the test is still a sort of black box.) For the foreseeable future, this sort of thing is firmly in the realms of fiction. Indeed, a world where robots were hard to distinguish from people was the basis for at least one very good film, Ridley Scott's 1982 classic *Blade Runner*, in which a young Harrison Ford spends his days carrying out cryptic tests with the aim of determining whether what appears to be a beautiful young woman is in fact a robot. Similar themes are explored in movies such as *Ex Machina* (2014).

Although *Blade Runner* scenarios are not in prospect, researchers have begun to ask whether there are variations of the Turing test which might meaningfully test for genuine intelligence, and which are resistant to trickery of the chatbot variety. One very simple idea is to test for *comprehension*, and one manifestation of this idea is the use of what are called

Winograd schemas. These are short questions, perhaps best illustrated by examples:[11]

> Statement 1a: The city councillors refused the
>   demonstrators a permit because they <u>feared</u>
>   violence.
> Statement 1b: The city councillors refused the
>   demonstrators a permit because they <u>advocated</u>
>   violence.
> Question: Who [feared/advocated] violence?

Notice that these two statements differ from each other in just one word (underlined in each case): but that small change dramatically alters their meaning. The point of the test is to identify who 'they' refers to in each case. In Statement 1a, 'they' clearly refers to the councillors (they are the ones that fear violence from the demonstrators), while in Statement 1b, 'they' refers to the demonstrators (the councillors are concerned about the fact that the demonstrators are advocating violence).

Here is another example:

> Statement 2a: The trophy doesn't fit into the brown
>   suitcase because it is too <u>small</u>.
> Statement 2b: The trophy doesn't fit into the brown
>   suitcase because it is too <u>large</u>.
> Question: What is too [small/large]?

Obviously, in Statement 2a, the suitcase is too small; in statement 2b, the trophy is too large.

Now, most literate adults would easily be able to handle these examples and others like them – but they resist the kind of cheap tricks used by chatbots and entries in the Loebner competition. To be able to give the correct answer, it is hard to avoid the conclusion that you really need to *understand* the text, and to have some *knowledge* about the kind of scenario in question. To understand the difference between Statements 1a and 1b, for example, you would need to know something about demonstrations (demonstrations often lead to violence), and councillors (that they have the power to grant or deny permits for demonstrations to take place, and that they will try to avoid situations that lead to violence).

Another similar challenge for AI involves understanding of the human world, and the unwritten rules that govern our relationships within it. Consider the following short dialogue from the psychologist and linguist Steven Pinker:

> Bob: 'I'm leaving you.'
> Alice: 'Who is she?'

Can you explain this dialogue? Of course you can. It's a staple of TV soap operas: Alice and Bob are in a relationship, and Bob's announcement leads Alice to believe that Bob is leaving her for another woman – and she wants to know who the other woman is. We might also speculate that Alice is pretty angry.

But how could a computer be programmed to understand such dialogues? Such a capability would surely be essential for understanding stories and indeed for writing them. This common-sense, everyday ability to understand the workings of human beliefs, desires and relationships would be an essential requirement for a computer program capable of following *EastEnders*. We all have this capability, and it would also seem to be a key requirement for both strong and weak AI. We have only vague ideas about how to achieve this capability, and none have been shown to be really successful. The ability for machines to comprehend and answer questions about such scenarios remains a long way off.

General AI

While the grand dream of AI seems intuitively obvious, as we have demonstrated, it is surprisingly hard to define what it means, or when we will know that we have found it. For this reason, although strong AI is an important and fascinating part of the AI story, it is largely irrelevant to contemporary AI research. Go to a contemporary AI conference, and you will hear almost nothing about it – except possibly late at night, in the bar.

A lesser goal is to build machines that have general-purpose human-level intelligence. Nowadays, this is usually referred to as **Artificial General Intelligence** (**AGI**) or just **General** AI. AGI roughly equates to having a computer that has the full range of intellectual capabilities that a person has – this would include the ability to converse in natural language (cf. the Turing test), solve problems, reason, perceive its environment and so on, at or above the same level as a typical person. A system capable of AGI would be capable of all the tasks shown in Figure 1, and more. The literature on AGI usually isn't concerned with issues such as consciousness or self-awareness, so AGI might be thought of as a weaker version of weak AI.[12]

However, even this lesser goal is on the margins of contemporary AI. Instead, what AI researchers usually focus on is building computer programs that can carry out tasks which currently require brains – progressively moving through the list of problems that we saw in Figure 1. This approach to AI – getting computers to do very specific tasks – is sometimes called **narrow** AI, but I have never heard this term used in the AI community. Indeed, if you used that expression at one of the major AI conferences, you would immediately identify yourself as an outsider. We don't refer to what we do as narrow AI – because narrow AI *is* AI. This might be disappointing to those of us that long for robot butlers, though it will perhaps be welcome news to those that have nightmares about the robot uprising.

So, now you know what AI is, and have some idea about why it's hard to achieve. But how, exactly, do AI researchers go about it?

Brain or Mind?

How might we go about producing human-level intelligent behaviour in a computer? Historically, AI has adopted one of two main approaches to this problem. Put crudely, the first possibility involves trying to model *the mind*: the processes of conscious reasoning, problem solving and so on, which we all make use of as we go about our lives. This approach is called **symbolic** AI, because it makes use of symbols that stand for things that the system is reasoning about. For example, a symbol 'room451' within a robot's control system might be the name that the robot uses for your bedroom, and a symbol 'cleanRoom' might be used as the name for the activity of cleaning a room. As the robot figures out what to do, it makes explicit use of these symbols, and so, for example, if the robot decides to carry out the action 'cleanRoom(room451)', then this means that the robot has decided to clean your bedroom. The symbols the robot is using *mean something* in the robot's environment.

For about 30 years, from the mid-1950s until the late 1980s, symbolic AI was the most popular approach to building AI systems. It has a lot of advantages, but perhaps the most important of these is that it is *transparent*: when the robot concludes that it will 'cleanRoom(room451)', then we can immediately understand what it has decided to do. But also, I think it was popular because it seems to reflect our conscious thought processes. We 'think' in terms of symbols – words – and when deciding what to do, we might have a mental conversation with ourselves about the pros and cons of various courses of action. Symbolic AI aspired to capture all this. As we will see in Chapter 2, symbolic AI peaked in the early 1980s.

The alternative to modelling the mind is to model the *brain*. One extreme possibility would be to try to simulate a complete human brain (and perhaps a human nervous system) within a computer. After all, human brains are the only things that we can say with certainty are capable of producing human-level intelligent behaviour. The problem with this approach is that the brain is an unimaginably complex organ: a human brain contains about 100 billion interconnected components, and we don't remotely understand the structure and operation of these well enough to duplicate it. It isn't a realistic possibility any time soon, and I suspect it is unlikely ever to be possible (although I'm sorry to say that hasn't stopped some people from trying).[13]

What we can do instead, however, is to take inspiration

from some structures that occur in the brain, and model these as components in intelligent systems. This research area is called **neural networks**, or **neural nets** – the name comes from the cellular information processing units called neurons that we find in the microstructure of the brain. The study of neural nets goes back to before the emergence of AI itself, and has evolved alongside the mainstream of AI. It is this area that has shown impressive progress this century, which has led to the current boom in AI.

Symbolic AI and neural nets are very different approaches, with utterly different methodologies. Both have moved in and out of fashion over the past 60 years, and as we will see, there has even been acrimony between the two schools. However, as AI emerged as a new scientific discipline in the 1950s, it was symbolic AI that largely held sway.

PART TWO

How Did We Get Here?

The Golden Age

Although Turing's article 'Computing Machinery and Intelligence', which introduced the Turing test, made what we now recognize as the first substantial scientific contribution to the discipline of AI, it was a rather isolated contribution, because AI as a discipline simply did not exist at the time. It did not have a name, there was no community of researchers working on it, and the only contributions at the time were speculative conceptual ones, such as the Turing test – there were no AI systems. Just a decade later, by the end of the 1950s all that had changed: a new discipline had been established, with a distinctive name; and researchers were able to proudly show off the first tentative systems demonstrating rudimentary components of intelligent behaviour.

The next two decades were the first boom in AI. There was a flush of optimism, growth and apparent progress, leading to the era called the **Golden Age of** AI, from about 1956 to 1974. There had been no disappointments yet; everything seemed possible. The AI systems built in this period are legends in the AI canon. Systems with quirky, geeky names like SHRDLU, STRIPS and SHAKEY – short names, all in upper-case, supposedly because those were the constraints of computer file names at the time (the tradition of naming AI systems in this way continues to the present day, although it has long since ceased to be necessary). The computers used to build these systems were, by modern standards, unimaginably limited, painfully slow and tremendously hard to use. The tools we take for granted when developing software today did not exist then and indeed could not have run on the computers of the time. Much of the 'hacker' culture of computer programming seems to have emerged at the time. AI researchers worked at night because then they could get access to the computers that were used for more important work during normal office hours; and they had to invent all sorts of ingenious programming tricks to get their complicated programs to run at all – many of these tricks subsequently became standard techniques, with their origins in the AI labs of the 1960s and 1970s now only dimly remembered, if at all.[1]

But by the mid-1970s, progress on AI stalled, having failed to progress far beyond the earliest simple experiments. The young discipline came close to being snuffed out by research funders and a scientific community that came to believe AI, which had promised so much, was actually going nowhere.

In this chapter, we'll look at these first two decades of AI. We'll look at some of the key systems built during this period, and discuss one of the most important techniques developed in AI at the time – a technique called a 'search', which to the present day remains a central component of many AI systems. We'll also hear how an abstract mathematical theory, called computational complexity and developed in the late 1960s and early 1970s, began to explain why so many problems in AI were fundamentally hard. Computational complexity cast a long shadow over AI.

We'll begin with the traditional starting point of the Golden Age: the summer of 1956, when the field was given its name by a young American academic by the name of John McCarthy.

The First Summer of AI

McCarthy belonged to that generation of academics who created the modern technological USA. With almost casual brilliance, throughout the 1950s and 1960s, he invented a range of concepts in computing that are now taken so much for granted that it is hard to imagine that they actually had to be invented. One of his most famous developments was a programming language called **LISP**, which for decades was the programming language of choice for AI researchers. At the best of times computer programs are hard to read, but even by the frankly arcane standards of my profession, LISP is regarded as bizarre, because in LISP (all (programs (look (like this)))) – generations of programmers learned to joke that LISP stood for 'Lots of Irrelevant Silly Parentheses'.[2]

McCarthy invented LISP in the mid-1950s, but astonishingly, nearly 70 years later, it is still regularly taught and used across the world. (I use it every day.) Think about that for a moment: when McCarthy invented LISP, Dwight D. Eisenhower was President of the United States, Nikita Khrushchev was First Secretary of the Communist Party of the Soviet Union and in China Chairman Mao Zedong was overseeing the implementation of his first five-year plan. There were no more than a handful of computers in the whole world. And the programming language McCarthy invented then is still routinely used today.

Born to immigrant parents in Boston, McCarthy demonstrated an unusual aptitude for mathematics at an early age. After graduating in mathematics from Caltech (California Institute of Technology), he was appointed to an associate professorship at Dartmouth College in New Hampshire while he was still in his twenties. McCarthy had become interested in computing before joining Dartmouth, and in 1955 he submitted a proposal to the Rockefeller Institute in the hope of obtaining funds to organize a summer school at Dartmouth. If you are not an academic, the idea of 'summer schools' for adults may sound a little strange, but they are a well-established and fondly regarded academic tradition even today. The basic idea is to bring together a group of researchers with common interests from across the world, and give them the opportunity to meet and work together for an extended period. They are held in summer because, of course, teaching has finished for the year, and academics have a big chunk of time without lecturing commitments. Naturally, the goal is to organize the summer school in an attractive location, and a lively programme of social events is essential.

Another essential requirement for a memorable summer school is a star-studded delegate list. With the benefit of hindsight, we can see that the Dartmouth summer school brought together most of the key individuals that would define the field of AI for decades ahead. One name on the invitation list is particularly poignant. The Princeton-based mathematician John Forbes Nash Jr had gained his PhD in mathematics six years earlier, introducing (in a thesis just 28 pages long) a concept called 'non-cooperative games'. The ideas Nash introduced became cornerstones of economic theory in the decades that followed, and ultimately earned him a Nobel Prize in 1994. But Nash was unable to enjoy the recognition his work was attracting. Just a few years after his PhD, Nash was consumed by episodes of paranoia and delusion, which took him out of academic life for decades. Happily, he recovered sufficiently that he was able to receive his Nobel Prize in 1994; his life was made the subject of the award-winning book and film *A Beautiful Mind*.[3]

The Dartmouth delegate list is also intriguing for another reason. Apart from the obvious presence of academics, the school hosted representatives from industry, government and the military (and even the RAND Corporation – the California-based thinktank made notorious in the 1960s for dispassionately debating how to 'win' a nuclear war). Only a decade earlier, the Manhattan Project had combined the capabilities of US academia, industry, government and military to develop the first atomic bomb – an unequivocal demonstration of US scientific and technological power. This combination – of academia, industry and the government/ military – was characteristic of the US development of computer technology in the decades that followed the Second World War, and was central to the establishment of the US as the international leader in AI over the next six decades.

When McCarthy wrote his funding proposal for the Rockefeller Institute in 1955, he had to give a name to the event, and he chose 'artificial intelligence'. In what would become something of a weary tradition for AI, McCarthy had unrealistically high expectations for his event: 'We think that a significant advance can be made [. . .] if a carefully selected group of scientists work on it together for a summer.'[4]

By the end of the summer school, the delegates had made no real progress but McCarthy's chosen name had stuck, and thus was a new academic discipline formed.

Unfortunately, many have subsequently had occasion to regret McCarthy's choice of name for the field he founded. For one thing, *artificial* can be read as *fake*, or *ersatz* – and who wants *fake intelligence*? Moreover, the word *intelligence* suggests that *intellect* is key. In fact, many of the tasks that the AI community has worked so hard on since 1956 don't seem to require *intelligence* when people do them. On the contrary, as we saw in the previous chapter, many of the most important and difficult problems that AI has struggled with over the past 60 years don't seem to be *intellectual* at all – a fact that has repeatedly been the cause of consternation and confusion for those new to the field.

But artificial intelligence was the name that McCarthy chose, and the name that persists to this day. From McCarthy's summer school, there is an unbroken thread of research by way of the participants in the summer school and their academic descendants, right down to the present day. AI in its recognizably modern form began that summer, and the beginnings of AI seemed to be very promising indeed.

The period following the Dartmouth summer school was one of excitement and growth. And, for a while at least, it seemed like there was rapid progress. Four delegates of the summer school went on to dominate AI in the decades that followed. McCarthy himself founded the AI lab at Stanford University in the heart of what is now Silicon Valley; Marvin Minsky founded the AI lab at MIT in Cambridge, Massachusetts; Alan Newell and his PhD supervisor Herb Simon went to Carnegie Mellon University (CMU). These four individuals, and the AI systems that they and their students built, are totems for AI researchers of my generation.

But there was a good deal of naivety in the Golden Age, with researchers making reckless and grandiose predictions about the likely speed of progress in the field, which have haunted AI ever since. By the mid-1970s, the good times were over, and a vicious backlash began – an AI boom and bust cycle destined to be repeated over the coming decades. But, however critically history may judge this period, it is hard for me to contemplate the characters of this time, and the work they did, with anything other than affection.

Divide and Conquer

As we've seen, General AI is a large and very nebulous target – it is hard to approach directly. Instead, the strategy adopted during the Golden Age was that of *divide and conquer*. Thus, instead of starting out trying to build a complete general intelligent system, the approach adopted was to identify the various individual *capabilities* that seemed to be required for general-purpose AI, and to build systems that could demonstrate these capabilities. The implicit assumption was that, if we could succeed in building systems that demonstrate each of these individual capabilities, then, later on, assembling them into a whole would be straightforward. This fundamental assumption – that the way to progress towards General AI was to focus on the component capabilities of intelligent behaviour – became embedded as the standard methodology for AI research. There was a rush to build machines that could demonstrate these component capabilities.

So, what were the main capabilities that researchers focused on? The first, and as it turned out one of the most stubbornly difficult, is one that we take for granted: **perception**. A machine that is going to act intelligently in a particular environment needs to be able to get information about it. We perceive our world through various mechanisms, including the five senses: sight, sound, touch, smell and taste. So, one strand of research involved building **sensors** that provide analogues of these. Robots today use a wide range of artificial sensors to give them information about their environment – radars, infrared range-finders, ultrasonic range-finders, laser radar and so on. But *building* these sensors – which in itself is not trivial – is only part of the problem. However good the optics are on a digital camera, and no matter how many megapixels there are on the camera's image sensor, ultimately all that camera does is break down the image it is seeing into a grid, and then assign numbers to each cell in the grid, indicating colour and brightness. So, a robot equipped with the very best digital camera will, in the end, only receive a long list of numbers. The second challenge of perception is therefore to interpret those raw numbers: to understand what it is seeing. And this challenge turned out to be far, far harder than the problem of actually building the sensors.

Another key capability for general intelligent systems seems to be the ability to learn from experience, and this led to a strand of AI research called **machine learning**. Like the name 'artificial intelligence' itself, 'machine learning' is perhaps an unfortunate choice of terminology. It sounds like a machine somehow bootstrapping its own intelligence: starting from nothing and progressively getting smarter and smarter. In fact, machine learning is not like human learning: it is about learning from and making predictions about data. For example, one big success in machine learning over the past decade is in programs that can recognize faces in pictures. The way this is usually done involves providing a program with examples of the things that you are trying to learn. Thus, a program to recognize faces would be trained by giving it many pictures labelled with the names of the people that appear in the pictures. The goal is that, when subsequently presented with solely an image, the program would be able to correctly give the name of the person pictured.

Problem solving and **planning** are two related capabilities that also seem to be associated with intelligent behaviour. They both require being able to achieve a goal using a given repertoire of actions; the challenge is to find the right sequence of actions. Playing a board game such as chess or Go would be an example: the goal is to win the game; the actions are the possible moves; the challenge is to figure out which moves to make. As we will see, one of the most fundamental challenges in problem solving and planning is that while they appear easy to do *in principle*, by considering all the possible alternatives, this approach doesn't work in practice, because there are far too many alternatives for it to be feasible.

Reasoning is perhaps the most exalted of all the capabilities associated with intelligence: it involves deriving new knowledge from existing facts in a robust way. To pick a famous example, if you know that 'All men are mortal', and you know that 'Michael is a man', then it is reasonable to conclude that 'Michael is mortal'. A truly intelligent system would be able to derive this conclusion, and then use the newly derived knowledge to make further conclusions. For example, knowing that 'Michael is mortal' should then allow you to conclude that 'at some point in the future, Michael will die' and that 'after Michael is dead, he will stay dead forever', and so on. Automated reasoning is all about giving computers this kind of capability: giving them the capability to reason *logically*. In Chapter 3, we will see that for a long time, it was believed that this kind of reasoning should be the main goal for AI, and although this is not a mainstream view any more, automated reasoning remains an important thread of the field.

Finally, **natural language understanding** involves computers interpreting human languages like English and Chinese. At present, when a programmer gives a computer a recipe to follow (an algorithm or program), she must do so using an *artificial* language: a language specially constructed accordingly to precisely defined unambiguous rules. These languages, of which Python, Java and C are perhaps the best-known examples, are *much* simpler than natural languages like English and Chinese. For a long time, the main approach to understanding natural languages involved trying to come up with precise rules that define these languages, in the same way that we have precise rules defining computer languages. But this turned out to be impossible. Natural languages are too flexible, vague and fluid to be rigorously defined in this way, and the way in which language is used in everyday situations resists attempts to give it a precise definition.

SHRDLU and the Blocks World

The **SHRDLU** system was one of the most acclaimed achievements of the Golden Age (the odd name derives from the

order in which letters were arranged on printing machines of the time – computer programmers enjoy obscure
jokes). Developed by Stanford University PhD student Terry
Winograd in 1971,[5] SHRDLU aimed to demonstrate two key
capabilities for AI: problem solving and natural language
understanding.

The problem-solving component of SHRDLU was based
around what became one of the most famous experimental
scenarios in AI: the **Blocks World**. The Blocks World was a
simulated environment containing a number of coloured objects (blocks, boxes and pyramids). The rationale for using
a simulated environment, rather than trying to build a real
robot, was simply to reduce the complexity of the problem
to something manageable. Problem solving in the SHRDLU
Blocks World involves arranging objects according to instructions from a user, using a simulated robot arm to manipulate
them. Figure 2 illustrates this: we see the initial configuration
of the Blocks World, and the goal configuration. The challenge
is to figure out *how* to transform the initial configuration to
the goal configuration.

To achieve this transformation, you are only allowed to
use a small repertoire of actions:

- *Pick up object x from the table.* Here, the robot arm picks
  up object *x* (which could be a block or pyramid) from
  the table. The robot arm will only be able to do this
  successfully if both object *x* is currently on the table,
  and the robot arm is currently empty.
- *Place object x on the table.* The robot arm will only be able
  to do this if it is currently carrying object *x*.

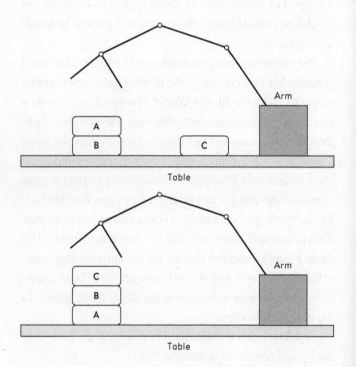

Figure 2

The Blocks World. Above is the initial configuration – below, the goal configuration. How do you get from one to the other?

- *Pick up object x from object y.* For the robot arm to be able to do this, the robot arm must be empty, object *x* must be currently on top of object *y* and object *x* must currently have nothing on top of it.
- *Place object x on top of object y.* For the robot arm to be able to do this, it has to actually be carrying object *x*, and there must be nothing currently on top of object *y*.

Everything that happens in the Blocks World reduces to these actions, and only these actions. Using these actions, a plan to achieve the transformation illustrated in Figure 2 could begin as follows:

- Pick up object A from object B
- Place object A on the table
- Pick up object B from the table

What would the Blocks World look like after these actions had been carried out? Can you figure the remaining part of the plan? (It isn't hard, but it is tedious.)

The Blocks World is probably the most studied scenario in the whole of AI, because tasks in the Blocks World – picking up packages and moving them around – sound like the kind of tasks we might envisage for robots in the real world. But the Blocks World as it appears in SHRDLU (and much subsequent research) has severe limitations as a scenario for developing practically useful AI techniques.

First, it is assumed that the Blocks World is *closed*. This means that the only thing that causes change in the Blocks World is SHRDLU. This is rather like saying that you live alone. If you live alone, you can safely assume that when you wake up, your keys will be where you left them the night before; if you don't live alone, there is always the possibility that someone else has moved them overnight. So, when SHRDLU places block x on top of block y, it can safely assume that block x remains on top of block y unless it has moved the block itself. The real world is not like that: any AI system that relies on the assumption that it is the only actor in its world is likely to get things wrong a lot of the time.

Second, and perhaps more importantly, the Blocks World is *simulated*. SHRDLU is not *actually* picking up objects and moving them around with a robot arm – it is just pretending to. It does this by maintaining a model of the world, and it models the effects of its actions on this world. It never actually looks at the world to build its model, or to check that the model it has is correct. This is a huge simplifying assumption, and researchers later argued that it therefore ignored most of the genuinely hard problems that a robot would face in the real world.

To better understand this point, consider the action 'Pick up object x from object y'. From the point of view of SHRDLU, this is a single action: the robot is assumed to carry out the *whole* of the action in a single indivisible step, and nowhere does it need to worry about what this action *actually involves*. Thus, all the program 'controlling' the arm has to do is to find the right order of such actions to carry out the required task. It doesn't need to worry about the messy business of actually carrying them out. But think about a robot in the physical world trying to undertake this action, perhaps in a warehouse. Here, the robot would have to be able to identify the two objects in question, successfully execute a complex locomotion problem to get the arm to the right place and grasp the relevant object. Even the final part of this 'atomic' action, grasping the relevant object, is, in reality, far from trivial – getting robots to manipulate even simple objects in the real world is phenomenally difficult, and remains a significant challenge to the present day. I gained a personal insight into this problem as a young academic in 1994, when I attended the American Association for AI Conference in Seattle. I vividly recall my astonishment at the apparent incompetence of robots that had been entered in a 'clean up the office' competition. The challenge was to build robots that could, as the name suggests, safely move through an office-like environment, identifying and collecting items of rubbish – something like a physical manifestation of the Blocks World, 20 years after SHRDLU. It seemed that even the best robots in the competition were comically slow and barely able to accomplish even an approximation of the task at hand. Of course, the problem was not with the robots, but with my naive underestimation of just how difficult such problems actually are. The fact that *we* find such tasks trivial leads us to believe, wrongly, that it must also be trivial to get machines to do them.

So, the Blocks World is appealing because it is intuitive and easy to explain, and seems to resemble a problem that we could imagine robots working on in the real world. But digging deeper, what it focuses on is the problem of finding a sequence of actions that will achieve a task; and while this is indeed a problem, it is only one of the problems that a robot would face in a 'real' blocks world – and it is by no means the most difficult of these.

One of the most lauded features of SHRDLU was that the user gave instructions to the system and received feedback from it in what seemed to be ordinary English. Here is a snippet of dialogue with SHRDLU (SHRDLU's responses are in italics):

PICK UP A BIG RED BLOCK.

OK. (Does so.)

GRASP THE PYRAMID.

I DON'T UNDERSTAND WHICH PYRAMID YOU MEAN.

FIND A BLOCK WHICH IS TALLER THAN THE ONE
    YOU ARE HOLDING AND PUT IT INTO THE BOX.

BY 'IT', I ASSUME YOU MEAN THE BLOCK WHICH IS
    TALLER THAN THE ONE I AM HOLDING.

OK. (Does so.)

WHAT DOES THE BOX CONTAIN?

THE BLUE PYRAMID AND THE BLUE BLOCK.

WHAT IS THE PYRAMID SUPPORTED BY?

THE BOX.

HOW MANY BLOCKS ARE NOT IN THE BOX?

FOUR OF THEM.

IS AT LEAST ONE OF THEM NARROWER THAN
    THE ONE WHICH I TOLD YOU TO PICK UP?

YES, THE RED CUBE.

IS IT SUPPORTED?

YES, BY THE TABLE.

CAN THE TABLE PICK UP BLOCKS?

NO.

CAN A PYRAMID BE SUPPORTED BY A BLOCK?

YES.

This dialogue is far beyond ELIZA – the system is much richer and more natural, able to cope with complex constructions ('IS AT LEAST ONE OF THEM NARROWER THAN THE ONE WHICH I TOLD YOU TO PICK UP?') and the use of words like 'it' to refer to things that appeared previously in the dialogue.[6] It was this aspect of the system – the way that a user interacted with it, via what seemed at first like ordinary English – that led to SHRDLU receiving a rapturous reception in the early 1970s. However, it later became clear that SHRDLU was able to generate rich dialogues only because those dialogues related to a very constrained scenario – the Blocks World. The dialogues were not quite 'canned' in the way that dialogues in ELIZA were canned, but they were, nevertheless, very constrained. There was hope, when the system first appeared, that the techniques it embodied might provide a route to much more general natural-language understanding systems, but this hope was not realized.

It is easy for us, 50 years later, to identify the limitations of SHRDLU. But it was hugely influential, and remains one of the landmark AI systems.

SHAKEY the Robot

Robots have always been closely associated with AI – particularly in the media. The 'machine man' in Fritz Lang's classic 1927 film *Metropolis* set the template for the endless portrayals of robotic AI that followed: a robot with two arms, two legs, a head . . . and a murderous temperament. Even today, it seems, every article about AI in the popular press is illustrated with a picture of a robot that could be a direct descendant of the *Metropolis* 'machine man'. It is, I think, no surprise that robots in general, and humanoid robots in particular, should become the public signifier for AI. After all, the idea of robots that inhabit our world, and work among us, is probably the most obvious manifestation of the AI dream – and most of us would be delighted to have robot butlers to do our every bidding.

It may therefore come as a surprise to learn that during the Golden Age robots were only a comparatively small part of the AI story. I'm afraid the reasons for this are rather mundane: building robots is expensive, time-consuming and, frankly, *difficult*. It would have been impossible for a PhD student working alone in the 1960s or 1970s to build a research-level AI robot. They would have needed an entire research lab, dedicated engineers and workshop facilities – and in any case, computers powerful enough to drive AI programs were too large and heavy to be carried by autonomous robots. It was easier and much cheaper for researchers to build programs like SHRDLU, which *pretended* to be working in the real world, than it was to build robots that *actually* operated in the real world, with all its complexity and messiness.

But although the roster of AI robots in the early period of AI is rather sparse, there was one glorious experiment with AI robots during this time: the **SHAKEY** project, which was carried out at the Stanford Research Institute (SRI) between 1966 and 1972.

SHAKEY was the first serious attempt to build a mobile robot that could be given tasks in the real world, and that could figure out on its own how to accomplish them. To do this, SHAKEY would be able to perceive its environment and understand where it was and what was around it; receive tasks from users, figure out for itself appropriate plans to achieve those tasks; and then actually carry out these plans, all the while making sure that everything was progressing as intended. The tasks in question involved moving objects such as boxes around an office environment. This may sound like SHRDLU but, unlike SHRDLU, SHAKEY was a real robot, manipulating real objects. This was a far bigger challenge.

To succeed, SHAKEY had to integrate a daunting array of AI capabilities. First, there was a basic engineering challenge: the developers needed to build the robot itself. It had to be small enough and agile enough to operate in an office, and needed sensors that were powerful and accurate enough that the robot could understand what was around it. For this, SHAKEY was equipped with a television camera, and laser range-finders for determining distance to objects; to detect obstacles, it had bump detectors, called 'cats' whiskers'. Next, SHAKEY had to be able to navigate around its environment. Then, SHAKEY needed to be able to plan how to carry out the tasks it was given. For this, the developers designed a system called **STRIPS** (for Stanford Research Institute Problem Solver),[7] which is now generally recognized as the ancestor of all AI planning techniques. And finally, all of these capabilities had to be made to work together in harmony. As any AI researcher will tell you, getting any one of these components to work is a challenge in itself; getting them to work as an ensemble is an order of magnitude harder.

But impressive as it was, SHAKEY also highlighted the limitations of the AI technology of the time. To make SHAKEY work, its designers had to greatly simplify the challenges faced by the robot. For example, SHAKEY's ability to interpret data from its TV camera was very limited – amounting to not much more than detecting obstacles. And even to enable this, the environment had to be specially painted and carefully lit. Because the TV camera required so much power, it was only switched on when it was needed, and it took about ten seconds after the power was turned on before it produced a usable image. And the developers constantly struggled with the limitations of computers at that time: it took up to 15 minutes for SHAKEY to figure out how to carry out a task, during which time SHAKEY would sit, immobile and inert, utterly isolated from its environment. Since computers with sufficient power to run SHAKEY's software were too large and heavy for SHAKEY to carry around, SHAKEY used a radio link to a computer that actually ran its software.[8] Overall, SHAKEY could not possibly have been put to use on any practical problem.

SHAKEY was arguably the first real autonomous mobile robot, and it pioneered an astonishing array of new AI technologies: like SHRDLU, it deserves a place of honour in the AI history books for these reasons. But SHAKEY's limitations demonstrated just how far AI actually was from the dream of practical autonomous robots, and just how daunting these challenges were.

Problem Solving and Search

The ability to solve problems is surely one of the key capabilities that distinguishes humans from other animals. While the Internet is full of videos of squirrels[9] and crows[10] who can apparently solve complex problems to get at food sources, no other animal comes close to us in terms of our ability to solve abstract problems (even when no food is involved). And problem solving, of course, seems like the kind of thing that requires intelligence – if we can build programs that can solve problems that people find hard, then surely this would be a key step on the road to AI? Problem solving was therefore studied intensely during the Golden Age, and a standard exercise for AI researchers of the time was to get a computer to solve a problem of the kind that you might come across on the puzzle page of a newspaper. Here is a classic example of such a puzzle, called the Towers of Hanoi:

In a remote monastery, there are three columns and 64 golden rings. The rings are of different sizes and rest over the columns. Initially, all the rings rested on the furthest left column, and since then, the monks have been moving the rings, one by one, between columns. Their goal is to move all the rings to the furthest right column. In doing so, the monks must obey two rules:

1. They may only move one ring at a time between columns.
2. At no time may any ring rest upon a smaller ring.

So, to solve the problem, you have to find the right sequence of moves, which will get all the rings from the furthest left column to the furthest right one, without breaking the rule that a ring can never be above a smaller ring.

In some versions of the story, the world is supposed to end when the monks complete their task – although, as we will see below, even if this story were true, we would not need to lose sleep over it, because the universe will surely end long before the monks are able to move all 64 rings. For this reason, the puzzle is usually deployed with far fewer rings.

Figure 3 illustrates the puzzle, showing the initial configuration of the puzzle (all rings are on the furthest left column), then the goal state (with all rings on the furthest right column), and finally an illegal configuration of the puzzle, for the three-ring version of the puzzle.

So, how do we go about solving problems like the Towers of Hanoi? The answer is to use a technique called **search**. At this point I should clarify that when we use the term 'search' in AI, we don't mean it in the sense of searching the web (e.g. Google or Baidu). Search in AI is a fundamental problem-solving technique, which involves systematically considering all possible courses of action. Any program that plays a game like chess will be based on search, as will the satellite navigation system in your car. It arises time and time again: it is one of the cornerstone techniques in AI.

All problems like the Towers of Hanoi have the same basic structure. As in the Blocks World, we want to find a sequence of actions that will take us from some **initial state** of the problem to some designated **goal state**. The term '**state**' is used in AI to refer to a particular configuration of a problem at some moment in time.

We can use search to solve problems like the Towers of Hanoi through the following procedure:

- First, starting from the initial state, we consider the effects of every available action on that initial state. The effect of performing an action is to transform the problem into a new state.
- If one of the actions has generated the goal state, then we have succeeded: the solution to the puzzle is the

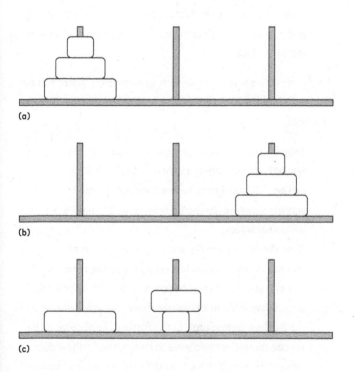

(a)

(b)

(c)

Figure 3
The Towers of Hanoi, a classic puzzle of the type studied in the
Golden Age of AI. Panel (a) shows the initial state of the puzzle and
(b) shows the goal state. Panel (c) shows a disallowed configuration
of the puzzle (it isn't allowed because a larger ring is on top of a
smaller ring).

sequence of actions that got us from the initial state to the goal state.

- Otherwise, we repeat this process for every state we just generated, considering the effect of each action on those states, and so on.

Applying this recipe for search generates a **search tree**: Figure 4 shows a fragment of the search tree for the Towers of Hanoi.

- Initially, we can only move the smallest ring, and our only choices are to move it to the middle or furthest right column. So, we have two possible actions available for the first move, and two possible successor states.
- If we chose to move the small ring to the centre column (shown via the left arrow emerging from the initial state), then we subsequently have three possible actions available to us: we can move the smallest ring to the furthest left column or the furthest right column, or we can move the middle-sized ring to the furthest right column (we can't move it to the centre column, because then it would be on top of the smallest ring, which violates the rules of the puzzle).
- . . . and so on.

Because we are systematically generating the search tree, level by level, we are considering all possibilities – and so if there is a solution, we will be guaranteed to eventually find it using this process. ('Eventually' is quite an important word in the previous sentence, for reasons which will become clear shortly.)

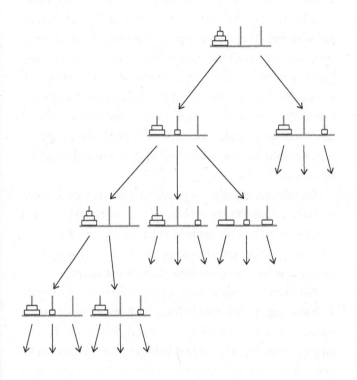

Figure 4
A small fragment of the search tree for the Towers of Hanoi puzzle.

So how many moves would you need to make to solve the Towers of Hanoi problem *optimally* (i.e. with the smallest possible number of moves from the initial state)? The answer, for three rings, turns out to be seven: you will never be able to find a solution that solves the puzzle in fewer than seven moves. There are solutions that solve it in more than seven moves (in fact there are *infinitely many* such solutions) but they are not optimal, because you could have done it in fewer. Now, because the search process we have described is exhaustive – in the sense that it will systematically unwind the search tree, considering all possibilities at every stage – it is guaranteed not just to find a solution, but to find the *shortest* solution.

So, this process of naive exhaustive search is guaranteed to find a solution to the problem if one exists, and it is also guaranteed to find the shortest solution. Moreover, as computational recipes go, exhaustive search is pretty simple – it is easy to write a program to implement this recipe.

But even a cursory study of the search tree in Figure 4 shows that, in the simple form we just described, naive exhaustive search is actually a pretty stupid process. For example, if you study the furthest left branch of the search tree, you will see that, after just two moves, we have returned to the initial state of the problem, which seems like a pointless waste of effort. If *you* were solving the Towers of Hanoi, you might make this mistake once or twice while looking for a solution, but you would quickly learn to spot and avoid such wasted effort. But a computer carrying out the recipe for naive exhaustive search does not: the recipe involves systematically generating all the alternatives, even if those alternatives are a waste of time, in the sense that they are re-visiting earlier failed configurations.

But apart from being hopelessly inefficient, exhaustive search has a much more fundamental problem. If you do a little experimentation, you will see that in almost all possible configurations of the Towers of Hanoi puzzle, you will have three possible moves available to you. We say that the **branching factor** of the puzzle is three. Different search problems will have different branching factors. In the board game Go, for example, the branching factor is 250, meaning that, on average, each player will have about 250 moves available in any given state of the game. So, let's look at how the *size* of a search tree grows with respect to the branching factor of the tree – how many states there will be in any given level of the tree. Consider the game of Go:[11]

- The first level of the tree will contain 250 states, because there are 250 moves available from the initial state of the game.
- The second level of the search tree will have 250 × 250 = 62,500 states, because we have to consider each possible move for each of the 250 states in the first level of the tree.
- The third level of the search tree will contain 250 × 62,500 = 15.6 million states.
- The fourth level of the search tree will contain 250 × 15.6 million = 3.9 billion states.

So, at the time of writing, a typical desktop computer would not have enough memory to be able to store the search tree for the game of Go for more than about four levels – and a typical game of Go lasts for about 200 moves. The number of states in the Go search tree for 200 moves is a number that is so large that it defies comprehension. It is hundreds of orders of magnitude larger than the number of atoms in our universe. No improvement in conventional computer technology is ever going to be able to cope with search trees this large.

Search trees grow fast. Ludicrously, unimaginably fast. This problem is called **combinatorial explosion**, and it is the single most important practical problem in AI, because search is such a ubiquitous requirement in AI problems.[12] If you could find a foolproof recipe for solving search problems quickly – to get the same result as exhaustive search, without all that effort – then you would make yourself very famous, and many problems that are currently very difficult for AI would suddenly become easy. But you won't, I'm afraid. We can't get around combinatorial explosion: we need to work with it.

Combinatorial explosion was recognized as a fundamental problem from the earliest days of AI – it was identified by McCarthy as one of the topics to be studied at his 1956 summer school on AI. Attention very quickly shifted to making search more efficient. To do this, there are several obvious lines of attack.

One possibility is to focus the search in some way. An obvious way of doing this is as follows: instead of developing the tree level by level, we instead build the tree along just one branch. This approach is called **depth-first search**. With depth-first search, we carry on expanding a branch until we get a solution or become convinced that we won't get a solution; if we ever get stuck (for example by re-creating a configuration that we already saw, as in the furthest left branch of

Figure 4), then we stop expanding that branch, and go back up the tree to start working on the next branch.

The main advantage that depth-first search has is that we don't have to store the whole of the search tree: we only need to store the branch we are working on. But it has a big disadvantage: if we pick the wrong branch to explore, then we may go on expanding our search along this branch without ever finding a solution. So, if we want to use depth-first search, we really want to know which branch to investigate. And this is what **heuristic search** tries to help us with.

The idea of heuristic search is to use 'rules of thumb' called **heuristics** which indicate where to focus our search. We can't typically find heuristics that are guaranteed to focus search in the best possible direction, but we can often find heuristics for the particular problems we are interested in solving, even though we know there will be some situations in which these heuristics won't perform well.

Heuristic search is such a natural idea that it has been re-invented many times over the years, and so it seems pointless to debate who invented it. But we can identify with reasonable confidence the first major application of heuristic search in an AI program: a program to play the game of checkers,[13] written by an IBM employee called Arthur Samuel in the mid-1950s. In writing his program, Samuel broke new ground for AI in many ways. Firstly, his checkers player established the tradition of using board games as a proving ground for AI techniques – a common technique even in the present day, although it is not without its critics. Secondly, as we have already mentioned, and are about to discuss in more detail, the program was based on heuristic search. And finally, although we will postpone discussion of this point until later, the program was arguably the first real machine learning program: his program taught itself how to play checkers.

Perhaps the key component of Samuel's program was a way of evaluating any given board position, to estimate how 'good' the position was for a particular player: intuitively, a 'good' board position for a particular player is one that would probably lead to a win for that player, whereas a 'bad' board position would probably lead to that player losing. To do this, Samuel used a number of features of the board position in order to compute its value. For example, one feature might be the number of pieces you have on the board: the more you have, the better you are doing. These different features were then aggregated by the program to give a single overall measure of the quality of a board position. Then, a typical heuristic would involve picking a move which leads to the best board position, according to this heuristic.

In practice, more was needed than this simple heuristic: because checkers is a game played against an adversary, you have to consider how your opponent is likely to act. Samuel's checkers player assumed that your opponent will make a move which is as bad for you as possible. This 'worst case reasoning' approach (you act so as to maximize your score under the assumption that your opponent will act so as to minimize it) is called **minimax search**, and is a fundamental idea in game playing.

Samuel's program played a credible game of checkers. This was an impressive achievement in many respects, but is all the more so when one considers the primitive state of practical computers of the time – the IBM 701 computer that

Samuel used could only handle programs that were the equivalent length of just a few pages of text. A modern desktop computer will have millions of times more memory than this, and will be millions of times faster. Given these restrictions, it is impressive that it could play the game at all, let alone play it competently.

Most early work on heuristic search, including Samuel's checkers player, used rather ad hoc heuristic approaches – a try-something-and-see-if-it-works approach. A breakthrough came in the late 1960s, with the work of Nils Nilsson and colleagues at SRI, who developed a technique called **A*** as part of the SHAKEY project that we discussed above. A* identified some simple rules that allow us to know when a heuristic is 'good'. Before A*, heuristic search was nothing more than a guessing game; afterwards, it was a mathematically well-understood process.[14] A* is now regarded as one of the foundational algorithms in computing, and is widely used in practice. Indeed, there is a pretty good chance you will have encountered A* today, since it is the algorithmic engine that drives software such as in-car satellite navigation systems. But, beautiful as it is, A* remains dependent on the specific heuristic used: a good heuristic will quickly lead to a solution, but a poor one will be of little value. And A* itself gives us no answer to the problem of how to find good heuristics for specific problems.

AI Crashes into the Complexity Barrier

We previously saw that computers were for all intents and purposes invented by Alan Turing in order to solve one of the great mathematical problems of his time. It is one of the

great ironies of scientific history that Turing invented computers in order to show that there are things which computers
are fundamentally incapable of doing – that some problems
are inherently undecidable.

In the decades following Turing's results, exploring the
limits of what computers can and cannot do became a small
industry in university mathematics departments across the
world. The focus in this work was on separating out those
problems that are inherently undecidable (cannot be solved
by computer) from those that are decidable (can be solved by
computer). One intriguing discovery from this time was that
there are *hierarchies* of undecidable problems: it is possible
to have a problem that is not just undecidable, but *highly* undecidable. (This kind of thing is catnip for mathematicians
of a certain type.)

But by the 1960s, it was becoming clear that whether a
problem is or is not decidable was far from being the end of
the story. The fact that a problem was decidable in the sense
of Turing's work did not mean that it was *practically* solvable
at all: some problems that were solvable according to Turing's theory seemed to resist all practical attempts to attack
them – they required impossible amounts of memory, or were
too impossibly slow to ever be practicable. And it was becoming uncomfortably obvious that many AI problems fell
into this awkward class.

Here's an example of a problem that is easily seen to be
solvable according to Turing's theory:

In your office you have four talented individuals working
for you: John, Paul, George and Ringo. For a particular

project, you need a team containing any three of these individuals. Unfortunately, personal rivalries mean that John and Paul cannot work together.

Can you form a suitable team?

In this case the answer is obviously 'yes': either John, George and Ringo, or Paul, George and Ringo will work. (Observe that these are the *only* solutions to this problem.)

Now suppose we add a further constraint: John and George can't work together. Can we still form a team? Yes: Paul, George and Ringo.

Now add one final constraint: Paul and George can't work together. With this final constraint, the answer to our problem becomes 'no': there is no team containing three members that satisfies the 'forbidden pairs' constraints.

Written a bit more generally, this is the problem we are considering:[15]

We are given a list of n individuals (in the above example, the individuals are John, Paul, George and Ringo, so $n = 4$), and a list of 'forbidden pairs' (e.g. 'John and Paul can't be together'). We are given a number, m, and we are asked whether it is possible to form a team containing exactly m of the listed individuals, which must satisfy the constraint that the team contains no forbidden pairing. (Obviously, for the problem to make sense, m must be smaller than n.)

It is important to emphasize that this problem is easily seen to be soluble *in principle*. Simply list all conceivable teams containing m members from our list of n individuals, and check whether each team satisfies the given constraints. This recipe is very easy to program on a computer. The problem is, therefore, trivially decidable according to Turing's classification.

But *how many* potential teams would you have to check using this recipe? If you have a pool of four individuals and you want a team of three, then you have exactly four possible teams to check. Easy. But let's look at what happens when the number of employees gets bigger.

If you have a pool of ten individuals and you want to choose five, you have 252 possibilities to look at. Tedious, but certainly feasible, I would say. Observe that the number of possible teams has grown much faster than the number of individuals or the size of target team.

Suppose you have a pool of 100 individuals and you need a team of 50. Then you would have to check 100 *billion billion billion* potential teams. A fast contemporary computer might be able to evaluate ten billion possible teams every second – which sounds a lot, until you realize that it would still need far, far more time to investigate all the alternatives than is available before the end of the universe. Waiting for the clever people at Intel to deliver a faster chip won't help you with this problem: no conceivable improvement in conventional computer technology will yield a machine that could check all these alternatives in any reasonable amount of time.

The phenomenon we are witnessing here is another example of combinatorial explosion. We were introduced to combinatorial explosion when looking at search trees, where each successive layer in the search tree multiplies the size of the tree. Combinatorial explosion occurs in situations where you must make a series of successive choices: each choice *multiplies* the total number of possible outcomes. In our team-building case, the choices we must make are whether to include an individual in the team: just adding one person to our pool of candidates can *double* the number of potential teams that we have to consider.

So, our naive approach, of exhaustively searching through all the candidate teams to see if any work, is not going to be feasible. It works *in principle* (given enough time, we will get the right answer) but it doesn't work *in practice* (because the amount of time required to consider all the alternatives quickly becomes impossibly large).

But as we noted earlier, naive exhaustive search is a very crude technique. We could use heuristics, but they aren't guaranteed to work. Is there a *smarter* way that is *guaranteed* to find an appropriate team, which doesn't involve exhaustively checking all the alternatives? *No!* You might find a technique that improves things marginally, but, ultimately, *you won't be able to get around that combinatorial explosion.* Any recipe you find that is guaranteed to solve this problem is not going to be feasible for most cases of interest.

The reason for this is that our problem is an example of what is called an **NP-complete** problem. I'm afraid the acronym is not helpful for the uninitiated: 'NP' stands for 'non-deterministic polynomial time', and the technical meaning is rather complex. Fortunately, the intuition behind NP-complete problems is simple.

An NP-complete problem is a combinatorial problem, like our team-building example, in which it is *hard to find solutions* (because there are too many of them to exhaustively check, as we discussed above) but where it is *easy to verify whether you have found a solution* (in our team-building example, we can check a possible solution by simply verifying that it doesn't contain any forbidden pairings).

There is one other important characteristic of NP-complete problems. To understand it, we need to introduce another problem (trust me, I'm doing this for a good reason). Our next problem is rather famous, as computational problems go, and you may have heard of it. It is called the *travelling salesman problem*:[16]

> A salesman must visit a group of cities in a road network, returning finally to his starting point. Not all the cities are connected by road, but for those that are, the salesman knows the shortest route. The salesman's car can drive for a certain, known number of miles on a single tank of petrol. Is there a route for the salesman, which will visit all the cities and return to the starting destination, which can be done on a single tank of petrol?

This problem has a combinatorial flavour, just like our team-building scenario. We can solve it, using brute force, just by listing all the possible tours of the cities, and checking whether each tour is possible on a single tank of petrol. However, as you might now guess, the number of possible tours increases very rapidly as the number of cities increases: for ten cities, you would have to consider up to 3.6 million possible tours; for 11 cities, you would have to consider up to 40 million.

So, the travelling salesman problem suffers from the combinatorial explosion problem, just like the team-building problem. But apart from this, they don't seem to have anything in common. And why should they? After all, what does team building have to do with finding the shortest tour in a road network? But now comes the really remarkable thing about NP-complete problems: although they appear to be completely different, they are, ultimately, *the same problem*.

To see what I mean by this, imagine I had ingeniously figured out a recipe that was guaranteed to quickly give me the correct answer to any team-building problem. Now suppose that you give me an instance of the travelling salesman problem. Then I can take the problem you gave me and quickly transform it into an instance of the team-building problem, which my recipe will quickly solve – *and the answer I obtain will then yield the answer to the problem you gave me*. What this means is, if you invent a quick technique to solve the team-building problem, then you will *also* have invented a quick technique to solve the travelling salesman problem. And this doesn't hold for just these two problems: the same is true for *all* NP-complete problems.

All NP-complete problems have this property: they can all easily be transformed into each other. This remarkable result means that all NP-complete problems stand or fall together. If you could find a quick recipe for solving *just one* NP-complete problem, *then you would also have found a quick recipe for solving all of them*. But, to date, nobody has found an efficient recipe for any NP-complete problem. And the question of whether NP-complete problems can be efficiently solved is, in fact, one of the most important open problems in science today. It is known as the **P vs NP problem**,[17] and if you can settle it one way or the other to the satisfaction of the scientific community, you stand to receive a prize of one million dollars from the Clay Mathematics Institute, who in the year 2000 identified it as one of the

'Millennium Problems' in mathematics. Smart money says that NP-complete problems *cannot* be solved efficiently; but smart money also says that we are a long way from knowing for certain whether this really is the case.

If you discover that a problem you are working on is NP-complete, then this tells you that conventional techniques to solve it are just not going to work: your problem is, in a precise mathematical sense, *hard*.

The basic structure of NP-complete problems was unravelled in a series of articles in the early 1970s: a 1971 paper by American-Canadian mathematician Stephen Cook established the central idea, and a subsequent paper by American Richard Karp demonstrated that the range of Cook's NP-complete problems was much wider than was first thought. Throughout the 1970s, researchers in AI started to look at the problems that they had been working on using the theory of NP-completeness. And the results were shocking. Everywhere they looked – in problem solving, game playing, planning, learning, reasoning – it seemed that key problems were NP-complete (or worse). The phenomenon was so ubiquitous that it became a joke – the term 'AI-complete' came to mean 'a problem as hard as AI itself' – if you could solve one AI-complete problem, so the joke went, you would solve them all.

Discovering that the problems you were working on were NP-complete – or worse – was a heavy blow. Before the theory of NP-completeness and its consequences were understood, there was always a hope that some sudden breakthrough would render these problems easy – **tractable**, to use the technical term. And technically, such a hope still remains, since we don't yet know for certain that NP-complete problems cannot be solved efficiently. But by the late 1970s the spectre of NP-completeness and combinatorial explosion began to loom large over the AI landscape. The field had hit a barrier, in the form of computational complexity, and progress ground to a halt. The techniques developed in the Golden Age seemed unable to scale up their applicability beyond scenarios with toys and microworlds like the Blocks World, and the optimistic predictions of rapid progress made throughout the 1950s and 1960s started to haunt the early pioneers.

AI as Alchemy

By the early 1970s, the wider scientific community was beginning to be more and more frustrated by the very visible lack of progress made on core AI problems, and by the continuing extravagant claims of some researchers. By the mid-1970s, the criticisms reached fever pitch.

Of all the critics (and there were many), the most outspoken, and most publicly vitriolic was surely the American philosopher Hubert Dreyfus. Dreyfus was commissioned by the RAND Corporation in the mid-1960s to write a report on the state of progress in AI. The title he chose for his report, *Alchemy and AI*, made very clear his disdain for the field and those who worked in it. Publicly equating the work of a serious scientist to alchemy is extraordinarily insulting. Re-reading *Alchemy and AI* now, I have to say I've never seen any other scientific report like it: the contempt is palpable and still rather shocking, more than half a century later.

While we might frown upon the way in which Dreyfus articulated his critique of AI, it is hard to avoid the conclusion that he had a few valid points – particularly about the inflated claims and grand predictions of AI pioneers. Herb Simon (later awarded a Nobel Prize in Economics) wrote in 1958:

> It is not my aim to surprise or shock you – but [. . .] there are now in the world machines that think, that learn and that create. Moreover, their ability to do these things is going to increase rapidly until – in a visible future – the range of problems they can handle will be co-extensive with the range to which the human mind has been applied.

There were many other similar claims at the time, and I cite Simon only because his turned out to be the best known. While an AI optimist, he was by no means the most unreasonable advocate of AI. In hindsight, it is painfully obvious that such claims and predictions were unrealistic. Some members of the AI community today believe that researchers at the time made such claims simply because they got carried away with their own excitement – others take the more cynical view that the hype was about trying to attract investment and research funding.

For what it's worth, my professional sense is that while there was naivety, there was no wholesale deliberate intent to deceive or misrepresent the state of AI. Researchers were excited by what they were doing, and, crucially, they *believed in it*. And they wanted others to believe in it too. They had built programs that could learn and plan and reason – albeit in a limited way – and they just assumed it was going to be easy to scale the application of these programs up.

So, I think at least some of the exuberance should be forgiven. In particular, there was no reason to suppose that the problems being tackled were *by their very nature* hard for computers to solve. Back then, there had always been the possibility that some breakthrough would render the difficult problems easy. But when understanding of NP-completeness began to spread, the community began to understand what it really meant for a computational problem to be *hard*.

The End of the Golden Age

In 1972, a key funding body for scientific research in the UK asked the eminent mathematician Sir James Lighthill to evaluate the state of and prospects for AI. Tradition has it that the request came after reports of academic in-fighting among members of the AI community at the University of Edinburgh, then and now one of the world's leading centres for AI research. Lighthill was at the time Lucasian Professor of Mathematics at the University of Cambridge, the most prestigious academic position that can be held by a UK mathematician (his successor in the post was Stephen Hawking). He had a wealth of experience in practical applied mathematics. However, reading the **Lighthill Report** today, he seems to have been left utterly bemused by his exposure to the AI culture of the time:

> able and respected scientists write [. . .] that AI [. . .] represents another step in the general process of evolution; that possibilities in the nineteen-eighties include an all-purpose intelligence on a human-scale knowledge base; that awe-inspiring possibilities suggest themselves based on machine intelligence exceeding human intelligence by the year 2000.

Lighthill's report was fiercely dismissive of mainstream AI – he specifically identified combinatorial explosion as a key problem that the AI community had failed to tackle. His report immediately led to severe funding cuts to AI research across the UK.

Over in the USA, the main funders of AI research historically had been the military funding agency the Defense Advanced Research Projects Agency (DARPA) and its predecessor, the Advanced Research Projects Agency (ARPA), but by the early 1970s they too were becoming frustrated with the failure of AI to deliver on its many promises. Funding cuts to AI research in the USA followed.

The decade from the early 1970s to the early 1980s later became known as the **AI winter**, although it should perhaps better be known as the *first* AI winter, because there were more to come. The stereotype was established, that of AI researchers making hopelessly overoptimistic and unwarranted predictions, only to fail to deliver. Within the scientific community, AI began to acquire a reputation somewhat akin to homeopathic medicine. As a serious academic discipline, it appeared to be in terminal decline.

CHAPTER 3

Knowledge Is Power

It is important not to underestimate the damage inflicted on AI during the mid-1970s. Many academics started to treat AI as a pseudo-science – the field has really only recently recovered from the reputational damage it suffered during the AI winter. But even as the Lighthill Report was being circulated and its consequences were being felt, a new approach to AI was beginning to gain attention, which promised to overcome the problems that had led to AI getting such a bad press. The problem with previous efforts, according to a new generation of researchers that burst onto the scene in the late 1970s and early 1980s, was that AI had focused too much on general approaches like search and problem solving. These 'weak' methods, it was argued, were missing a key ingredient that must surely be a crucial part of any intelligent activity: *knowledge*. 'Scientia potentia est,' wrote the seventeenth-century philosopher Francis Bacon – 'Knowledge is power'. The proponents of **knowledge-based AI** took Bacon's dictum literally: they were convinced that explicitly capturing and using human knowledge was the key to progress in AI.

A new class of knowledge-based AI systems began to emerge. These so-called **expert systems** used human expert knowledge to solve specific, narrowly defined problems. Expert systems provided evidence that AI systems could outperform humans in certain tasks, and perhaps more importantly, for the first time, they showed that AI could be applied to problems of commercial interest – AI suddenly showed the potential to make money. And it was possible to teach the techniques of knowledge-based AI to a wide audience – a generation of graduates emerged determined to apply their practical AI skills.

Expert systems made no claim to be General AI. Rather, the aim was to build systems that could solve very narrow, very specific problems that required considerable human expertise. Typically, these were problems in which a human expert had acquired expertise over a long period of time, and where that human expertise was scarce.

For the next decade, knowledge-based expert systems were the main focus of AI research. Enormous investment from industry flowed into the field. By the early 1980s, the AI winter was over – another, much bigger AI boom was underway.

In this chapter, we'll look at the expert systems boom, which lasted from the late 1970s to the late 1980s. We'll start by seeing how human expert knowledge can be captured and given to computers, and I'll tell you the story of MYCIN – one of the most celebrated expert systems of the period. We'll see how researchers looked to try to build richer ways of capturing knowledge, using the power and precision of mathematical logic – and how this goal ultimately foundered. We'll then hear the story of one of the most ambitious and notorious failed projects in AI history – the Cyc project, which tried to use human expert knowledge to solve the biggest problem of them all: General AI.

Capturing Human Knowledge Using Rules

The idea of using knowledge in AI systems was arguably not a new one. Heuristics, as we saw in the previous chapter, were widely used in the Golden Age as a means to focus problem solving in promising directions. Such heuristics can be understood as embodying knowledge about a problem. But heuristics only capture knowledge *implicitly*. Knowledge-based AI was based on an important new idea: that human knowledge about a problem should be *explicitly* captured and *represented* within an AI system.

The most common scheme adopted for what came to be called **knowledge representation** was based on **rules**. A rule in the context of AI captures a discrete chunk of knowledge, in the form of an 'if . . . then . . .' expression. Rules are actually rather simple, and best explained by way of an example, so below are some rules (written in English), which are part of the folklore of AI.[1] They capture knowledge for an expert system that assists a user in the task of classifying animals (see Appendix A for a little more detail on how rules are used):

IF animal gives milk THEN animal is mammal

IF animal has feathers THEN animal is bird

IF animal can fly AND animal lays eggs THEN animal is bird

IF animal eats meat THEN animal is carnivore

The way we interpret such rules is as follows: each rule has an **antecedent** (the part after the 'IF') and a **consequent** (the part after the 'THEN'). For example, in the following rule –

> IF animal can fly AND animal lays eggs THEN animal is bird

the antecedent is 'animal can fly AND animal lays eggs', while the consequent is 'animal is bird'. The usual interpretation of such a rule is that if the information that we currently have correctly matches the antecedent, then the rule **fires**, meaning that we may then conclude the consequent. For this rule to fire, we would therefore require two pieces of information: that the animal we are trying to classify can fly, and the animal we are trying to classify lays eggs. If we do indeed have this information, then the rule fires, and we conclude that the animal is a bird. This conclusion gives us more information, which can then be used in subsequent rules to obtain more information, and so on. Usually, expert systems interacted with a user, in the form of a consultation. The user would be responsible for providing information to the system, and answering questions posed by the system.

Figure 5 illustrates the structure of a typical expert system. The **knowledge base** contains the knowledge that the system has – the rules – while the **working memory** contains the information the system currently has about the problem currently being solved (e.g. 'animal has hair'). Finally, the **inference engine** is the part of the system that actually applies the knowledge the system has during problem solving.

Given a knowledge base like our animals example above,

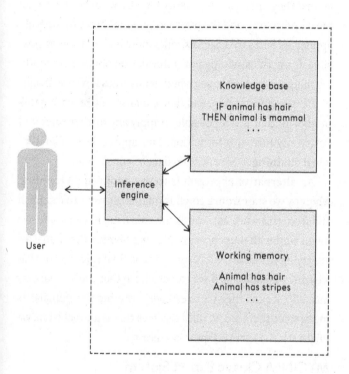

Figure 5
The structure of a typical expert system.

an inference engine can operate in one of two ways. The first is that the user tells the system everything they know about the particular problem at hand (in this case, whether the animal they are trying to classify has stripes, whether it eats meat and so on), and the inference engine then exhaustively applies its rules to derive as much new information as possible, firing rules, adding new information obtained to working memory, looking to see whether any rules now fire in light of the new information, and then exhaustively repeating this process until it is not possible to apply any further rules and derive any further information. This approach is called **forward chaining**: we work from data to conclusions.

An alternative approach is to use **backward chaining**, whereby we start from a conclusion that we want to establish and from this work backwards towards data. For example, we might start with the goal of establishing whether the animal we are trying to classify is a carnivore. The final rule tells us that we can conclude this if we can establish that the animal eats meat. So, we can then try to establish whether the animal eats meat; since there are no rules that give this as a conclusion, we might ask the user this question directly.

MYCIN: A Classic Expert System

Of the first generation of expert systems that emerged in the 1970s, perhaps the most iconic was **MYCIN**[2] (the name derives from the fact that many antibiotics have 'mycin' as a suffix). MYCIN demonstrated, for the first time, that AI systems could outperform human experts in important problems, and provided the template for countless systems that followed.

MYCIN was intended to be a doctor's assistant, providing expert advice about blood diseases in humans. The system was developed by a team of researchers at Stanford University, including experts from Stanford's AI labs, led by Bruce Buchanan, and experts from Stanford's medical school, led by Ted Shortliffe. The fact that the project benefitted directly from the commitment of the people who actually knew the stuff the expert system was supposed to be expert in was a key factor in the success of MYCIN. Many later expert system projects failed because they lacked the necessary buy-in from the relevant human experts.

MYCIN's knowledge about blood diseases was represented using a slightly richer form of rules than we used in the animals example above. A typical MYCIN rule (expressed in English) is as follows:

IF:
1) The organism does not stain using the Gram method AND
2) The morphology of the organism is rod AND
3) The organism is anaerobic
THEN:
There is evidence (0.6) that the organism is bacteroides.

This is the rule expressed in the language actually used by MYCIN:

RULE036:
PREMISE: ($AND (SAME CNTXT GRAM GRAMNEG)
(SAME CNTXT MORPH ROD)
(SAME CNTXT AIR ANAEROBIC))

ACTION: (CONCLUDE CNTXT IDENTITY
  BACTEROIDES TALLY 0.6)

MYCIN's knowledge about blood disease was encoded and refined over a period of about five years. In its final version, the knowledge base contained hundreds of rules.

MYCIN became iconic because it embodied all the key features that came to be regarded as essential for expert systems.

First, the operation of the system was intended to resemble a consultation with a human user – a sequence of questions to the user, to which the user provides responses. This became the standard model for expert systems, and MYCIN's main role – diagnosis – became a standard task for expert systems.

Second, MYCIN was able to *explain* its reasoning. This issue – the transparency of reasoning – became crucially important for applications of AI. If an AI system is operating on a problem that has significant consequences (in the case of MYCIN, potentially life or death consequences), then it is essential that those who are asked to follow the system's recommendations have confidence in them, and for this the ability to explain and justify a recommendation is essential. Experience shows that systems which operate as 'black boxes', making recommendations without the ability to justify them, are treated with great suspicion by users.

Crucially, MYCIN was able to answer questions relating to why it had reached a particular conclusion. It did this by producing the chain of reasoning that led to the conclusion – the rules that were fired and the information that had been obtained leading to these rules being fired. In practice, the explanation capabilities of most expert systems ultimately boiled down to something similar. While not ideal, such explanations are easy to produce, and give at least some mechanism through which to understand the system's conclusions.

Finally, MYCIN was able to cope with **uncertainty**: situations in which the information provided was not known to be true with certainty. Handling uncertainty turned out to be a ubiquitous requirement for expert system applications and AI systems more generally. In systems like MYCIN, for example, it is rarely the case that a definite conclusion can be drawn on the basis of a particular piece of evidence. For example, when a user has a blood test which comes back positive, then that provides some useful evidence that can be taken into consideration by the system, but there will always be the possibility of a faulty test (a 'false positive' or 'false negative'). Alternatively, if a patient displays some symptom, then this may be *indicative* of a particular ailment, but not enough to conclude with certainty that the patient suffers from the ailment (coughing is one of the symptoms of lassa fever, but the fact that a patient is coughing would be nowhere near enough evidence to conclude that the patient has lassa fever). To be able to make good judgements, expert systems need to be able to take such evidence into account in a principled way.

In order to handle uncertainty, MYCIN used a technique called certainty factors – numeric values indicating the degree of belief or disbelief in a particular piece of information. Certainty factors were a rather ad hoc solution to the problem of capturing uncertainty, and for this reason they subsequently came in for a good deal of criticism. The problem of handling and reasoning with uncertainty became a major topic of research in AI, and remains so to the present day. We shall hear much more about this issue in Chapter 4.

In trials carried out in 1979, MYCIN's performance in diagnosing blood diseases was shown to be at a comparable level to human experts when evaluated on ten real cases, and above the level of general practitioners. This was one of the first times that an AI system demonstrated capabilities at or above human expert level in a task of real significance.

Boom Times Again

MYCIN was just one of a number of high-profile expert systems that appeared in the 1970s. The **DENDRAL** project, also from Stanford University, was led by Ed Feigenbaum, who became one of the best-known advocates of knowledge-based systems, and is often regarded as the 'father of expert systems'. DENDRAL aimed to help chemists determine the chemical structure of a compound from the information provided by mass spectrometers. By the mid-1980s, DENDRAL was being used by hundreds of people every day.

The **R1/XCON** system was developed by the Digital Equipment Corporation (DEC) in order to help configure their VAX range of computers. By the mid-1980s, DEC claimed it had processed more than 80,000 orders. The system at the time had more than 3,000 rules relating to 5,000 different system components. By the end of the 1980s, the system had about 17,500 rules, and the developers claimed it had saved the company about $40 million.

DENDRAL showed that expert systems could be useful; MYCIN showed they could outperform human experts at their own game; and R1/XCON showed that they could make serious money. These success stories attracted a lot of interest: AI, it seemed, was ready for business. This was a compelling story, and, not surprisingly, investment flowed in – massive investment. A flurry of start-up companies rushed to cash in on the boom. A typical product offering from such a company was a software platform for building expert systems, together with the support services to develop and deploy them. Alternatively, you could buy computers that were specially designed to quickly execute LISP, the programming language of choice for building expert systems. These LISP machines remained available until the early 1990s, when ordinary PCs became cheap enough and powerful enough that spending $70,000 on a computer that could only run LISP didn't seem like very good value for money any longer.

Companies across the world scrambled to get in on the expert systems boom, and not just software companies. By the 1980s industry was beginning to understand that knowledge and expertise were important assets that could be nurtured and developed, to profitable advantage. Expert systems seemed to make this intangible asset tangible. The concept of a knowledge-based system resonated with the then prevailing view that Western economies were entering a post-industrial period, in which new opportunities for economic development would come primarily from the so-called knowledge-based industries and services, rather than from manufacturing and other traditional industries.

If we look back at the experience of expert systems, we can see that there was more to the emergence of the boom than just the success stories of MYCIN, DENDRAL and the like. Expert systems made AI *accessible*. You didn't need a PhD to build an expert system (I bet you could easily follow the animal rules I gave above). Anybody comfortable with programming could be taught the principles of expert systems, and, indeed, building expert systems seemed somehow easier than building conventional programs. A grand new job title emerged: **knowledge engineer**.

Ironically, given the Lighthill Report that nearly killed British AI just a decade before, in 1983 the UK government launched an ambitious research funding initiative for computer technology, called the Alvey programme, which had AI at its heart. But given the bad press that AI had received so recently, it seemed everyone involved wanted to avoid actually calling it AI. Instead, they called it *Intelligent Knowledge-Based Systems*. The future of AI seemed bright indeed – as long as you didn't call it AI.

Logic-based AI

Although rules became the dominant approach to capturing human knowledge, a huge range of other schemes were proposed. For example, Figure 6 shows a (simplified) version of a knowledge representation scheme called **scripts**, which was developed by psychologists Roger Schank and Robert P. Abelson. Their work built on a psychological theory of human understanding, which proposed that our behaviour is partly governed by stereotypical patterns ('scripts'), which we also use to understand our world. They suggested that the same idea might be used in AI. Consider the script in Figure 6, for example: this describes a stereotypical restaurant scenario. The script describes (in English) the various roles

Name: RESTAURANT

Roles: Customer, Waiter, Cook, Cashier

Entry condition: Customer is hungry

Props: Food, table, money, menu, tip

Events:
1. Customer enters restaurant
2. Customer goes to table
3. Waiter brings menu
4. Customer orders food
5. Waiter brings food
6. Customer eats food
7. Customer asks waiter for bill
8. Waiter brings bill to customer
9. Customer gives money to cashier
10. Customer leaves restaurant

Main concept: 6

Results: Customer not hungry,
   Customer has less money,
   Restaurant has more money

Figure 6
A script describing a stereotypical restaurant eating experience.

of participants in the script (customer, waiter, cook, cashier), what is typically required for the script to be initiated (the customer is hungry), the different physical items that will be manipulated by the script (food, table, money, menu, tip), and, crucially, the stereotypical sequence of events that are associated with the script – in Figure 6, these events are numbered 1 to 10. Schank and Abelson speculated that such a script might be used as part of an AI program to understand stories. They suggested that stories become interesting (funny, frightening, surprising) when events in the story *differ* from the stereotypical script. For example, a funny story might include a situation where the script stalls after step 4: the customer orders food, but it never arrives. A crime story might omit step 9: the customer orders and eats food, but leaves the restaurant without paying. There were several attempts to build systems that could understand stories using scripts as their basis, although with limited success.[3]

Another scheme that attracted a lot of attention was **semantic nets**.[4] Semantic nets are such an intuitive and natural scheme that they are regularly reinvented in the present day – indeed, if you were asked to invent a knowledge representation scheme, then I think it's quite possible you would come up with something like it yourself. Figure 7 shows a simple semantic net, which represents some knowledge about me (my date of birth, place of residence, gender and children) as well as some more general knowledge about the world (a female human is a person, a cathedral is both a building and a place of worship, and so on).

At one point in the emergence of knowledge-based AI, it seemed that everyone had their own personal scheme for

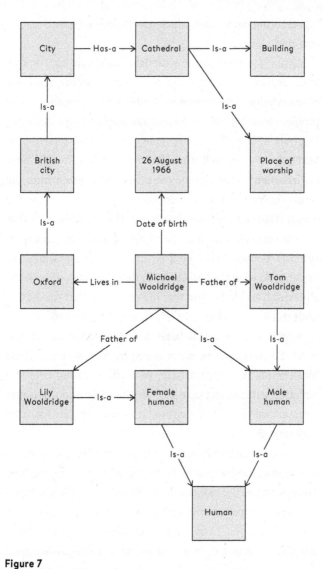

Figure 7

A simple semantic network, capturing some information about me, my children and the place I live in.

representing knowledge, which was incompatible with everyone else's.

Although rules became established as the de facto knowledge representation scheme for expert systems, the issue of knowledge representation troubled AI researchers. One problem was that rules were just too simple to capture knowledge about complex environments. Rules of the type used in MYCIN were not well suited to capturing knowledge about environments that change over time, or contain multiple actors (human or AI), or where there is uncertainty about the actual state of the environment. Another problem was that the various schemes used to capture knowledge in expert systems seemed, well, a bit *arbitrary*. Researchers wanted to understand what the knowledge in their expert systems actually *meant*, and to be sure that the reasoning that the system undertook was robust. In short, they wanted to provide a proper mathematical basis for knowledge-based systems. The issues were summarized by AI researcher Drew McDermott in a 1978 article, with the punning title 'No Notation without Denotation'.[5] 'It is not just important that a system be correct,' he wrote, 'it is also crucial that it be understood.'

The solution that began to emerge in the late 1970s was to use **logic** as a unifying scheme for knowledge representation. To understand the role that logic played in knowledge-based systems, it helps to know a little about what logic is and why it was developed. Logic was developed in order to understand reasoning and, in particular, what distinguishes good (**sound**) **reasoning** from bad (**unsound**) **reasoning**. Let's see some examples of reasoning, both sound and unsound.

All humans are mortal.

Emma is human.

Therefore, Emma is mortal.

This example illustrates a particular pattern of logical reasoning called a **syllogism**. And I hope you will agree that the reasoning here is perfectly reasonable: if all humans are mortal, and Emma is human, then Emma is indeed mortal.

Now consider the following example:

All professors are good-looking.

Michael is a professor.

Therefore, Michael is good-looking.

You may be less comfortable with this example, because while you were happy to accept the statement 'All humans are mortal', you would probably balk at the statement 'All professors are good-looking' – it obviously isn't true. However, from a *logical* point of view, there is nothing at all wrong with the reasoning in this example: it is perfectly sound. If it was indeed the case that all professors are good-looking, and it was also the case that Michael is a professor, then it would be entirely reasonable to conclude that Michael was good-looking. Logic is not concerned with whether the statements you start from (the **premises**) are *actually* true or not, simply whether the pattern of reasoning you use, and the conclusions you draw, would be reasonable if the premises were indeed true.

The next example, however, shows some unsound reasoning:

All students are hard-working.

Sophie is a student.

Therefore, Sophie is rich.

The pattern of reasoning here is not sound because it is not reasonable to draw the conclusion that Sophie is rich given the two premises. Sophie *may* be rich, but that isn't the point, which is that you can't reasonably derive this conclusion from the two given premises.

So, logic is all about patterns of reasoning, of which syllogisms as shown in the first two examples above are perhaps the simplest useful examples. Logic tells us when we can safely draw conclusions from premises, and the process through which this is done is called **deduction**.

Syllogisms were introduced by the Ancient Greek philosopher Aristotle, and for more than a millennium they provided the main framework for logical analysis. However, they capture a very limited form of logical reasoning, completely inappropriate for many forms of argument. From early on, mathematicians have had a strong interest in trying to understand the general principles of sound reasoning, as mathematics is, ultimately, all about reasoning: the job of a mathematician is to derive new mathematical knowledge from existing knowledge – making deductions, in other words. By the nineteenth century, mathematicians were troubled about the principles of what they were doing. What does it mean, they wondered, for something to be true? How can we be sure that a mathematical proof represents a reasonable deduction? How can we even be sure that $1 + 1 = 2$?

From about the mid-nineteenth century, mathematicians started to investigate these questions in earnest. In Germany, Gottlob Frege developed a general logical calculus within which we can for the first time start to see something resembling the full framework of modern mathematical logic. Augustus de Morgan in London, and George Boole in Cork, Ireland, started to show how the same kinds of techniques that are used for problems of algebra can be applied to logical reasoning. (In 1854, Boole published some of his findings under the gloriously immodest title of *Laws of Thought*.)

By the start of the twentieth century, the basic framework of modern logic had been largely established, and a logical system had emerged that to the present day provides the language that underpins almost all work in mathematics. The system goes by the name of **first-order logic**. First-order logic is the *lingua franca* of mathematics and reasoning. Within this one framework we can capture all the types of reasoning studied by Aristotle, Frege, de Morgan, Boole and others. And in just the same way, within AI, first-order logic seemed to offer a unifying framework for the endlessly varied and mostly ad hoc knowledge representation schemes that were floating around at the time.

The paradigm of **logic-based AI** was thus born, and one of its earliest and most influential advocates was John McCarthy – the same John McCarthy that hosted the Dartmouth Summer School in 1956, and gave the field its name. McCarthy described his vision for logical AI as follows:[6]

> The idea is that an agent can represent knowledge of its world, its goals and the current situation by sentences in logic and decide what to do by [deducing] that a certain action or course of action is appropriate to achieve its goals.

The 'agent' here is the AI system; the 'sentences in logic' that McCarthy refers to are precisely the statements like 'All humans are mortal' and 'All professors are good-looking' that we saw above. First-order logic provides a rich, mathematically precise language with which such statements may be expressed.

A (rather stylized) illustration of McCarthy's vision for logical AI is shown in Figure 8. We see a robot operating in a Blocks World type of environment. The robot is equipped with a robot arm, and with a perception system which is used to obtain information about its environment. Within the robot, we see a logical description of the environment, with statements like On(A, Table), On(C, A), and so on. These statements are in fact expressions of first-order logic, and for the scenario shown in Figure 8, it is pretty obvious what they are intended to mean:

- On(x, y) means that the object x is on top of object y;
- Clear(x) means that there is nothing on top of object x; and
- Empty(x) means that x is empty.

In logical AI, one of the key tasks is to come up with a vocabulary of expressions like On(x, y), Clear(x) and so on, in order to be able to represent the scenario at hand.

The role of the internal logical representation for the robot is to capture all the information that the agent has about its environment. It became common to refer to this representation as the **beliefs** of the system. The fact that the robot's belief system contains the expression 'On(A, Table)' is then taken to mean that 'The robot believes that block A is on the table'. We need to be careful with such terminology, though. While it is helpful to use a vocabulary that we are familiar with when we populate the robot's belief system ('On(x, y)'

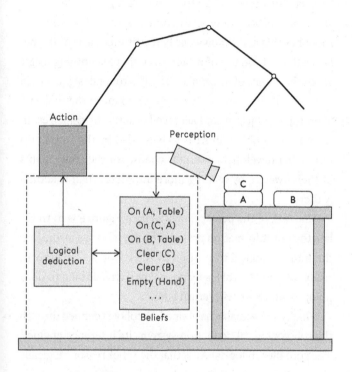

Action

Perception

On (A, Table)
On (C, A)
On (B, Table)
Clear (C)
Clear (B)
Empty (Hand)
. . .

C
A
B

Logical
deduction

Beliefs

Figure 8
McCarthy's vision for logic-based AI. A logic-based AI system
explicitly represents its beliefs about the environment via logical
statements, and intelligent decision making is broken down into a
process of logical reasoning.

is pretty self-explanatory for human readers), the *meaning* of an expression such as this, when present in the robot's belief base, is ultimately derived from the *role it plays in the behaviour of the robot*. It only really counts as a belief if, when the robot has this in its knowledge base, the robot acts as if it believes that x is on top of y. Moreover, there is nothing magic about the choice of terms like 'On'. The robot designer could just as easily have used 'Qwerty(x, y)' to mean that object x is on top of object y, and achieved exactly the same result. A common problem in AI is to be misled by the suggestive terms that developers naturally choose for the components of their system, by reading more into them than is actually there.

The task of the perception system in Figure 8 is to translate the raw information provided by the robot's sensors into the internal logical form used by the robot. As we have already mentioned, this is by no means a trivial thing to do, a point to which we will return later.

Finally, the actual behaviour of the robot is defined through the robot's logical deduction system (its inference engine). The core idea in logical AI is that the robot reasons logically about what it should do: it *deduces* what it should do next.

Overall, we can envisage the robot continually operating on a cycle of observing its environment through its sensors, updating its beliefs about its environment, deducing what the next action to perform should be, performing this action and then starting the whole process again.

It is important to understand why logic-based AI was so influential. Perhaps the most important reason is that it makes everything so *pure*. The whole problem of building an intelligent system is reduced to one of constructing a logical description of what the robot should do. And such a system is *transparent*: to understand *why* it did something, we can just look at its beliefs and its reasoning.

There are, I think, other, less obvious reasons why the logical approach was so influential. For one thing, it is appealing to imagine that reasoning provides the basis for the decisions that *we* make. And when we reason, we seem to do so in *sentences*: when contemplating the merits of various courses of action, we might have a mental conversation with ourselves, discussing the pros and cons of each. Logic-based AI seems to reflect this idea.

Programs as Logic

Throughout the late 1970s through to the mid-1980s the paradigm of logic-based AI grew in influence: by the early 1980s, it was the mainstream of AI. It was so influential that researchers began to speculate that it might be useful not just in AI, but across the whole of computing. **Logic programming**, as it became known, proposed to fundamentally change the way that people wrote computer programs. The sales pitch for logic programming went something like this: Programming is fiddly, time-consuming and error-prone, because it forces us to think down to the level of detailed recipes, which are hard for people to cope with. Logic programming frees us from this curse. With logic programming, you use the power of logic to express what you know about the problem – logical deduction will do the rest. There would be no need to write a recipe. A logic program would, in effect, deduce what it needed to do.

Logic programming was realized in an influential language called **PROLOG**,[7] which is probably the most prominent legacy of the era of logic-based AI – the language is still widely taught and used today. The language came about largely through the work of Bob Kowalski, an American-born researcher working in the UK, and two French researchers, Alain Colmerauer and Philippe Roussel, who were based in Marseille. In the early 1970s, Kowalski realized that rules expressed in first-order logic could form the basis of an actual programming language. While Kowalski had the idea for the new language, he didn't work out the details – this was done by Colmerauer and Roussel after Kowalski visited them in 1972.

PROLOG is a very intuitive language, so let's see an example. Here is how we might express the 'All humans are mortal' example that we saw earlier:

human(emma).
mortal(X) :- human(X).

The first line is a PROLOG 'fact', which expresses the fact that Emma is human. The second line is a PROLOG rule, which says that X is mortal if X is human.

To actually get PROLOG to do anything, we need to give it a goal. In this case, a relevant goal would be to try to determine whether Emma is mortal, which we would express as:

mortal(emma).

In presenting this as a goal to PROLOG, we are asking 'Is it the case that Emma is mortal?', or more specifically, 'Can you deduce that Emma is mortal, given the facts and rules you have been granted?' Provided with this goal, PROLOG uses logical deduction to establish that this is indeed the case.[8] (For a more in-depth explanation of PROLOG, have a look at Appendix B.)

The example above only hints at the power of PROLOG. For some problems, it turns out that you can write incredibly succinct and elegant PROLOG programs. The WARPLAN planning system, written by David Warren in 1974 which could solve planning problems including the Blocks World and far beyond that, required just 100 lines of PROLOG code;[9] writing the same system in a language like Python would be likely to require thousands of lines of code, and months of effort. Moreover, the programs you wrote in PROLOG were not just programs: *they were logical formulae.* Thus, programs in PROLOG looked like McCarthy's vision for logic-based AI.

Throughout the late 1970s and early 1980s, PROLOG rose in prominence, until it was challenging McCarthy's venerable LISP as the programming language of choice for AI hackers. In the early 1980s, it became the subject of massive investment by the Japanese government, in what was called the Fifth Generation Computer Systems Project. At the time, the Japanese economy was booming in comparison to the US and European economies – a cause of concern to US and European governments. But at the same time, the Japanese government was worried that, while Japanese industry was adept at refining and commercializing technology, it was much less successful at fundamental innovation, particularly in computing. The Fifth Generation project was intended to change this, establishing Japan as a centre of global computing innovation – and logic programming was one of the key technologies earmarked for investment. Some $400 million was ploughed into the Fifth Generation project over the next decade. But while it seems to have played an important role in building up Japan's computer science base, Japan's computing industry did not leapfrog past the USA as a consequence. And PROLOG did not take off as a general language for computing in the way that some in the logic programming community had believed it might.

While PROLOG didn't conquer the programming world, it would be wrong to call it a failure. After all, every day, across the world, programmers happily write productive PROLOG programs, and are grateful for the elegance and power of the language. But for me, the most important legacy of PROLOG is an intangible one: logic programming provides a *different way of thinking about computing* – a completely different perspective on computational problems and how to solve them. Generations of programmers have benefitted from this new perspective.

Cyc: The Ultimate Expert System

The so-called **Cyc project** was arguably the most famous experiment in the period of knowledge-based AI. Cyc was the brainchild of Doug Lenat, a gifted AI researcher who combined outstanding scientific ability with unwavering intellectual conviction and a decided ability to persuade others to buy into his vision. Lenat rose to prominence in the 1970s with a series of impressive AI systems, which in 1977 earned him the Computers and Thought Award, the most prestigious award that can be given to a young AI scientist.

In the early 1980s, Lenat became convinced that the

'Knowledge is power' doctrine had applications far beyond the construction of narrowly focused expert systems. He was convinced it provided the key to General AI – the Grand Dream. Here is what he wrote (with co-author Ramanathan Guha) in 1990:[10]

> We don't believe there is any short-cut to being intelligent, any yet-to-be-discovered Maxwell's equations of thought . . . [N]o powerful formalism can obviate the need for a lot of knowledge. By knowledge, we don't just mean dry, almanac-like or highly domain-specific facts. Rather, most of what we need to know to get by in the real world is . . . too commonsensical to be included in reference books; for example, animals live for a single solid interval of time, nothing can be in two places at once, animals don't like pain . . . Perhaps the hardest truth to face, one that AI has been trying to wriggle out of for 34 years, is that there is probably no elegant, effortless way to obtain this immense knowledge base. Rather, the bulk of the effort must (at least initially) be manual entry of assertion after assertion.

And so, in the mid-1980s, Lenat and colleagues set themselves the task of creating this 'immense knowledge base', and the Cyc project was born.

The ambition in the Cyc project was mind-boggling. To operate as Lenat envisaged, Cyc's knowledge base would need a complete description of 'consensus reality' – the world as we understand it. Pause for a moment to reflect on this challenge. Somebody would have to explicitly tell Cyc that, for example:

an object dropped on Planet Earth would fall to the ground,
and that it would stop moving when it hit the ground;

but that an object dropped in space would not fall;

a plane that runs out of fuel will crash;

people tend to die in plane crashes;

it is dangerous to eat mushrooms you don't recognize;

red taps usually produce hot water, while blue taps usually
produce cold water;

. . . and so on.

All the everyday knowledge that a reasonably educated person unwittingly carries with them would need to be *explicitly* written down in Cyc's own special language and fed to the system.

Lenat estimated the project would require 200 person years of effort, and the bulk of this was expected to be in the manual entry of knowledge – telling Cyc all about our world, and our understanding of it. Lenat was optimistic that, before too long, Cyc would be able to educate itself. A system capable of educating itself in the way Lenat envisaged would imply that General AI was effectively solved. Thus, the **Cyc hypothesis** was that the problem of General AI was primarily one of knowledge, and that it could be solved by a suitable knowledge-based system. The Cyc hypothesis was a bet; a high-stakes bet, but one that, if it proved successful, would have world-changing consequences.

One of the paradoxes of research funding is that, sometimes, it is the absurdly ambitious ideas that win out. Indeed, some research funding agencies go out of their way to encourage world-vaulting ambition over safe but plodding proposals. Perhaps this was the case with Cyc. In any case, in

1984, Cyc received funding from the Microelectronics and Computer Consortium (MCC) in Austin, Texas, and the project was launched.

Of course, it didn't work.

The first problem was that nobody had ever tried to organize the whole knowledge of human consensus reality before – where on earth do you *begin*? For a start, you need to agree all the vocabulary that you are going to use, and how all the terms you use relate to one another. This problem – defining your basic terms and concepts, and organizing your knowledge around them, goes by the grand name of **ontological engineering**, and the ontological engineering challenge posed by Cyc was exponentially larger than any other project that had been attempted previously. Lenat and colleagues rapidly discovered that their original ideas about how to structure the knowledge that Cyc would use, and the way in which this knowledge would be captured, were simply too naive and imprecise, and, some way into the project, they found they had to start again.

Despite these setbacks, a decade into the project, Lenat was still full of cheerful optimism, and in April 1994 his optimism caught the attention of Vaughan Pratt, a computer science professor at Stanford University.[11] Pratt is one of computing's leading theoreticians, used to thinking about the fundamental nature of computing using the precise and pedantic language of mathematics. He was intrigued by a presentation on Cyc, and asked for a demo. Lenat agreed.

In advance of the visit, Pratt wrote to Lenat to outline his expectations. He gave a list of the kinds of capabilities he was expecting to see, based on published scientific articles about

Cyc. 'I'm assuming the demo will work best if my expectations are well matched to Cyc's current capabilities,' Pratt
wrote. 'If I arrive expecting too much I may go away disappointed, but if my expectations are set too low [. . .] we may
spend too long on things that don't do justice to Cyc's full
range of abilities.' He did not receive a reply.

Pratt went to see Cyc on 15 April 1994. The demonstration
itself started with some straightforward illustrations of modest
but genuine technical accomplishments that Cyc was capable
of – identifying some inconsistencies in a database that required some reasoning on behalf of Cyc. So far, so good. Then
Lenat started to stretch Cyc's capabilities a little. The second
demonstration involved Cyc retrieving images according
to requirements that were written in ordinary English. The
query 'someone relaxing' resulted in a picture of three men
in beachwear holding surfboards – Cyc had correctly made a
link between surfboards, surfing and relaxing. Pratt scribbled
down the chain of reasoning that Cyc took to get to this link.
It required nearly 20 rules, involving some that seem slightly
strange to us – 'All mammals are vertebrates' was one of the
rules required to get there. (The version of Cyc that Pratt
saw had half a million rules.)

Pratt then wanted to explore one of the most central features of Cyc: its practical knowledge of our world. For example, Pratt asked whether Cyc knew that bread was food.
His host translated the query into the rule language used
by Cyc. 'True,' responded Cyc. 'Does Cyc consider bread to
be a drink?' asked Pratt. This time Cyc got stuck. They tried
telling it explicitly that bread is not a drink. It still didn't
work: 'after a bit of fiddling we dropped this question', Pratt

reported. They went on. Cyc seemed to know that various activities caused death, but not that starvation was a cause of death. In fact, Cyc didn't seem to know anything about starvation. Pratt went on to explore questions about planets, the sky and cars, but it rapidly became clear that Cyc's knowledge was sketchy and unpredictable. For example, it didn't know that the sky was blue, or that cars typically have four wheels.

Based on his expectations raised by Lenat's presentation, Pratt had prepared a list of more than a hundred questions to ask Cyc, which he hoped would start to explore the extent of Cyc's common-sense understanding of our world. For example:

> If Tom is 3 inches taller than Dick, and Dick is 2 inches
>> taller than Harry, how much taller is Tom than Harry?
> Can two siblings each be taller than the other?
> Which is wetter, land or sea?
> Can a car drive backwards? Can a plane fly backwards?
> How long can people go without air?

These are all pretty basic questions to ask about our world, but they could not be meaningfully asked of or answered by Cyc. Reflecting on his experience, Pratt was careful with his critique of Cyc. Perhaps Cyc had made some progress towards the goal of general intelligence, he speculated; the problem was, it was impossible to tell *how far*, because Cyc's knowledge was so patchy and unevenly distributed.

What can we learn from Cyc about the road to general artificial intelligence? If we ignore the inflated expectations, then Cyc stands up as a technically sophisticated exercise in large-scale knowledge engineering. It didn't deliver General

AI, but it taught us a lot about the development and organization of large knowledge-based systems. And to be strictly accurate, the Cyc hypothesis – that General AI is essentially a problem of knowledge, which can be solved via a suitable knowledge-based system – has been neither proved nor disproved yet. The fact that Cyc didn't deliver General AI doesn't demonstrate that the hypothesis was false, merely that this particular approach didn't work. It is conceivable that a different attempt to tackle General AI through knowledge-based approaches *might* deliver the goods.

In some ways, Cyc was just ahead of its time. Three decades after the Cyc project began, Google announced the **knowledge graph** – a large knowledge base, which Google use to augment their search services. The knowledge graph has a vast array of facts about real-world entities (places, people, movies, books, events), which are used to enrich the search results that Google finds. When you type in a query to Google, it typically contains names and other terms which refer to real things in the world. For example, suppose you search Google with the query 'Madonna'. A simple web search would respond with web pages that contain the word 'Madonna'. But a search engine can be much more helpful if it understands that the character string 'Madonna' refers to a popular singer (real name: Madonna Louise Ciccone). So, if you search for 'Madonna' on Google, you will find that the response for your query includes an array of information about the singer, which will answer most routine questions that people ask about her (date and place of birth, children, most popular recordings and so on). One key difference between Cyc and the Google knowledge graph is that knowledge in the knowledge graph is not hand-coded, but is automatically extracted from web pages such as Wikipedia – in 2017, it was claimed the system contained about 70 billion facts about 500 million entities. Of course, the knowledge graph does not aspire to general intelligence – and it isn't clear to what extent it involves actual reasoning of the kind that was so central to the knowledge-based systems view of the world. But, nevertheless, I think there is some Cyc DNA in the knowledge graph.

However we might try to justify it retrospectively, the sad fact is that Cyc's main role in AI history is as an extreme example of AI hype, which very publicly failed to live up to the grand predictions that were made for it. Lenat's role in AI has been mythologized in a piece of computing folklore. A 'micro-Lenat', so the joke goes, is the scientific unit for measuring how bogus something is. Why a *micro*-Lenat? Because nothing could be as bogus as a whole Lenat.

Cracks Appear

Like so many versions of AI that are beautiful in theory, knowledge-based AI proved to be limited in practice. The approach struggled even with some reasoning tasks which seem absurdly trivial to us. Consider the task of **common-sense reasoning**, one classic example of which is given by the following scenario:[12]

> You are told Tweety is a bird, so you conclude Tweety can fly. Later, though, you are told that Tweety is a penguin, so you retract your earlier conclusion.

At first sight, it looks like this problem ought to be easy to capture in logic. It looks, in fact, very much like the syllogisms that we saw earlier should do the job – as long as our AI system had the knowledge 'if x is a bird then x can fly', then given the information that 'x is a bird', it should be able to deduce that 'x can fly'. Well, so far, so good. The difficulty comes with what happens next, when we are told that Tweety is a penguin. Then, we need to retract – take back – our earlier conclusion that Tweety can fly. But logic cannot cope with this. In logic, adding more information never eliminates any of the conclusions you obtained earlier. But that is precisely what is going on here: the additional information ('Tweety is a penguin') causes us to eliminate our earlier conclusion ('Tweety can fly').

Another problem in common-sense reasoning arises when we encounter contradictions. Here is a standard example from the literature:[13]

> Quakers are pacifists;
> Republicans are not pacifists;
> Nixon is a Republican and a Quaker.

Try to capture this scenario in logic and a disaster ensues, because we end up concluding that Nixon both is and is not a pacifist – a contradiction. Logic fails utterly in the presence of such contradictions: it cannot cope, and can tell us nothing useful at all. Yet this is the kind of contradictory situation we all encounter every day of our lives. We are told that taxes are good and we are told that taxes are bad; we are told that wine is good for us and that wine is bad for us; and so on. It's ubiquitous. The problem once again is that we are trying to use logic for something it was not intended for – in mathematics, if you encounter a contradiction then that means you made a mistake.

These problems seem almost comically trivial, but they were major research challenges for knowledge-based AI in the late 1980s – they attracted some of the smartest people in the field. And they were never really solved.

It also turned out to be harder to build and deploy successful expert systems than it first appeared. The main difficulty was what became known as the **knowledge elicitation** problem. Put simply, this is the problem of extracting knowledge from human experts, and encoding it in the form of rules. Human experts often find it hard to articulate the expertise they have – the fact that they are good at something does not mean that they can tell you how they actually do it. And human experts, it transpired, were not necessarily all that eager to share their expertise. After all, if your company had a program that could do what you do, why would they keep you? Concerns about AI replacing people are nothing new.

By the end of the 1980s, the expert systems boom was over. The technology of knowledge-based systems could not be said to have failed, because many successful expert systems were built in this period, and many more have been built since. But once again, it seemed, the reality of what AI had actually produced had not lived up to the hype.

Robots and Rationality

Those who will not reason, perish in the act.
Those who will not act, perish for that reason.
— W. H. Auden

In his 1962 book *The Structure of Scientific Revolutions*, the philosopher Thomas Kuhn argued that, as scientific understanding advances, there will be times when established scientific orthodoxy can no longer hold up under the strain of manifest failures. At such times of crisis, he argued, a new orthodoxy will emerge and replace the established order: the scientific paradigm will change. By the late 1980s, the boom days of expert systems were over, and another AI crisis was looming. Once again, the AI community was criticized for overselling ideas, promising too much, and delivering too little. This time, the paradigm being questioned was not just the 'Knowledge is power' doctrine that had driven the expert systems boom, but the basic assumptions that had underpinned AI since the 1950s, symbolic AI in particular. The fiercest critics of AI in the late 1980s, though, were not outsiders, but came from within the field itself.

The most eloquent and influential critic of the prevailing AI paradigm was the Australian-born roboticist Rodney

Brooks. Born in 1954, Brooks seemed like an unlikely candidate to be a vocal critic of AI. He had studied and worked at the three leading centres of AI research: Stanford University, Massachusetts Institute of Technology and Carnegie Mellon University. Brooks' main interest was in building robots that could carry out useful tasks in the real world. Throughout the early 1980s, he began to be frustrated with the then-prevailing idea that the key to building such robots was to encode knowledge about the world in a form that could be used by the robot as the basis for reasoning and decision-making. He took up a faculty position at MIT in the mid-1980s and began his campaign to rethink AI at its most fundamental level.

The Brooksian Revolution

To understand Brooks' arguments, it is helpful to return to the Blocks World. Recall that the Blocks World is a simulated domain consisting of a table top, on which are stacked a number of different objects – the task is to rearrange the objects in certain specified ways. At first sight, the Blocks World seems perfectly reasonable as a proving ground for AI techniques: it sounds like a warehouse environment, and I dare say exactly this point has been made in many grant proposals over the years. But for Brooks, and those that came to adopt his ideas, the Blocks World was bogus, for the simple reason that it is *simulated*, and the simulation glosses over everything that would be difficult about a task like arranging blocks in the real world. A system that can solve problems in the Blocks World, however smart it might appear to be, would be of no value in a warehouse, because the *real* difficulty in the physical world comes from dealing with issues like perception, which are completely ignored in the Blocks World. The Blocks World was held up as a symbol of all that was wrong and intellectually bankrupt about the AI orthodoxy of the 1970s and 1980s. This did not stop research into the Blocks World, however: you can still regularly find research papers using it to the present day; I confess to have written some myself.

Brooks set out his stall with three key principles. Firstly, he was convinced that meaningful progress in AI could only be achieved with systems that were **situated** in the real world: that is, systems that were directly in some environment, perceiving it and acting upon it. Secondly, he argued that intelligent behaviour can be generated without explicit knowledge and reasoning of the kind promoted by knowledge-based AI in general, and logic-based AI in particular. Finally, he argued that intelligence is an **emergent property** that arises from the interaction of an entity in its environment.

Brooks made his case in a satirical parable, published in 1991:[1]

Suppose it is the 1890s. Artificial Flight (AF) is the glamour subject in science, engineering and venture capital circles. A bunch of AF researchers are miraculously transported by a time machine to the 1980s for a few hours. They spend the whole time in the passenger cabin of a commercial passenger Boeing 747 on a medium duration flight. Returned to the 1890s, they feel invigorated, knowing that AF is possible on a grand scale. They immediately set to work duplicating what they have seen. They make great progress in designing pitched seats, double pane windows and know that if only they can figure out those weird 'plastics' they will have their grail within their grasp.

The point here is that, when we contemplate *human* intelligence, we tend to focus on its more glamorous and tangible aspects: reasoning, for example, or problem solving, or playing chess. *Intellectual* activities. These are the things that academics tend to value, and want to be good at – so the fact that the AI research agenda was skewed towards such activities was perhaps a consequence of this prejudice. Reasoning and problem solving might have a role in intelligent behaviour, but Brooks and others argued that they were not the right *starting point* from which to build AI.[2]

Returning to Brooks' parable, he also took issue with the 'divide and conquer' assumption that had underpinned AI since its earliest days: the idea that progress in AI research could be made by decomposing intelligent behaviour into its constituent components (reasoning, learning, perception), with no attempt to consider how these components worked together –

> [The artificial flight researchers] agree that the project is too big to be worked on as a single entity and that they will need to become specialists in different areas. After all, they had asked questions of fellow passengers on their flight and discovered that the Boeing Company employed over 6,000 people to build such an aeroplane. [. . .] Everyone is busy but there is not a lot of communication between the groups.

Finally, he pointed out the naivety of ignoring the issue of 'weight'. His parable tells us that:

The people making the passenger seats used the finest solid steel available as the framework. There was some muttering that perhaps they should use tubular steel to save weight, but the general consensus was that if such an obviously big and heavy airplane could fly then clearly there was no problem with weight.

The 'weight' which Brooks alludes to here is *computational effort*. In particular, he took issue with the idea that all decision-making processes should be reduced to ones such as logical reasoning, which require exorbitant amounts of computer-processing time and memory.

The title Brooks chose for his parable was 'Intelligence Without Representation'. As an undergraduate studying AI in the mid-1980s, in the middle of the expert systems boom, I had been taught that knowledge representation and reasoning were central to AI. Brooks' article seemed to deny everything I thought I knew about my field. It felt like heresy. In 1991, a young colleague returning from a large AI conference in Australia told me, wide-eyed with excitement, about a shouting match that had developed between PhD students from Stanford (McCarthy's home institute) and MIT (Brooks'). On one side, there was established tradition: logic, knowledge representation and reasoning. On the other, the outspoken, disrespectful adherents of a new AI movement – not just turning their backs on hallowed tradition, but loudly ridiculing it.

While Brooks was probably the highest-profile advocate of the new direction, he was by no means alone. Many other researchers were reaching similar conclusions, and while they did not necessarily agree on the smaller details, there were a number of commonly recurring themes in their different approaches.

The most important was the idea that knowledge and reasoning were deposed from their role at the heart of AI. McCarthy's vision of an AI system that maintained a central symbolic, logical model of its environment (as in Figure 8), around which all the activities of intelligence orbited, was firmly rejected. Some moderate voices argued that reasoning and representation still had a role to play, although perhaps not a *leading* role; but more extreme voices rejected them completely.

It is worth exploring this point in a little more detail. Remember that the McCarthy view of logical AI assumes that an AI system will continually follow a particular loop: perceiving its environment, reasoning about what to do and then acting. But, in a system that operates in this way, the system is *decoupled* from the environment.

Take a second to stop reading this book, and look around. You may be in an airport departure lounge, a coffee shop, on a train, in your home, or lying by a river in the sunshine. As you look around, you are not *disconnected* from your environment and the changes that the environment is undergoing. You are *in the moment*. Your perception – and your actions – are embedded within, and in tune with your environment. Of course, there will be occasions where you pause to reason, and disconnect from your environment, but these situations are the exception, rather than the norm.

The problem is that the knowledge-based approach doesn't seem to reflect this. Suppose I present you with a robot designed according to the McCarthy model of logical AI. The robot continually operates through a continual *perceive–reason–act* loop, processing and interpreting the data it receives from its sensors and using this perceptual information to update its beliefs; reasoning about what to do; performing the action it then selects; and starting its decision loop again. I proudly tell you that I designed the robot so that it always chooses the *best* action to perform, for whatever task it is that the robot is supposed to do. Let's consider the way the robot operates over time – see Figure 9.

At time t_0 through to time t_1, the robot senses its environment, then it takes from t_1 to t_2 to process this sensor data and update the robot's beliefs. Between t_2 and t_3 the robot reasons about what action to perform, and finally, at time t_3, the robot starts to act upon its decision.

Now, the claim was that the robot always made the *best* decision about what to perform; but is the action that it chooses the best thing at time t_1 or time t_3? The information

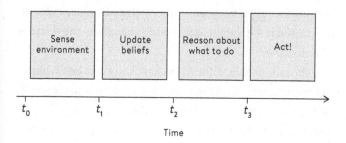

Figure 9
The robot chooses the best time to perform. But *when* is it the best action to perform? At the time at which it observes its environment or at the time when it finally concludes which action to perform?

the robot has about its environment was obtained no later than t_1, but the robot only starts to act on this information at t_3. This approach is unrealistic in practice, but, perhaps surprisingly, until the late 1980s, it was implicit in almost all AI research: AI had focused on building machines which could make the best decision *in principle* (assuming the world doesn't change while figuring out what to do) rather than the best decision *in practice*.[3]

For these reasons, another key theme at the time was the idea that there should be a close-coupled relationship between the *situation* that the system finds itself in, and the *behaviour* that it exhibits.

Behavioural AI

If Brooks had been just another critic of AI, it is unlikely that his ideas would have gained much traction. After all, by the mid-1980s, the AI community was accustomed to ignoring its critics, and carrying on regardless. What raised Brooks' critiques from being yet another Dreyfus-style attack was that he convincingly articulated an alternative paradigm, and demonstrated it with some impressive systems in the decades that followed.

The new paradigm for AI became known as **behavioural AI** because, as we shall see, it emphasized the role of the specific individual behaviours that contribute to the overall operation of an intelligent system. The particular approach adopted by Brooks was called the **subsumption architecture**, and of all the approaches from the period, this seems to have had the most lasting impact. So, let's see how the subsumption architecture can be used to build a modest but useful robotic application: a vacuum cleaning robot. (Brooks was a founder of the company iRobot, manufacturer of the popular Roomba robot vacuum cleaners, the design of which was based on his work.)[4] Our robot will be required to travel around a building, avoiding obstacles and vacuuming when it detects dirt – when the robot has a low battery, or its dirt container is full, we want it to return to its docking station and shut down.

The basic methodology for the subsumption architecture requires identifying the individual component behaviours that are required for the robot. We then start to build our robot by getting it to exhibit one of the behaviours, and then progressively add further behaviours. The key challenge is to think about how these behaviours are interrelated, and to organize them in such a way that the robot is exhibiting the right behaviour at the right time. This typically requires experimenting with the robot extensively, to ensure that the behaviours are organized in the right way.

Our vacuum cleaning robot requires six behaviours:

- **Avoid obstacles:** If I detect an obstacle, then change direction, choosing a new direction at random.
- **Shut down:** If I am at the docking station and have a low battery, then shut down.
- **Empty dirt:** If I am at the docking station and am carrying dirt, then empty dirt container.
- **Head to dock:** If the battery is low or dirt container is full, then head to docking station.
- **Vacuum:** If I detect dirt at the current location then switch on vacuum.

- **Walk randomly:** choose a direction at random and move in that direction.

The next challenge is to organize these behaviours. For this, Brooks suggested using what he called a **subsumption hierarchy** – see Figure 10. The subsumption hierarchy determines the precedence for behaviours: those that appear lower in the hierarchy take precedence over those that appear further up. Thus, obstacle avoidance is the highest priority behaviour: the robot will *always* avoid obstacles if it ever encounters one. It is not difficult to see how these behaviours, organized into the hierarchy in Figure 10, will solve the problem: the robot will search for dirt, and vacuum when it finds dirt, as long as it is not low on power or the dirt container is full; it will return to its docking station if the battery is low or the dirt container is full.

Although the behaviours in our vacuum cleaning robot look like rules, they are in fact much simpler. To implement them within a robot requires nothing like as much effort as logical reasoning. In fact, they can be directly implemented in the form of simple electrical circuits, and as a consequence, our robot will react to changing sensor data very quickly: it will be in tune with its environment.

In the decades that followed, Brooks built a string of influential robots, using the subsumption architecture as the basic development framework. His Genghis robot, for example, which now resides in the Smithsonian Air and Space Museum, used 57 behaviours arranged into a subsumption architecture to control a six-legged mobile robot.[5] It would have been ludicrously hard to build Genghis using knowledge-based

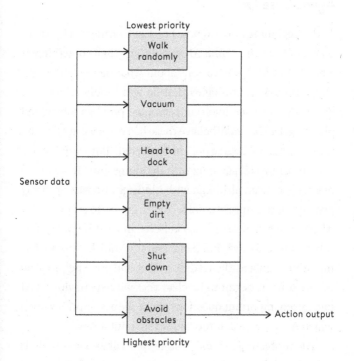

Figure 10
A simple subsumption hierarchy for a robot vacuum cleaner.

AI techniques – if it had been possible at all. These developments propelled robotics back into the mainstream of AI, after decades on the sidelines.

Agent-based AI

At the beginning of the 1990s, I met one of the chief protagonists of the behavioural AI revolution – then something of a hero of mine. I was curious about what he really thought about the AI technologies that he was loudly rejecting – knowledge representation and reasoning, problem solving and planning. Did he *really* believe these had no place at all in the future of AI? 'Of course not,' he answered. 'But I won't make a name for myself agreeing with the status quo.' It was a depressing answer, although with hindsight he was probably just trying to impress a naive young graduate student. But whether this professor really believed in what he was doing, others certainly did, and behavioural AI quickly became as mired in dogma as the traditions that had gone before. And before long, it began to be clear that while behavioural AI had raised important questions about the assumptions upon which AI was based, it too had severe limitations.

The problem was *it didn't scale up*. If all we want to do is to build a robot to vacuum an apartment, then behavioural AI is all we need. A vacuum-cleaning robot doesn't need to reason or be able to converse in English or solve complex problems. Because it doesn't need to do those things, we can build autonomous robot vacuum cleaners using the subsumption architecture (or something like it – there were lots of similar approaches at the time) and we will get a beautifully efficient solution. But while behavioural AI was very successful for some problems – mainly robotics – it provided no silver bullet for AI. It is hard to design behavioural systems with more than just a few behaviours, because understanding the possible interactions between behaviours becomes very difficult. Building systems using behavioural approaches was a black art – the only way to really know whether such a system was going to work was to try it out, and this was time-consuming, costly and unpredictable. And the solutions developed with a behavioural approach, beautifully efficient as they were, tended to be minutely tailored to a very specific problem. It was hard to take what had been learned from solving one problem and to apply it in another.

Brooks was correct to point out that capabilities such as knowledge representation and reasoning are not the right foundations upon which to build intelligent behaviour, and his robots demonstrated what could be achieved with purely behavioural approaches. But the dogmatic insistence that reasoning and knowledge representation have no role to play was, I think, a misstep. There *are* situations that naturally call for reasoning (whether strictly logical or otherwise), and to try to deny this makes no more sense than trying to build a vacuum cleaning robot that decides what to do by logical deduction.

While some proponents of the new AI took a hard-line view – anything like logical representation and reasoning were strictly *verboten* – others adopted a more moderate line, and it is this more moderate line that seems to have prevailed through to the present day. Moderates accepted the key lessons of behavioural AI, but argued that the right solution was a *combination* of behavioural and reasoning approaches. A new direction for AI began to emerge, which took on board the key lessons of Brooks, while at the same time embracing what had previously proved to be successful in AI's reasoning and representation heritage.

Once again the focus of activity in AI began to change, away from *disembodied* AI systems like expert systems and logical reasoners, towards building **agents**. An agent was intended to be an AI system that was 'complete' in the sense that it was a self-contained, autonomous entity, situated in some environment and carrying out some specific task on behalf of a user. An agent was supposed to provide a complete, integrated set of capabilities, rather than just some isolated disembodied capability like logical reasoning. By focusing on building *complete* intelligent agents, rather than just the *components* of intelligence, it was hoped that AI could avoid the fallacy that so irked Brooks – the idea that AI can succeed by separating out the components of intelligent behaviour (reasoning, learning and so on) and developing these in isolation from one another.

The agent-based view of AI was directly influenced by behavioural AI, but softened the message. The movement began to emerge in the early 1990s. It took the community a while to agree on what they were really talking about when they talked about 'agents', but by the mid-1990s, a consensus emerged that agents had to have three important capabilities. Firstly, they had to be reactive: they had to be attuned to their environment, and able to adapt their behaviour appropriately when changes in the environment demanded it. Secondly, they had to be proactive: capable of systematically working to achieve their given task on behalf of their user. Finally, agents were social: capable of working with other agents when required. The Golden Age of AI had emphasized proactive behaviour – planning and problem solving; while behavioural AI had emphasized the importance of being reactive – embodied in and attuned to the environment. Agent-based AI demanded both, and in addition threw something new into the mix: the idea that agents would have to work with other agents, and for this, they would need *social* skills – the ability not just to communicate, but to cooperate, coordinate and negotiate with other agents in the further- ance of their tasks.

It was this latter consideration – that agents need to be *social* – that marked out the agent-based AI paradigm from those that had preceded it. With hindsight, it seems some- what strange that it took AI so long to start seriously thinking about how AI systems might interact with each other, and what issues would arise when they did so. While the Turing test emphasized a kind of social ability, this was the ability to interact with people via natural languages like English and engage in ordinary conversation. In agent-based AI, commu- nication with *people* was not the main concern, whereas the idea that agents would work with *other agents* was.

A typical design for an agent is shown in Figure 11. This agent architecture, called **TouringMachines**,[6] divided over- all control of the agent into three sub-systems. The reactive sub-system operated like a Brooksian subsumption architec- ture: it was responsible for situations that required a quick response and no reasoning, such as obstacle avoidance. The planning sub-system was responsible for figuring out how to achieve the agent's goals; and the modelling layer handled interactions with other agents. The three control layers were

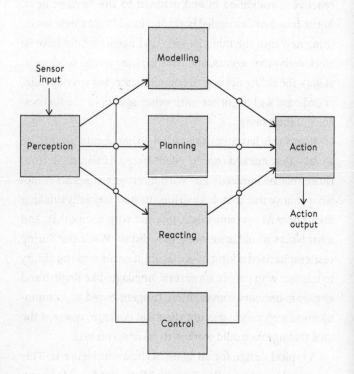

Figure 11
A typical agent's architecture: TouringMachines.

mediated by a control sub-system, which listened to the recommendations coming from each of the three layers and decided which recommendation to follow. This was often a very straightforward decision: if the reactive layer says 'STOP!', then you should probably listen. Many similar agent architectures were developed in the early 1990s.

HOMER: A Complete Agent

My favourite example of an agent from this time was **HOMER**, a simulated robot submarine, which existed in a two-dimensional 'sea world'.[7] HOMER was given tasks to accomplish in the sea world, which typically related to collecting packages and moving them from one location to another. HOMER is clearly a spiritual descendant of SHRDLU, and shared with SHRDLU one of its key limitations – it was only a simulation. But it was considerably more sophisticated.

HOMER took instructions from a user within a limited subset of English with about an 800-word vocabulary. HOMER could plan how to achieve its instructions, and could then carry out its plans, adapting them as circumstances required. To get a feel for HOMER's capabilities, let's look at some dialogues with it. The first concerns a floating log that HOMER could see (the user's input is in a normal font; HOMER's responses are in italics; my comments are in parentheses).

What is in front of you?
A log.
Do you own the log?
No, I don't.
The log belongs to you.

Oh. (Used by HOMER to indicate it has been told
   something it didn't know previously.)
[. . .]
Turn away from your log.
OK, I am turning.
(Log is moved by the user.)
Turn around.
OK, I'm turning.
I've lost the log!

This dialogue demonstrates some simple but important
common-sense reasoning: HOMER remembered about the
log, expected to see the log when it turned around and was
surprised when it discovered that the log had disappeared.

The next scenario starts with HOMER waiting at a pier,
which has a package on it: HOMER's task was to collect the
package and deliver it to a barge.

Drop the package at the barge next Saturday at 9 p.m.
OK.
(HOMER generates plan.)
Are you going to the pier next Saturday?
Yes.
Why are you going to go to the pier?
I'll go to the pier in order to pick up the package.
What time are you going to pick it up?
8.56 p.m.
Where will the package be next Sunday?
At the barge.
Will the package be at the pier a week from now?
No.

Here we see HOMER demonstrating some common-sense understanding of time, and how its actions affect its environment – that after it has dropped off the package at the barge, the package will no longer be at the pier. It also demonstrates an understanding that its own plans will take time to accomplish – it needs to leave the pier at 8.56 p.m. in order to be at the barge for 9 p.m.

AI Assistants

Although agent-based AI had its origins in robotics, many researchers quickly realized that the paradigm of agent-based AI had useful applications in the software world. There was no claim that this was General AI – as was the case with expert systems, the idea was that **software agents** could be built to do useful tasks on our behalf. Software agents operated in software environments, such as desktop computers and the Internet. The big idea was to have AI-powered software agents working alongside us as assistants on routine everyday tasks like processing emails and surfing the web.

To understand how this idea of software agents emerged, we need to know a little bit about the way in which we interact with computers, and how thinking on this subject has evolved over time.

Users of the earliest computers were, like Alan Turing, very often the scientists and engineers that had helped to design and build them. And the interfaces to the computers they built were crude – on the Manchester Baby computer that Turing used when he arrived in Manchester in the late 1940s, each individual bit of computer memory had to be set by flipping a switch to indicate a '1' or '0'. Nothing was hidden from the user – users had to understand how the machine worked in order to program it. Very few people had the technical skills to program in this way, and any skills you acquired on the Manchester Baby would be of no use whatsoever if you wanted to program the computer at Cambridge, because they were entirely different machines.

By the late 1950s, this situation had begun to change. The main innovation at this time was the development of **high-level programming languages**. These languages were high-level in the sense that they hid some of the low-level machine details from programmers, so a programmer was no longer required to understand how a particular computer worked in order to program it. These high-level languages were *machine independent*, in the sense that a program written in (say) COBOL on one computer could be expected to run – more or less – on another computer. Programming skills became transferable. These innovations dramatically increased the usability of computers and marked the beginning of a shift in the way that we interact with computers from a 'computer-oriented' mindset to a 'human-oriented' mindset.

This trend has continued throughout the subsequent six decades, with a steady progression away from machine-oriented modes of human–computer interaction towards ever more human-oriented modes. The 1980s saw a huge leap forward in this respect, with the introduction in 1984 of the Macintosh ('Mac') computer by the Apple Computer company. The Mac was the first mass-market computer explicitly intended to be usable without specialist computer training, and its main selling point was its user interface. The Mac had a graphical user interface (GUI) based on a desktop metaphor.

What this means is that the Mac user interface was (and still is) populated with graphical icons representing documents and folders, all manipulated by moving a mouse that controlled a pointer on the screen. Although you have probably heard the term 'desktop' to describe your computer interface, it may not have occurred to you that this term is used because your screen is supposed to resemble a real physical desk – the documents on your desktop are supposed to be analogues of the documents that you might find on a physical desktop, and the folders are supposed to be analogues of the physical folders that you might use to collect together physical documents; the metaphor continues, for example, with the idea of a trash can, where you drag documents that you want to remove. (The metaphor is a bit stretched these days, and I suspect many young people will be only dimly aware of it.)

Desktop-based graphical user interfaces of the type pioneered by the Mac in 1984 are still standard today.[8] Indeed, it is remarkable how little the basic ideas have changed during this time, given the huge advances in hardware over the same period: I suspect a Mac user from 1984 would have no difficulty navigating a modern Mac or Microsoft Windows interface.

The point about these interfaces, therefore, is that the user interacts with the computer using *concepts that are familiar to them* (desktops, documents, folders, trash cans), in the hope that this makes the process of interaction more natural, and therefore makes the computer more accessible.

By the late 1980s, following the success of the Mac, the then CEO of Apple, John Sculley, was contemplating what the next Mac-like innovation in human–computer interaction might be. He settled upon an idea that he called the **Knowledge Navigator**, a vision of computing that anticipated several nascent technologies (notably the World Wide Web, which at that time lay a couple of years in the future). To illustrate the Knowledge Navigator, Apple commissioned a concept video to be made, which went by the same name and which was released in 1987.[9] The video was highly speculative – intended to demonstrate a vision, rather than form the basis of a product road-map.

In the video, we see a college professor using a computer that bears a strong resemblance to a modern tablet computer. The tablet's user interface looks like a conventional desktop interface, with one important exception: the professor's interaction with the tablet is mediated by a software agent. Like HOMER, the agent interacts using ordinary English, although unlike HOMER, the agent is illustrated on the tablet display as an animated human figure. The agent politely reminds the professor of his daily schedule, handles some queries about material for a lecture the professor is planning and manages phone calls.

The video is fanciful (and it includes quite a lot of rather lame humour), but it has an important historical role, for several reasons. The first is that it hints at the way in which the Internet would become a routine part of our working environment. At the time the video was made, the Internet did not really exist for private individuals, or even most companies – it was largely the preserve of universities and government (mostly military) organizations. And the video anticipated the tablet computer. But, for the AI community, the most important point about the video is that it established the idea of *interacting with a computer via an agent*.

The **agent-based interface** represented a completely different mode of human–computer interaction to what had gone before. When we use an application like Microsoft Word or Internet Explorer, the application takes a passive, responsive role. These applications never take control, or take the initiative. When Microsoft Word does something, it does it because you selected a menu item, or clicked on a button. There is only one agent in the interaction between you and Microsoft Word, and that agent is you.

The agent-based interface changed that. Instead of the computer passively waiting to be told what to do, an agent would take an active role, in the same way that a human collaborator would. The agent would *work with you* as an assistant, actively cooperating with you to do whatever it was that you wanted to do.

The agent in the Knowledge Navigator video is animated, and is shown as if it were a person in a video conference call, speaking in fluent English. These capabilities were well beyond the AI technology of the time, and remain so to the present day. But these aspects were not essential to the main idea – that AI could make software an active collaborator rather than a passive servant. This central idea took hold, and by the mid-1990s, spurred on by the rapid expansion of the World Wide Web, interest in software agents grew rapidly.

The title of a widely read article of the time, published by Belgian-born MIT Media Lab Professor Pattie Maes, captured the zeitgeist: 'Agents That Reduce Work and Information Overload'.[10] The article described a number of prototype agents developed in Pattie's lab – agents for email management, meeting scheduling, filtering news and music recommendation. The email assistant, for example, would observe a user's behaviour when receiving an email (read the email immediately; file it; immediately delete it; and so on), and, using a machine-learning algorithm, would try to predict what the user would do when a new email arrived. When the agent was sufficiently confident in its predictions, then it would start to take the initiative, and process the email according to its prediction.

In the decade that followed, hundreds of similar agents were developed. Many of these were based around the Internet. In the early days of the World Wide Web, search tools were in their infancy, and Internet connections were far slower than today. Many routine tasks on the web were very time-consuming, and it was hoped that agents might be able to automate the drudge work.[11] By the end of the 1990s, interest in the World-Wide Web was exploding. Software agents seemed like an obvious technology for the rapidly growing web, and a slew of agent start-up companies were launched as part of what became the dot-com bubble.

I was actually part of this story. In the summer of 1996, some colleagues asked me to join an ambitious start-up company based in London. They offered me three times my academic salary. I thought about it for about half a second and agreed immediately. Our plan was to use agents to enhance web search. We would, we hoped, turn the World Wide Web into a library. But we knew nothing about business, and to be honest, not much more about building commercial software. And it rapidly became clear that, although we were burning through our investor's money at a jaw-dropping rate, we really didn't know how we were ultimately going to make this money back. It was a miserable time, and I left the company nine months after joining. The company itself folded only eight months later.

As it happened, my grim start-up experience presaged what was to happen on a global scale a few years later. The dot-com bubble, as it became known, lasted from 1995 to early 2000. As income for the ambitious and expensive new Internet start-ups failed to materialize, they began to run out of money. In early 2000, the dot-com market collapsed.

Software agents were just a small part of the dot-com story, but they were the most visible AI component of it. But the dream being promoted by AI researchers was not wrong, in this case; it was simply premature. Two decades later, an app called Siri was launched for the Apple iPhone. Siri was developed at SRI International – the same institute that had developed SHAKEY three decades earlier. Siri was a direct descendent of the work on software agents from the 1990s, and many in the AI community immediately drew parallels with Apple's Knowledge Navigator video. Siri was envisaged as a software agent that users could interact with in natural language, and that could carry out simple tasks on their behalf. Other mass-market software agents rapidly followed: Amazon's Alexa, Google's Assistant and Microsoft's Cortana are all realizations of the same vision. They all trace their heritage to agent-based AI. They could not, realistically, have been built in the 1990s because the hardware available at the time was not up to the task. To make them viable, they needed the computer power that only became available on mobile devices in the second decade of this century.

Acting Rationally

The agent paradigm provided yet another way of thinking about AI: *building agents that can act effectively on our behalf*. But this raised an intriguing question. The Turing test established the idea that the goal of AI was to produce behaviour that was indistinguishable from that of humans. But if we want agents to act on our behalf and do the best for us, then whether they make *the same choices that a human would make* is irrelevant. Surely what we really want is for them to make *good* choices – the best choices possible. The goal of AI thus began to shift from building agents that make *human* choices to agents that make *optimal* choices.

The theory of optimal decision-making that underpins most work in AI goes back to the 1940s, and the work of John von Neumann – the same John von Neumann whom we met in Chapter 1, who did seminal work on the design of the earliest computers. Along with his colleague Oskar Morgenstern, he developed a mathematical theory of rational decision-making. This theory showed how the problem of making a rational choice could be reduced to a mathematical calculation.[12] In agent-based AI, the idea was that the agent would use their theory to make optimal decisions on your behalf.

The starting point of their theory is your **preferences**. If your agent is to act on your behalf, then it needs to know what your wishes are. You then want the agent to act in order to bring about your preferred choices as best it can. So, how do we give an agent our preferences? Suppose your agent has to choose between getting an apple, orange or pear. If your agent is going to do its best for you, then it needs to know your desires with respect to these outcomes. For example, your preferences might be the following:

> Oranges are preferred to pears;
> pears are preferred to apples.

In this case, if your agent was given a choice between an apple and an orange, and chose an orange, you'd be happy – if it gave you an apple, you would be disappointed. This is a simple example of a **preference relation.** Your preference relation describes how you rank every pair of alternative outcomes. Von Neumann and Morgenstern required preference relations to satisfy certain basic requirements of consistency. For example, suppose you claimed your preferences were as follows:

> Oranges are preferred to pears;
> pears are preferred to apples;
> apples are preferred to oranges.

Your preferences here are rather odd, because the fact that you prefer oranges to pears and pears to apples would lead me to conclude you preferred oranges above apples, which contradicts the last statement. Your preferences are therefore inconsistent. It would be impossible for an agent given such preferences to make a good decision for you.

Their next step is to see that consistent preferences can be given a *numeric* representation, using what are called **utilities**. The basic idea of utilities is that each possible outcome is associated with a number: the larger the number, the more preferred the outcome. For example, we can capture the preferences in the first example above by assigning the utility of an orange to be 3, the utility of a pear to be 2 and the utility of an apple to be 1. Since 3 is bigger than 2 and 2 is bigger than 1, these utilities correctly capture our first preference relation. Equally well, we could have chosen utilities so that oranges have value 10, pears have value 9 and apples have value 0. The *magnitude* of the values doesn't matter in this case: all that is important is the *ordering* of outcomes that is induced by the utility values. Crucially, it is *only* possible to represent preferences via numeric utility values if they satisfy the consistency constraints – see if you can assign numeric values to apples, oranges and pears in order to represent the example with inconsistent preferences above!

The sole purpose of using utility values to represent preferences is that it reduces the problem of making the best choice to a mathematical calculation. Our agent chooses an action whose outcome maximizes utility on our behalf; which is the same as saying that it chooses an action in order to bring about our most preferred outcome. Problems like this are called optimization problems, and they have been extensively studied in mathematics.

Unfortunately, most choices are trickier than this because they involve uncertainty. Settings of **choice under uncertainty** deal with scenarios where actions have multiple possible outcomes, and all we know about these outcomes is the *probability* that each will result.

To understand what I mean by this, let's look at a scenario in which your agent has to make a choice between two options.[13] Here is the scenario:

Option 1: A fair coin is tossed. If it comes up heads your
agent is given £4. If it comes up tails your agent is
given £3.

Option 2: A fair coin is tossed. If it comes up heads your
agent is given £6. If it comes up tails your agent is
given nothing.

Which option should your agent choose? I claim that Option 1
is a better choice. But why, exactly, is it better?

To understand why this is, we need a concept called **expected utility**. The expected utility of a scenario is the utility
that would be received *on average* from that scenario.

So, consider Option 1. The coin we are tossing is fair (not
weighted to either heads or tails), and so we would expect
heads and tails to come up, on average, an equal number of
times – heads half the time, tails half the time. So, half the
time your agent would receive £4 and half the time it would
receive £3. On average, therefore, the amount you would
expect to earn from Option 1 would be $(0.5 \times £4) + (0.5 \times £3) =$
£3.50; this is the expected utility of the option.

Of course, if your agent chose Option 1, then *in practice*
it would never actually receive £3.50; but if you had the opportunity to make this choice enough times, and you always
chose Option 1, then on average you would receive £3.50 each
time you made the choice.

Following the same reasoning, the expected utility of
Option 2 is $(0.5 \times £6) + (0.5 \times £0) = £3$, so on average choosing Option 2 would give you £3.

Now, the basic principle of rational choice in von Neumann
and Morgenstern's theory says that a rational agent would

make a choice **maximizing expected utility**. In this case, the choice which maximizes expected utility would be Option 1, since this gives expected utility of £3.50 against the expected utility of £3 with Option 2.

Note that Option 2 offers the tantalizing possibility of getting £6, which is more than would be received with any outcome associated with Option 1; but this attractive possibility has to be weighed against the equally likely possibility of getting nothing in Option 2, which is why the expected utility of Option 1 is larger.

The idea of maximizing expected utility is often grossly misunderstood. Some people find the idea of reducing human preferences and choices to a mathematical calculation distasteful. This distaste often arises from the mistaken belief that utilities are money, or that utility theory is in some sense selfish (since presumably an agent that maximizes expected utility must be acting only for itself). But utilities are nothing more than a numeric way of capturing preferences: von Neumann and Morgenstern's theory is completely neutral with respect to what an individual's preferences are or should be. The theory copes equally well with the preferences of angels and devils. If all you care about is other people, then that's fine: if your altruism is captured in your preferences, utility theory will work for you just as well as it does for the most selfish person in the world.

By the 1990s, the idea of AI as the paradigm of building agents that would act rationally on our behalf, with rationality defined according to the Von Neumann and Morgenstern model, had become the new orthodoxy in AI and remains so today:[14] if there is any common theme that unites the various strands of contemporary AI, it is this. Inside almost all AI systems today, there is a numeric utility model, representing the preferences of the user, and the system will try to maximize expected utility according to this model – to act rationally on behalf of the user.

Coping with Uncertainty

One long-term problem in AI, which became much more crisply defined in the 1990s, was that of dealing with uncertainty. Any realistic AI system has to deal with uncertainty, and sometimes a lot of it. To pick an example, a driverless car obtains streams of data from its sensors, but sensors are not perfect. For example, there is always a chance that a range-finder will simply be wrong when it says 'No obstacle'. The information the range-finder has is not useless – it has some value – but we can't just assume it is correct. So how should we make use of it, taking into account the possibility of error?

Many ad hoc schemes for dealing with uncertainty were invented and re-invented throughout the history of AI, but by the 1990s, one approach had come to dominate. The approach is called **Bayesian inference**. Bayesian inference was invented by an eighteenth-century British mathematician, the Reverend Thomas Bayes. He formulated a version of a technique that we now call **Bayes' Theorem** in his honour. It is concerned with how we should rationally adjust our beliefs in the presence of new information. In the case of our driverless car example, the beliefs relate to whether there is an obstacle in front of us; the new information is the sensor data.

Apart from anything else, Bayes' Theorem is interesting because it highlights how poorly people cope with cognitive decisions involving uncertainty. To better understand this, consider the following scenario:

> A deadly new flu virus infects one in every thousand people. A test for the flu is developed, which is 99% accurate. On a whim you take the test, and it comes out positive.
>
> How concerned should you be?

After the test came back positive, I think it is a safe bet that most people would be *extremely* concerned. After all, the test is *99 per cent accurate*! So, if I asked what the probability was that you had flu after the positive test, I suspect most people would say 0.99 (corresponding to the accuracy of the test).

In fact, this answer is hopelessly wrong. You would only have about a *one in ten* chance of having the flu. This seems completely counterintuitive, so what on earth is going on here?

Imagine that we select 1,000 people at random and give them the flu test. We know that only about one person in this 1,000 will actually have the flu, so let's assume that in our test this is indeed the case: one person has the flu, and 999 don't.

First let's consider the poor soul who has the flu. Since the test is 99 per cent accurate, it will correctly identify someone who actually has the flu 99 per cent of the time. So, we can expect this test to come out positive (with probability 0.99).

Now think about the lucky 999 souls who *don't* have the flu. Again, the test is 99 per cent accurate, so it will only misdiagnose someone who doesn't have the flu about one time in every 100 tests. But we are testing 999 people who don't have the flu; so we can expect something like nine or ten of those tests to come back positive. In other words, about nine or ten of those people can be expected to test positive for the flu *even though they don't have it*.

So, if we test 1,000 people for the flu, we can expect about 10 or 11 of those tests to come back positive; but we can also expect that only one of the people who tests positive actually has the flu.

In short, since so few people do have the flu there will be far more *false positives* than *true positives*. (This, incidentally, is one reason why doctors don't like to rely on a single test to make a diagnosis.)

Let's look at an example of how Bayesian reasoning can be used in robotics. Let's suppose we have a robot that is exploring some unknown territory – a distant planet, or a building that has been devastated by an earthquake. We want our robot to explore the new territory and construct a map of it. The robot can perceive its environment through its sensors, but there is a catch: the sensors are noisy. Thus, when the robot makes an observation and the sensors say 'There is an obstacle in this location', they may be right or they may be wrong. We don't know for sure. If our robot just assumes its sensor data is always correct, then at some point it will make a decision based on incorrect information and crash into an obstacle.

Bayes' Theorem here is used as follows. Just as in the test for flu, we can use the probability that the sensor reading is correct to update our beliefs that there is an obstacle at the relevant location. By making multiple observations, we can progressively refine our map of the environment.[15] And over time, we become increasingly confident about where the obstacles are.

Bayes' Theorem is important because it gives us the right way of handling imperfect data: we neither discard the data nor accept it without question. Instead, we use it to update our probabilistic beliefs about how the world is.

Powerful though it is, much work was needed to make Bayesian reasoning usable in AI, because AI systems often have to deal with *lots* of complex interconnected data. To capture such interconnections, AI researchers developed **Bayesian networks**, or Bayes nets for short. These are a graphical representation of the relationships that exist between data. They were put forward in their contemporary form largely through the work of Judea Pearl, a hugely influential researcher who has done perhaps more than anyone else to understand and articulate the role of probability in AI.[16] Consider the simple Bayes net in Figure 12. This Bayes net captures the relationships between three hypotheses: *You have a common cold*; *You have a runny nose*; and *You have a headache*. The arrows from one hypothesis to another indicate influence relationships between these hypotheses. Roughly speaking, an arrow from hypothesis X to hypothesis Y would mean that the truth of X would have some influence on the truth of Y. Thus, for example, whether you have a common cold will influence whether you have a runny nose; and, if you have a runny nose, then this tells you something about the likelihood that you have a common cold. The relationships between these various probabilities are captured using Bayesian reasoning; if you would like to dig a little deeper into the details, see Appendix C.

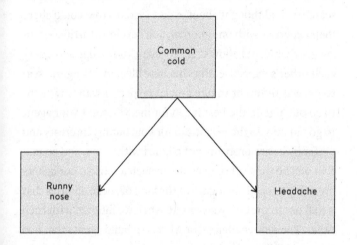

Figure 12
A simple Bayesian network.

When Siri Met Siri

Although the dot-com boom ended in 2000, interest in agents didn't, and attention began to focus on a new twist to the agent story. What could we do, researchers began to wonder, *if our software agents could talk to each other*? The idea was not a wholly new one: back in the days of knowledge-based AI, researchers had thought about expert systems that could share their expertise with one another, and developed artificial languages that would allow them to share knowledge and query each other's expertise. But this new idea, **multi-agent systems**, was different in one crucial respect: I want my agent to go out and do the best it can for me; you want your agent to go out and do the best it can for you; but my interests and preferences are probably not aligned with yours, and so neither will be those of our agents. In such a setting, our agents are going to need analogues of the kind of social abilities that we all use in the everyday world, when we interact with each other. The new challenge for AI was to build agents that had these capabilities.[17]

With hindsight, it seems odd that these *social* aspects of AI had not been considered before. But, before the emergence of multi-agent systems, the focus had been on developing individual agents, without any consideration as to how they might interact with other AI agents. And the assumption that there could be *multiple* agents, rather than just one, changed the AI story quite fundamentally. The problem an agent has to solve is that of knowing what to do – what action to perform on my behalf. I will be happy with an agent if it makes a *good* choice of action on my behalf. But if there are multiple agents around, then whether the action chosen by my agent is good or not will probably depend, at least in part, *on what other agents choose to do*. My agent should therefore take into account what these other agents are likely to do when making its decision; and those other agents in turn will need to take into account the actions of my agent when they are making theirs.

This kind of reasoning – where agents need to mutually consider each other's preferences and probable choice of action when deciding what to do – had in fact been previously studied in the field of **game theory**, the branch of economics that studies strategic decision-making.[18] Although, as the name suggests, game theory had its origins in the study of games like chess and poker, in fact it has applications everywhere that decisions are to be made in the presence of multiple agents.

Probably the most famous idea in game theory, and an idea that came to form the bedrock for decision-making in multi-agent systems, is that of **Nash equilibrium**. The idea of Nash equilibrium was formulated by John Forbes Nash Jr, whom we met earlier as someone invited to John McCarthy's summer school on AI at Dartmouth College in 1956. He was jointly awarded the 1994 Nobel Prize in Economics (along with John Harsanyi and Richard Selten), for his work on Nash equilibrium.

The basic idea of a Nash equilibrium is easy to understand. Suppose we have just two agents, each of whom has to make a choice. Suppose Agent One chooses to do x and Agent Two chooses to do y. Then how can we say whether they were good decisions? The idea is that their decisions will have been good ones (technically, they form a Nash equilibrium) if *neither agent regrets their choice*. That is:

Agent One is satisfied that, given that Agent Two did *y*, doing *x* was the best thing for Agent One; and

Agent Two is satisfied that, given that Agent One did *x*, doing *y* was the best thing for Agent Two.

Nash equilibria are called *equilibria* because they capture a kind of stability in decision-making: neither agent has any incentive to do anything else.

The multi-agent systems community rapidly adopted game theory ideas such as the Nash equilibrium as the basis for decision-making in their systems – but a now-familiar difficulty appeared. When Nash formulated his Nobel Prize-winning idea in the 1950s, he was not concerned with *computing* Nash equilibria. But if we want to have agents that can use this idea when they make decisions, then this is, of course, a central problem. And, perhaps predictably, it turned out that Nash equilibria are hard to compute. Finding efficient ways to compute Nash equilibria remains a major topic in AI today.

AI Reaches Maturity

By the end of the 1990s, the agent paradigm had become established as the orthodoxy in AI: we build agents and delegate our preferences to them; these agents act rationally on our behalf to carry them out, using rational decision-making as exemplified by von Neumann and Morgenstern's expected utility theory; and these agents rationally manage their beliefs about the world using Bayesian reasoning, with their understanding of the world captured using a Bayes net, or some variation of it; and if there are multiple agents, then we look to game theory to provide a decision-making framework. This was not General AI, and it didn't give any road-map for how to get to General AI. But by the end of the 1990s, the increasing acceptance of these tools led to an important change in the perception of AI within the AI community itself. For the first time, it really felt like we were not just groping in the dark, desperately clutching on to whatever we found: we had a well-established scientific basis for our field, one that was firmly grounded in respected and proven techniques from probability theory and the theory of rational decision-making.

Two achievements in this period signalled the maturity of the discipline. The first made headlines around the world; the second, equally if not more important, is unknown to all but AI insiders.

The headline breakthrough was made by IBM, who, in 1997, were able to show that an AI system, by the name of DeepBlue, was able to beat Russian grand master Garry Kasparov in the game of chess. DeepBlue took its first match from Kasparov in February 1996 in a six-game tournament, but Kasparov won overall, four games to two. An upgraded version of the system played Kasparov just over a year later, and this time, Deep-Blue defeated Kasparov overall. It seems Kasparov was very unhappy about it at the time, apparently suspecting IBM of cheating, but he has since enjoyed a good side-line to his brilliant chess career by speaking about the experience. From that point on, chess was, to all intents and purposes, a solved game: AI systems existed which could reliably beat the very best players.

DeepBlue's success derived from two main ingredients.

The first was heuristic search: Arthur Samuel, author of the seminal checkers-playing program in the 1950s, would have had no difficulty understanding the core techniques, albeit they had been refined over a forty-year period. But the second ingredient was rather controversial: DeepBlue was essentially a super-computer. It relied on enormous computer power to do its work. This led to criticisms that the system was really not AI at all, but nothing more than brute computational force. But this dramatically understates the importance of the AI techniques that made use of all this computer power. With the same computing power, a naive approach to chess, such as an exhaustive search of the type that we looked at for the Towers of Hanoi puzzle in Chapter 2, would simply not have worked.

While you may well have heard of DeepBlue's victory over Kasparov, I think it is unlikely that you will have heard of the second major achievement of the time, although its ramifications are probably more profound. You may recall from Chapter 2 that certain computational problems are intrinsically hard – NP-complete, to use the technical term – and that many problems of interest in AI fall into this category. By the early 1990s, it was beginning to be clear that progress on algorithms for NP-complete problems was such that this no longer represented the fundamental barrier that it had appeared two decades before.[19] The first problem shown to be NP-complete was called SAT (short for 'satisfiability'). This is the problem of checking whether simple logical expressions are consistent – whether there is any way they could be true. SAT is the most fundamental of all NP-complete problems, and you will recall that, if you have an efficient way to solve just one type of NP-complete problem, then you have automatically found a way to solve them all. By the end of the 1990s, 'SAT solvers' – programs to solve SAT problems – were sufficiently powerful that they began to be used on industrial-scale problems. At the time of writing, SAT solvers are so efficient that they are now routinely used throughout computing – they are just another tool that we call on when faced with NP-complete problems. This doesn't mean that NP-complete problems can now always be solved efficiently: there will always be cases that bring even the best SAT solvers to their knees. But we are no longer afraid of NP-completeness, and this is one of the major unsung achievements of AI over the past four decades.

For all its newfound respectability, not everyone was happy about what mainstream AI had become by the end of the 1990s. In July 2000, I was at a conference in Boston, watching a presentation by one of the bright young stars of the new AI. I was sitting next to a seasoned AI veteran – someone who had been in AI since the Golden Age, a contemporary of McCarthy and Minsky. He was contemptuous. 'Is this what passes for AI nowadays?' he asked. 'Where did the magic go?' And I could see where he was coming from: a career in AI now demanded a background, not in philosophy or cognitive science or logic, but in probability, statistics and economics. It doesn't seem as, well, *poetic*, does it? But the fact is, it worked.

AI had changed direction again, but this time the future seemed much more settled. Had I been writing this book in the year 2000, I would have confidently predicted that this would be the future of AI for the rest of my career. There would be no drama: we would use these tools, and with them, progress would be slow but steady. I had no inkling that, just around the corner, dramatic new developments were about to shake AI to its core once again.

CHAPTER 5

Deep Breakthroughs

In January 2014, something unprecedented happened in the UK technology industry. Google acquired a small company in a deal that, while unremarkable by the standards of Silicon Valley, was extraordinary by the standards of the UK's rather modest computer technology sector. The company they acquired was DeepMind, a start-up company which at the time employed fewer than 25 people, for the reported sum of £400 million.[1] At the time of acquisition, it looked from the outside as though DeepMind had no products, technology or business plan. They were virtually unknown, even within the specialist area in which they had chosen to operate: AI.

The acquisition of this tiny AI company for a huge sum made headlines – the world wanted to know who this mystery outfit were, and why Google thought an unknown company could possibly be worth so much.

Artificial intelligence was suddenly big news – and big business. Interest in AI exploded. The press noticed the buzz, and stories about AI began to appear in the media daily. Governments across the globe also noticed, and started to ask how they should respond; a string of national AI initiatives quickly followed. Technology companies scrambled to avoid being left behind, and an unprecedented wave of investment followed. While DeepMind was the highest-profile AI acquisition, there were many others. In 2015, Uber acquired no fewer than 40 researchers from Carnegie Mellon University's machine learning lab in a single deal.

In less than a decade, AI had been transformed from a quiet backwater of computing into the hottest and most hyped area of science. The sudden sea change in attitudes to AI was driven by rapid progress in one core AI technology: machine learning. Machine learning is a subfield of AI, but for much of the last 60 years, it had evolved on a separate path, and as we will see in this chapter, the relationship between AI and its suddenly glamorous offspring has at times been strained.

In this chapter we will hear how the twenty-first-century machine learning revolution happened. We'll begin by briefly reviewing what machine learning is, and then look at how one particular approach to machine learning – neural networks – came to dominate. Like the story of AI itself, the story of neural networks is a troubled one: there have been two 'neural net winters', and as recently as the turn of the century, many in AI regarded neural networks as a dead or dying field. But neural nets ultimately triumphed, and the new idea driving their resurgence is a technique called **deep learning**. Deep learning is the core technology of DeepMind. I will tell you the DeepMind story, and how the systems that DeepMind built attracted global adulation. But while deep learning is a powerful and important technique, it isn't the end of the story for AI, so, just as we did with other AI technologies, we'll discuss its limitations in detail too.

Machine Learning, Briefly

The goal of machine learning is to have programs that can compute a desired output from a given input, *without being given an explicit recipe for how to do this*. An example is in order. One classic application of machine learning is text recognition: taking handwritten text and transcribing it. Here, the input is a picture of the handwritten text; the desired output is the string of characters represented by the handwritten text.

Text recognition is hard, as any postal worker will tell you. We all write differently, and many of us write unclearly; we use pens that leak ink on to the paper; and the paper itself becomes dirty and battered. Returning to Figure 1 in our first chapter, text recognition is an example of a problem for which we don't know how to come up with an appropriate recipe. It isn't like playing board games, where we have recipes that work in principle but need heuristics to make them practical: we just don't know what a recipe for text recognition might be. We need something else entirely – which is where machine learning comes in.

A machine learning program for text recognition would typically be **trained** by giving it many examples of handwritten characters, with each example labelled with the actual text that was written. Figure 13 illustrates this.

The type of machine learning we have just described is called **supervised learning**, and it illustrates a crucially important point: *machine learning needs data*. Lots and lots of data. In fact, as we will see, the provision of carefully curated sets of training data was crucial to the current success of machine learning.

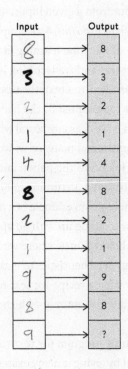

Figure 13

Training data for a machine learning program to recognize handwritten characters (in this case, numbers). The goal is that the program will be able to identify handwritten numbers on its own.

When we train a machine learning program, we have to be very careful about the training data that we use. First, we can usually only train the program with a tiny fraction of the possible inputs and outputs. In our handwriting example, we can't show the program all possible handwritten characters – that's impossible. If we *could* train the program with the complete set of possible inputs, then there would be no need for any clever machine learning techniques: our program could just remember each input and corresponding desired output. Whenever it was then presented with an input all it would have to do would be to look up the corresponding output. This is not machine learning. So, a program will have to be trained using only a small part of the overall set of possible inputs and outputs. But if the training data set is too small, then the program may not have enough information to learn the desired mapping from inputs to outputs.

Another fundamental problem with training data is called **feature extraction**. Suppose you are working for a bank, which wants a machine learning program that will learn to identify bad credit risks. The training data for your program will probably consist of lots of records of past customers, each customer record being labelled with whether that customer in fact turned out to be a good or bad risk. The customer record will typically include their name, date of birth, residential address, annual income, along with records of transactions, loans and corresponding repayments and so on. These components are called the **features** that can be used for training. But does it make sense to include *all* these features in your training data? Some of them may be completely irrelevant to whether someone is a bad credit risk. If you don't know in advance which features are going to be relevant for your problem, then you might be tempted to include everything. But there is a big problem with this, called the **curse of dimensionality**: the more features you include, the more training data you are going to have to give the program, and the more slowly the program is going to learn.

The natural response is to only include a small number of features in your training data. But this presents problems of its own. For one thing, you may accidentally omit features that are necessary for the program to be able to learn appropriately – the features that actually indicate a poor credit risk. For another, if you make a poor choice of which features to include, then you also run the risk of introducing bias into your program. For example, if the only feature that you decided to include for your bad-risk program was the address of the customer, then this is likely to lead to the program learning to discriminate against people from certain neighbourhoods. The possibility that AI programs may become biased, and the problems this raises, are explored in more detail later.

In **reinforcement learning**, we don't give the program any explicit training data: it experiments by making decisions, and receives feedback on those decisions as to whether they were good or bad. For example, reinforcement learning is widely used to train programs to play games. The program plays the game, and gets positive feedback if it wins or negative feedback if it loses. The feedback it gets, whether positive or negative, is called the **reward**. The reward is taken into account by the program the next time it plays. If it receives a positive reward, then that makes it more likely to play the same way; a negative reward would make it less likely to do so.

A key difficulty with reinforcement learning is that in many situations, rewards may be a long time in coming, and this makes it hard for the program to know which actions were good and which were bad. Suppose our reinforcement-learning program loses a game. What does that loss tell it, or indeed, us, about any individual move made during the game? Concluding that *all* the moves were bad would probably be an over-generalization. But how does it and how do we know which were the bad moves? This is the **credit assignment** problem. We encounter the credit assignment problem in everyday life. Suppose you choose to smoke cigarettes. Then it is likely, at some point in the future, that you will receive feedback on this choice: in this case, negative feedback, in the form of health problems. But this negative feedback is only received long after you made the decision to smoke (decades, usually). Such delayed feedback makes it hard for you to learn not to smoke. If smokers received negative feedback (in the form of life-threatening ill health) *immediately* after they made the decision to smoke, then I think it is a safe bet that far fewer people would choose to do so.

So far, we have said nothing about *how* a program might learn. Machine learning as a field is as old as AI itself, and just as large. Many techniques have been proposed over the past 60 years. But the recent successes of machine learning have been based around one particular technique: neural networks (usually abbreviated to 'neural nets'). Neural nets are in fact one of the oldest techniques in AI – they were part of the original proposal by John McCarthy for his AI summer school in 1956. But they have seen a huge resurgence of interest this century.

Neural nets, as the name suggests, were inspired by the networks of nerve cells – **neurons** – that are found in the microstructure of the brain and nervous system. Neurons are cells that can communicate with each other in a simple way, through fibres in the brain called **axons** to other neurons via 'junctions' called **synapses**. Typically, a neuron receives electro-chemical signals via its synaptic connections, and depending on the signals received, will generate an output signal that will in turn be received by other neurons via their synaptic connections. Crucially, the inputs that a neuron receives are differently weighted: some inputs are more important than others, and some inputs may inhibit the neuron, preventing it from generating an output. In animal nervous systems, networks of neurons are massively interconnected: the human brain is made up of about 100 billion neurons, and neurons in the human brain typically have thousands of connections.

The idea of neural nets in machine learning, then, is to use these kinds of structures in a computer program; after all, the human brain provides proof that neural structures can learn very effectively.

Perceptrons (Neural Nets Version 1)

The study of neural networks had its origins in the work of US researchers Warren McCulloch and Walter Pitts in the 1940s. They realized that neurons could be modelled as electrical circuits – more specifically, simple logical circuits – and they used this idea to develop a straightforward but very general mathematical model of them. In the 1950s, this model was refined by Frank Rosenblatt in a neural net model that he called the **perceptron model**. It is significant because it was the first neural net model to actually be implemented, and is still of relevance today.

Rosenblatt's perceptron model is shown in Figure 14. The square indicates the neuron itself; the arrows going into the square correspond to the inputs of the neuron (corresponding to its synaptic connections), and the arrow coming out to the right indicates the output of the neuron (corresponding to an axon). In the perceptron model, each input is associated with a number called its **weight**: in Figure 14, the weight associated with Input 1 is w_1, the weight associated with Input 2 is w_2, and the weight associated with Input 3 is w_3. Each input to the neuron is either active or inactive: if an input is active, then it 'stimulates' the neuron by the corresponding weight. Finally, each neuron has an **activation threshold**, which is another number (written as T in Figure 14). The idea is that if the neuron is stimulated beyond its activation threshold, T, then it will 'fire', which means making its output active. In other words, we add together the weights of all the inputs that are active; and if the total meets or exceeds T, then the neuron produces an output.

To make this idea concrete, suppose that each weight in the neuron shown in Figure 14 is 1, and the threshold is 2. Then the neuron will fire if any two of its inputs are active. In other words, the neuron fires if a *majority* of its inputs are active.

Alternatively, suppose the weight of Input 1 is 2 while the weight on Inputs 2 and 3 are both 1, and the threshold, T, is 2. In this case, the neuron will fire if either Input 1 is active, or both of Inputs 2 and 3 are active, or all three inputs are active.

Of course, the neural nets that we see in nature contain

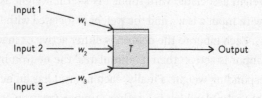

Figure 14
A single neural unit in Rosenblatt's perceptron model.

many neurons. Figure 15 shows a perceptron consisting of three artificial neurons. Notice that each neuron operates completely independently. Moreover, each neuron can 'see' each input – however, the weights for the same input may be different for different neurons. Thus, the weight associated with Input 1 may be different for each of the three neurons to which it provides an input. Also, each neuron may have a different activation threshold (these are the values T_1, T_2, and T_3). So, we can think of these three neurons each computing something different.

However, the arrangement shown in Figure 15 does not reflect the highly interconnected structure of the brain, where the output of one neuron will feed into many others. To reflect more clearly the complexity of the structures in the human brain, artificial neural networks are usually organized in **layers**, as shown in Figure 16 – in what is known as a **multi-layer perceptron**. This network consists of nine neurons, arranged into three layers of three neurons each. Every neuron in each successive layer receives all the outputs from the layer preceding it.

One immediate point to note is that even in this very small network, things have started to get complicated: we now have a total of 27 connections between neurons, each with their own weight, and all nine neurons have their own activation threshold. Although multiple layers for neural nets were envisaged as far back as the work of McCulloch and Pitts, in Rosenblatt's time, attention was focused on networks with a single layer, for the simple reason that nobody had any idea how to train neural networks with more than one layer.

The weights associated with each connection are crucial

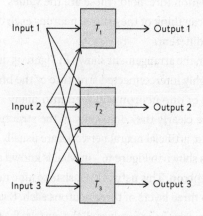

Input 1 → T_1 → Output 1

Input 2 → T_2 → Output 2

Input 3 → T_3 → Output 3

Figure 15

A perceptron consisting of three artificial neurons organized into a single layer.

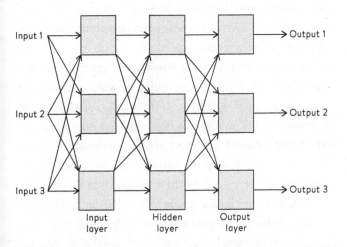

Figure 16
A perceptron with nine neurons in three layers.

to the operation of a neural net. In fact, that is really all a neural net breaks down into: this list of numbers. (For any reasonably sized neural network, it will be a *long* list of numbers.) Training a neural network therefore involves finding appropriate numeric weights somehow. The usual approach is to adjust the weight after each training episode, trying to make the network correctly map inputs to outputs. Rosenblatt experimented with a few different techniques for doing this, and found one for a simple perceptron model which he called an error correction procedure.

Nowadays, we know that Rosenblatt's approach is guaranteed to work: it will always train a network correctly, but there is one very big caveat. In 1969, Marvin Minsky and Seymour Papert published a book entitled *Perceptrons*,[2] in which they showed that there are quite dramatic limits to what single-layer perceptron networks can do. In fact, single-layer perceptron models of the type shown in Figure 15 are very limited: they are incapable of learning many simple relationships between inputs and outputs. But what most readers of the time seem to have fixated on was that Minsky and Papert showed that perceptron models cannot learn a very simple concept, one called 'exclusive OR' ('XOR'). To give you an example, imagine your network has just two inputs. Then the XOR function should produce an output when exactly *one* of the inputs is active (but not when both are active). It is easy to show that simple (single-layer) perceptrons can't capture XOR. (The interested reader can find more about these issues in Appendix D.)

It seems that quite sweeping conclusions were drawn from Minsky and Papert's book, which remain controversial even to the present day. Theoretical results which demonstrated the fundamental limitations of *certain classes* of perceptron seem to have been taken to imply limitations for the perceptron model *in general*. In particular, *multi-layer* perceptrons, of the type shown in Figure 16, are *not* subject to these limitations: in a precise mathematical sense, they can be shown to be completely general. However, at the time, nobody had any idea how to train a network with multi-layer perceptrons: they were a theoretical possibility, rather than a working reality. It would take two decades before the science was developed that made this possible.

I wonder whether the negative reaction to perceptron models at this time was in part a response to some rather overexcited publicity about them previously. For example, a 1958 *New York Times* article had breathlessly reported that:[3]

> The [US] Navy revealed the embryo of an electronic computer today that it expects will be able to walk, talk, see, write, reproduce itself and be conscious of its existence.

We can debate the precise causes, but whatever they may have been, the fact is that research into neural nets declined sharply at the end of the 1960s in favour of the symbolic AI approaches championed by McCarthy, Minsky, Newell and Simon (ironically, this decline came only a few years before the onset of the AI winter that we heard about in Chapter 2). In 1971, Rosenblatt died in a sailing accident, leaving the neural nets community without one of its main champions. Perhaps, had he survived, the history of AI might have been different; but following his death, research into neural nets went into abeyance for more than a decade.

Connectionism (Neural Nets Version 2)

The field of neural nets was largely dormant until a revival began in the 1980s. The revival was heralded by the publication of a two-volume book entitled *Parallel Distributed Processing* (or PDP, for short).[4] The choice of title is intriguing. Parallel and distributed processing is a mainstream area of computing, concerned with building computer systems that can operate in parallel. It doesn't, on a first reading, suggest AI or neural networks, and I suspect some who bought the book based on the title alone would have been bewildered to discover that it was about neural networks. So perhaps the choice of title was an attempt to distance the new wave from previous neural net research.

Probably the most important element of the new body of work was, in a sense, not so new: it was focused around neural nets with multiple layers, which could be shown to easily overcome the limitations of simple perceptron systems that were identified by Minsky and Papert. But there was one key difference. Work on perceptron models had previously focused on single-layer networks because, at the time, nobody had any idea how to 'train' multi-layer neural networks – how to find out what the 'weights' of the connections between neurons should be. And PDP provided a solution to this problem in the form of an algorithm called **backpropagation**, more commonly referred to as **backprop** – probably the single most important technique in the field of neural nets.

As is often the case in science, backprop seems to have been invented and reinvented a number of times over the years, but it was the specific approach introduced by the PDP researchers that definitively established it.[5]

Unfortunately, a proper explanation of backprop would require university-level calculus, and is far beyond the scope of this book. But the basic idea is simple enough. Backprop works by looking at cases where a neural net has made an error in its classification: this error manifests itself at the output layer of the network. (Imagine that the network has been shown a picture of a cat, and the output layer has classified it as a dog.) The backprop algorithm propagates the error backwards through the network through each preceding layer (hence the name – **back**ward **prop**agation). It does this by first computing a landscape of errors: for each possible weight, we know the error, and this error value then gives a kind of contour map of errors. We can then find the steepest way to descend in the map, in stages, all the way from the current error down to the lowest error of all – the steepest route will give the fastest way to resolve the error. This process is called **gradient descent**. It then moves progressively on to the preceding layer, and so on.

PDP also provided much more general models of neurons than were provided by perceptron models. For example, perceptrons are essentially binary (on-or-off) computational units: PDP presented much more general models.

The development of backprop and the other innovations introduced by the PDP community made possible a whole slew of applications for neural nets, which went far beyond the simple demonstrations of perceptron models of 20 years earlier. Interest in neural nets exploded – but the PDP bubble proved to be short-lived. By the mid-1990s, neural net research was once more out of favour. With hindsight, we can see that the wheels came off the PDP wagon not because of any inherent fundamental limitations of the basic ideas, but for a much more prosaic reason: computers of that time were just not powerful enough to handle the new techniques. And, at the same time that advances in PDP seemed to be flat-lining, other areas of machine learning seemed to be making rapid progress. Mainstream interest in machine learning began to turn away from neural models once again.

Deep Learning (Neural Nets Version 3)

I recall being on an appointment panel for an academic AI post in around the year 2000. Another member of the panel tried to persuade us that we shouldn't consider applicants working in neural nets. 'It's a niche field', he argued, 'why would we hire someone researching in a declining area?' I think we ignored him, but to be fair, in the year 2000, you would have had to be very far-sighted indeed to understand that neural nets were about to undergo another resurgence. But a resurgence did indeed begin, around the year 2006, and it led to the biggest and most highly publicized expansion ever in the history of AI.

The big idea that drove the third wave of neural net research went by the name of deep learning.[6] I would love to tell you that there was a single key idea which characterizes deep learning, but in truth the term refers to a collection of related ideas. Deep learning means deep in at least three different senses.

Of these, perhaps the most important, as the name suggests,

is simply the idea of having *more layers*. Each layer can process a problem at a different level of abstraction – layers close to the input layer handle low-level concepts in the data (such as the edges in a picture), and as we move deeper into the network, we find more abstract concepts being handled.

As well as being deep in the sense of more layers, deep learning was able to enjoy the benefits of having larger numbers of neurons. A typical neural network from 1990 might only have about one hundred neurons (the human brain, you will recall, has about 100 billion). No surprise, then, that such networks are very limited in what they can achieve. A state-of-the-art neural net from 2016 would have about one million neurons[7] (about the same number as a bee).

Finally, deep learning uses networks that are deep in the sense that the neurons themselves have many connections. In a highly connected neural network from the 1980s, each neuron might have 150 connections with other neurons. A neuron in a state-of-the-art neural network at the time of writing would have about as many connections as there are in a cat brain; a human neuron has on average about 10,000.

So, deep neural networks have more layers, and more, better-connected neurons. To train such networks, techniques beyond backprop were needed, and these were provided in 2006 by Geoff Hinton, a British-Canadian researcher who, more than anyone else, is identified with the deep learning movement. Hinton is, by any reckoning, a remarkable individual. He was one of the leaders of the PDP movement in the 1980s, and one of the inventors of backprop. What I find personally so remarkable is that Hinton didn't lose heart when PDP research began to lose favour. He stuck with it, and saw it through to its next incarnation, in the form of deep learning – for which he has received international acclaim. (Hinton is also, as it happens, the great-great-grandson of George Boole, who we met in Chapter 3 as one of the founders of modern logic; although, as Hinton has pointed out, that is probably the only thing that connects him to the logical tradition in AI.)

Deeper, bigger, more interconnected neural nets were one key ingredient in the success of deep learning; and work by Hinton and others on new techniques for training neural nets was another. But there were two further ingredients required to make deep learning a success: *data* and *computer power*.

The importance of data to machine learning can be illustrated no better than by the story of the **ImageNet** project.[8] ImageNet was the brainchild of Chinese-born researcher Fei Fei Li. Born in Beijing in 1976, Li moved to the US in the 1980s, and studied physics and electrical engineering. She joined Stanford University in 2009, and headed the AI lab at Stanford from 2013 to 2018. Li's insight was that the entire deep learning community would benefit from having large, well-maintained data sets that would provide a common baseline against which new systems could be trained, tested and compared. To this end, she started the ImageNet project.

ImageNet is a large online archive of images – about 14 million images at the time of writing. The images themselves are nothing more than photographs which you can download in common digital formats, such as JPEG. Crucially, though, the images have been carefully classified into 22,000 different categories, using an online thesaurus called WordNet,[9] which contains a large number of words that have been carefully arranged into categories, for example, identifying words that have the same or opposite meanings, and so on. Looking into the ImageNet archive now, I can see it has about 1,032 pictures in the category of 'volcanic crater'; it has about 122 pictures in the category of 'frisbee', and so on. It is important to understand that the images of a particular category in the database are not artificial; and nor were they chosen because they look similar – on the contrary. If you look at the 'frisbee' category, then you'll see that really the only thing they feature in common is, well, frisbees. In some images, of course, the frisbees are being thrown from one person to another, but in some, the frisbee is on a table, with nobody in view. They are all different – except that they all feature frisbees.

The eureka moment for image classification came in 2012, when Geoff Hinton and two colleagues, Alex Krizhevsky and Ilya Sutskever, demonstrated a system called **AlexNet**, a neural net that dramatically improved performance in an international image recognition competition.[10]

The final ingredient required to make deep learning work was raw computer-processing power. Training a deep neural net requires a huge amount of computer-processing time. The work that needs to be done in training is not particularly complex – but there is an enormous amount of it. A new type of computer processor that became common earlier this century proved to be ideal for the computational heavy lifting. Graphics Processing Units (GPUs) were originally developed to handle computer graphics problems, such as providing high-quality animations in computer games. But these chips turned out to be perfect for training neural nets. Every deep learning lab worth its name now has a stock of GPUs – but however many they have, their students will complain it is not enough.

For all their undoubted successes, deep learning and neural nets suffer from some well-publicized drawbacks.

First, the intelligence they embody is **opaque**. The expertise that a neural network has captured is embodied in the numeric weights associated with the links between neurons, and, as yet, we have no way of getting at or interpreting this knowledge. A deep learning program that tells you it sees cancerous tumours in an X-ray scan cannot justify its diagnosis; a deep learning program that declines a bank loan for a customer cannot tell you why it does so. In Chapter 3, we saw that expert systems like MYCIN were capable of a crude form of explanation – retracing the reasoning that was used to reach a conclusion or recommendation – but neural networks are not even capable of this crude form of explanation. There is a lot of work underway currently to try to deal with this issue. But, at present, we have no idea how to interpret the knowledge and representations that neural networks embody.

Another key problem for deep learning is that, in a subtle but very important way, neural networks are not robust. For example, it is possible to make slight changes to images, which are undetectable to humans, but which result in neural nets completely misclassifying them. Figure 17 illustrates this.[11] On the top is the original image of a panda; on the bottom, a doctored image. I hope you will agree that the two images appear to be the same, and in particular, they both seem to be pictures of a panda. While a neural net correctly classifies

(a)

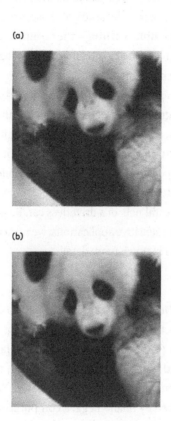

(b)

Figure 17
Panda or gibbon? A neural network correctly classifies image
(a) as a panda. However, it is possible to adjust this image in a way
that is not detectable to a human so that the same neural network
classifies the resulting image (b) as a gibbon.

the image on the top as a panda, the image on the bottom is classified as a gibbon. The study of these issues is known as **adversarial machine learning** – the terminology arises from the idea that an adversary is deliberately trying to obfuscate or confuse the program.

While we might not be overly concerned if our image classification program incorrectly classified our collection of animal images, adversarial machine learning has thrown up much more disturbing examples. For example, it turns out that road signs can be altered in such a way that, while a human has no difficulty interpreting them, they are completely misunderstood by the neural nets in a driverless car. Before we can use deep learning in sensitive applications, we need to understand these problems in much more detail.

DeepMind

The story of DeepMind, which I referred to earlier in this chapter, perfectly epitomizes the rise of deep learning. The company was founded in 2010 by Demis Hassabis, an AI researcher and computer games enthusiast, together with his school friend and entrepreneur Mustafa Suleyman, and they were joined by Shane Legg, a computational neuroscientist that Hassabis met while working at University College London.

As we heard, Google acquired DeepMind early in 2014; I can recall seeing stories in the press about the acquisition, and starting in surprise when I saw that DeepMind were an *AI* company. It was obvious at the time of the acquisition that AI was big news again, but the idea that there was an AI company in the UK *which I had never heard of* that was worth (apparently) £400 million was utterly bewildering. Along with many others, I immediately went to the DeepMind website, but, frankly, it didn't give me much more information. There were no details at all about the company's technology, products or services. It did, however, present one rather intriguing titbit: the publicly stated mission of DeepMind, it said, was *to solve intelligence*. I have already mentioned that the wildly varying fortunes of AI over the past 60 years have taught me to be wary of ambitious predictions about progress in AI: you can imagine how startled I was to see such a bold statement from a company that had just been acquired by one of the world's technology giants.

But the website offered no more detail, and I could find nobody who knew any more than I did. Most colleagues in AI regarded the announcement with scepticism, possibly tinged with a little professional jealousy. I heard little more about DeepMind until later that year, when I happened to meet a colleague, Nando de Freitas. Nando is one of the world leaders in deep learning, and at the time, he was a professor alongside me at Oxford University (he later left to work with DeepMind). He was on his way to a seminar with his students, and, under his arm, he was clutching a pile of scientific papers. He was obviously excited about something. He told me: 'This group in London, they've trained a program to play Atari video games from scratch.'

I have to say, I was not impressed. Programs that can play video games are nothing new. It's the sort of challenge we might give to an undergraduate student as a project – which is what I told Nando, dismissively. So, he patiently explained what was going on – and then I understood why he was so excited, and it slowly began to dawn on me that we really *were* entering a new era of AI.

The Atari system that Nando referred to was the Atari 2600 games console dating from the early 1980s. The platform was one of the first successful video game platforms: it supported video at the grand resolution of a 210 × 160 pixel grid, with up to 128 different colours; user input was through a joystick equipped with a single button. The platform used plug-in cartridges for game software, and the version that DeepMind used had 49 games in total. They described their aim as follows:[12]

> Our goal is to create a single neural network agent that is able to successfully learn to play as many of the games as possible. The network was not provided with any game-specific information or hand-designed visual features, and was not privy to the internal state of the emulator; it learned from nothing but the video input, the [score] . . . and the set of possible actions – just as a human player would.

To understand the significance of DeepMind's achievement, it is important to understand what their program did and didn't do. Perhaps most importantly, *nobody told the program anything at all about the games it was playing*. If we were trying to build an Atari-playing program using knowledge-based AI of the type we discussed in Chapter 3, then the way we would probably proceed would be by extracting knowledge from an expert Atari player, and trying to encode it using rules or some other knowledge representation scheme. (Good luck with that, if you want to try.) But DeepMind's program was given *no* knowledge about the game at all. The only information the program was given was the image that would appear on the screen of the console (in the form of a 210 × 160 colour-pixel grid), and the current score of the game. That was it – the program had nothing else to go on whatsoever. What is particularly significant here is that the program was not given information such as 'object A is at location (x, y)' – any information like this would have to be somehow extracted from the raw video data *by the program itself*.

The results were remarkable.[13] The program taught itself to play using reinforcement learning: playing a game repeatedly, experimenting in each game and getting feedback, and learning which actions led to rewards versus those that didn't. The program learned to play 29 of the 49 games at above human-level performance. With some games, it achieved super-human levels of performance.

One game in particular attracted a lot of interest. The game of Breakout was one of the first video games to be developed in the 1970s: it involves the player controlling a 'bat', which is used to bounce a 'ball' up to a wall, which is made up of coloured 'bricks'. Every time the ball hits a brick, the brick is destroyed, and the goal is to destroy the whole wall as quickly as possible. Figure 18 shows the program at an early stage of learning to play (after it has played the game about a hundred times) – at this stage, it misses the ball frequently.

But after a few hundred more training rounds, the program becomes expert: it doesn't *ever* miss the ball. And then something remarkable happened. The program learned that the most efficient way to accumulate points was to 'drill'

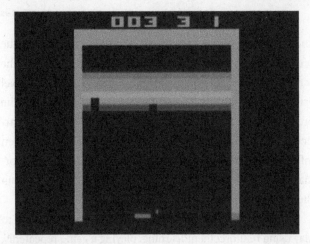

Figure 18
DeepMind's Atari player missing the ball at an early stage of learning to play Breakout.

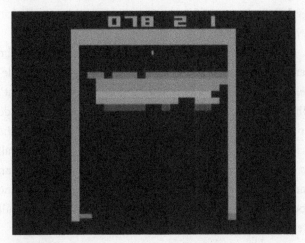

Figure 19
Eventually, the program learns that the best way to quickly accumulate a good score is to 'drill' a hole through the wall, so that the ball bounces above it. Nobody told the program to do this, and this behaviour took the developers completely by surprise.

a hole down the side of the wall, so that the ball was above the wall: the ball would then quickly bounce between the wall and the top barrier, without the player having to do anything (see Figure 19). This behaviour was not anticipated by DeepMind's engineers: it was autonomously learned by the program. The video of the game is readily available online: I have used it in my lectures dozens of times. Every time I show the video to a new audience, there is an audible gasp of amazement as the audience understands what the program had learned to do.

Again, just to underscore the point, DeepMind did *not* write a program to play an Atari video game: that would be easy. What they did was to write *one* program that *learned to play* 29 out of 49 Atari games at *better* than human-level ability; and the *only* inputs that the program received were the video feed and the score.

As I have already mentioned, the main technique used in the Atari player was reinforcement learning, which was implemented using a neural network with three hidden layers. The inputs to the neural network were pre-processed, having reduced the image from its raw 210 x 160 colour format to an 84 x 84 format, with a grey-scale replacing the colour. The program took a sample from its available inputs, only using every fourth image rather than using every single image produced. The neural network was trained using classic deep learning techniques ('stochastic gradient descent').

The program was by no means perfect: with some games, it performed very poorly, and it is interesting to look at why this was the case. One particularly problematic game for it was called Montezuma's Revenge. The difficulty with

Montezuma's Revenge is that rewards are very sparse: a player has to carry out a complex sequence of tasks before getting a reward (unlike, for example, the game of Breakout, where the reward follows more or less immediately). More generally, problems where the reward comes a long time after the relevant action are typically hard for reinforcement learning: this is the credit assignment problem discussed earlier, which is the problem of knowing which of your actions led to the reward you received.

If their Atari-playing program was the only thing that DeepMind had ever accomplished, then they would have earned a respectable place in AI history. But the company followed it up with a further series of stunning successes.

The most famous of these – and, at the time of writing, probably still the most famous AI system built to date – was called **AlphaGo**. It was a program to play the ancient Chinese board game Go.

Go is an intriguing target for AI. On the one hand, the rules of Go are *extremely* simple – much simpler than chess, for example. And yet, on the other, in 2015, Go-playing programs were well below the level of human expert performance. So why was Go such a difficult target? The answer is simply that the game is *big*. The board is a 19 × 19 grid, giving a total of 361 places where pieces may be laid; chess is played on an 8 × 8 grid, with therefore only 64 places for pieces. As we saw in Chapter 2, the branching factor for Go (the average number of moves available to a player at any given point in the game) is about 250, while chess has a branching factor of about 35. In other words, *Go is much larger than chess in terms of its board size and branching factor.*

And games of Go can last for a long time: 150 moves in one game is common.

The size of the game is what makes it hard for human players: thinking about a board of that size is at, or even beyond the limit of what human players can manage. This makes *explicit* strategizing in Go very difficult. For machines, too, this is a problem. The board size and branching factor seem to rule out naive search techniques – something else is required.

AlphaGo used two neural networks: the value network was solely concerned with estimating how good a given board position was, while the policy network made recommendations about which move to make, based on a current board position.[14] The policy network contained 13 layers, and was trained by using supervised learning first, where the training data was examples of expert games played by humans, and then reinforcement learning, based on self-play. Finally, these two networks were embedded in a sophisticated search technique, called Monte Carlo tree search.

Before the system was announced, DeepMind hired Fan Hui, a European Go champion, to play against AlphaGo: the system beat him five games to zero. This was the first time a Go program had beaten a human champion player in a full game. Shortly after, DeepMind announced that AlphaGo was going to be pitted against Lee Sedol, a world champion Go player, in a five-match competition to be held in Seoul, Korea, in March 2016.

The science of AlphaGo is fascinating, and AI researchers – myself included – were intrigued to see what would happen. (For the record, my guess was that AlphaGo might win one or two matches at most, but that Sedol would decisively win the competition overall.) What none of us expected was the completely unprecedented wave of publicity that surrounded the competition. The event made headlines across the world, and the story of the competition was even made into a feature film.[15]

In the event, AlphaGo beat Lee Sedol four games to one: Lee lost the first three, came back to win the fourth, but lost the fifth. By all accounts, Lee was stunned to lose the first game – he expected to win easily. More than one person joked at the time that AlphaGo deliberately lost the fourth match so that Lee wouldn't feel so bad.

At various points in the competition, human commentators remarked on what seemed to be strange moves made by AlphaGo. They were, apparently, 'not the kind of moves that a human would make'. Of course, when we try to analyse how AlphaGo played, we do so from a very human standpoint: we instinctively look for the kind of motives and strategies that *we* would use when we play the game: we anthropomorphize. Trying to understand AlphaGo in this way is pointless: AlphaGo is a program that was optimized to do one single thing – to play the game of Go. We want to attribute motives and reasoning and strategy to the program, but there are none of these: AlphaGo's extraordinary capability is captured in the weightings in its neural nets. These neural nets are nothing more than very long lists of numbers, and we have no way of extracting or rationalizing the expertise that they embody. AlphaGo can't tell us why it made its moves, and this, as we will see, is one of the key challenges with deep learning.

AlphaGo was widely touted as a triumph for the new AI of deep learning and big data – and indeed it was. But if you dig beneath the surface, you will find that an awful lot of the clever engineering in AlphaGo is classic AI search. Arthur Samuel, who in the 1950s developed the checkers-playing program we discussed in Chapter 2, would have had no difficulty in understanding the search techniques used in Alpha-Go: there is an unbroken thread from his work in the 1950s through to the most celebrated AI system of the modern era.

One might think that two landmark achievements were enough, but, just 18 months later, DeepMind were in the news again, this time with a generalization of AlphaGo called AlphaGo Zero. The extraordinary thing about AlphaGo Zero is that it learned how to play to a super-human level without any human supervision at all: *it just played against itself.*[16] To be fair, it had to play itself a *lot*, but nevertheless it was a striking result, and it was further generalized in another follow-up system called AlphaZero, which learned to play a range of other games, including chess: after just nine hours of self-play, AlphaZero was able to consistently beat or draw against Stockfish, one of the world's leading dedicated chess-playing programs. Veterans from the computer chess community were astonished. The idea that AlphaZero had played itself for nine hours and taught itself to be a world-class chess player was almost beyond belief. The exciting thing here was the *generality* of the approach: AlphaGo could only play Go, and for all its cleverness at this, it had required considerable effort to build the system specifically for that. Alpha-Zero, it seemed, could be turned to many different types of board games.

Of course, we need to be careful not to read too much into these results. For one thing, although AlphaZero embodies an impressive degree of generality (it is a far more general expert game-playing program than any other program before it), it does not in itself represent a major advance towards general intelligence. It doesn't remotely have the same kind of generality of intelligent capabilities that we all have. It can play board games superbly, but it can't converse or make a joke or cook an omelette or ride a bicycle or tie a pair of shoelaces. Its remarkable abilities are still actually very narrow. And of course, board games are highly abstract – they are a long way from the real world, as Rodney Brooks would be quick to remind us.

But whatever niggles and caveats one might have, I believe the simple truth is that DeepMind's work, starting with their Atari player through to AlphaZero, represented an extraordinary series of breakthrough achievements in AI. And in doing all this, they managed to capture the imagination of millions.

Towards General AI?

Deep learning has proved to be enormously successful, in the sense that it has enabled us to build programs that we could not have imagined a few years ago. But laudable as these achievements genuinely are, they are not a magic ingredient that will propel AI towards the Grand Dream. Let me try to explain why. To do this, we'll look at two widely used applications of deep learning techniques: image captioning and automated translation.

In an image-captioning problem, we want a computer to be able to take an image and give a textual description of it. Systems that have this capability to some degree are now in widespread usage – the last update of my Apple Mac software gave me a photo-management application that does a decent job of being able to classify my pictures into categories like 'Beach scene', 'Party', and so on. At the time of writing, several websites are available, typically run by international research groups, which allow you to upload photos and will attempt to provide captions for them. To better understand the limitations of current image-captioning technology – and hence deep learning – I uploaded a family picture to one (in this case, Microsoft's CaptionBot)[17] – the photo is shown in Figure 20.

Before examining CaptionBot's response, pause for a moment to look at the picture. If you are British, or a fan of science fiction, then you will very probably recognize the gentleman on the right of the picture: he is Matt Smith, the actor who played the eponymous Doctor Who from 2010 to 2013 in the BBC television show. (You won't recognize the gentleman on the left – he is my late grandfather-in-law.)

CaptionBot's interpretation of the picture was as follows:

> I think it's Matt Smith standing posing for a picture and they seem :-) :-)

CaptionBot correctly identified a key element of the picture, and went some way to recognizing the setting (standing; posing for a picture; smiling). However, this success can easily mislead us into thinking that CaptionBot is doing something which it most certainly is not: and what it is not doing is *understanding*. To illustrate this point, think about what it means for the system to identify Matt Smith. As we saw previously, machine learning systems like CaptionBot are trained by

Figure 20
What is going on in this picture?

giving them a very large number of training examples, each example consisting of a picture together with a textual explanation of the picture. Eventually, after being shown enough pictures containing Matt Smith, together with the explanatory text 'Matt Smith', the system is able to correctly produce the text 'Matt Smith' whenever it is presented with a picture of the man himself. This is a very useful capability – the culmination of decades of diligent research, with endless possible applications.

But CaptionBot is not 'recognizing' Matt Smith in any meaningful sense. To understand this, suppose I asked *you* to interpret what you see in the picture. You might come back with an explanation like this:

> I can see Matt Smith, the actor who played Doctor Who, standing with his arm around an older man – I don't know who he is. They are both smiling. Matt is dressed as his Doctor Who character, so he is probably filming somewhere. In his pocket is a rolled-up piece of paper, so that is likely to be a script. He is holding a paper cup, so he is probably on a tea break. Behind them, the blue box is the Tardis, the space ship/time machine that Doctor Who travels around in. They are outdoors, so Matt is probably filming on location somewhere. There must be a film crew, cameras and lights somewhere close by.

CaptionBot wasn't able to do any of that. While it was able to identify Matt Smith, in the sense of correctly producing the text 'Matt Smith', it wasn't able to *use* this knowledge to then interpret and understand what is going on in the picture. And the absence of understanding is precisely the point here.

Apart from the fact that systems like CaptionBot only have a limited ability to interpret the pictures they are shown, there is another sense in which they do not, and currently cannot, demonstrate understanding of the kind that we can.

When you looked at the picture of Matt Smith dressed as Doctor Who, you would probably have experienced a range of thoughts and emotions, above and beyond simply identifying the actor and interpreting what was going on. If you were a Doctor Who fan, you might have found yourself reminiscing fondly about your favourite episode of *Doctor Who* with Matt Smith in the title role ('The Girl Who Waited', I hope we can all agree). You might have remembered watching Matt Smith as Doctor Who with your parents or your children. You might have remembered being scared by the monsters in the programme, and so on. It might remind you of an occasion where you were on a film set, or saw a film crew.

Your *understanding* of the picture is therefore grounded in your *experiences* as a person in the world. Such an understanding is not possible for CaptionBot, because CaptionBot has no such grounding (and nor, of course, does it purport to). CaptionBot is completely *disembodied* from the world, and as Rodney Brooks reminded us, intelligence is *embodied*. I emphasize that this is not an argument that AI systems cannot demonstrate understanding, but rather that understanding means more than being able to map a certain input (a picture containing Matt Smith) to a certain output (the text 'Matt Smith'). Such a capability may be *part* of understanding, but it isn't by any means the whole story.

Automated translation from one language to another is another area in which deep learning has led to rapid progress over the past decade. Looking at what these tools can and cannot do helps us to understand the limitations of deep learning. Google Translate is probably the best-known automated translation system.[18] Originally made available as a product in 2006, the most recent versions of Google Translate use deep learning and neural nets. The system is trained by giving it large volumes of translated texts.

Let's see what happens when the 2019 iteration of Google Translate is given an unreasonably difficult problem: translating the first paragraph of *À la recherche du temps perdu* (*In Search of Lost Time*), the classic early-twentieth-century novel by the French author Marcel Proust. Here is the first paragraph, in the original French:

> *Longtemps, je me suis couché de bonne heure. Parfois, à peine ma bougie éteinte, mes yeux se fermaient si vite que je n'avais pas le temps de me dire: 'Je m'endors.' Et, une demi-heure après, la pensée qu'il était temps de chercher le sommeil m'éveillait; je voulais poser le volume que je croyais avoir encore dans les mains et souffler ma lumière; je n'avais pas cessé en dormant de faire des réflexions sur ce que je venais de lire, mais ces réflexions avaient pris un tour un peu particulier; il me semblait que j'étais moi-même ce dont parlait l'ouvrage: une église, un quatuor, la rivalité de François Ier et de Charles Quint.*

I'm embarrassed to say that, despite the decade-long efforts of a hard-working group of language teachers, I understand very little French: I can make out only the odd isolated phrase in the above text, and without help, I have no sense whatsoever of what the entire text means.

Here is that first paragraph, translated into English by a professional translator:[19]

> For a long time I used to go to bed early. Sometimes, when I had put out my candle, my eyes would close so quickly that I had not even time to say 'I'm going to sleep.' And half an hour later the thought that it was time to go to sleep would awaken me; I would try to put away the book which, I imagined, was still in my hands, and to blow out the light; I had been thinking all the time, while I was asleep, of what I had just been reading, but my thoughts had run into a channel of their own, until I myself seemed actually to have become the subject of my book: a church, a quartet, the rivalry between François I and Charles V.

Much better! But interestingly, although this is beautifully written English, the *meaning* is still not completely transparent, not to me, at least. What does the author mean when he writes 'I . . . seemed actually to have become the subject of my book: a church, a quartet, the rivalry between François I and Charles V'? How can you 'become' a church? What does he mean by a 'quartet'? What 'rivalry' between François I and Charles V is he referring to? And, for someone that uses electric lighting: what does it mean to 'blow out' a light?

Now let's see what Google Translate made of it:

> Long time, I went to bed early. Sometimes, when my candle, my eyes would close so quickly that I had no time to say: 'I fall asleep.' And half an hour later the thought that it was time to go to sleep would awaken me; I wanted

to ask the volume that I thought I had in my hands and blow my light; I had not ceased while sleeping to reflections on what I had read, but these reflections had taken a rather peculiar turn; I felt that I myself was what spoke the book: a church, a quartet, the rivalry between Francis I and Charles V.

This is recognizably the same text as the professional translation, and so Google Translate is doing something sophisticated. But you don't have to be a professional translator, or an expert on literature, to see its limitations. The expression 'blow my light' makes no sense in English; and the sentences that follow don't make sense either; indeed, they are rather comical. And the translation includes phrasings that a native English speaker would never use. The overall impression that we are getting is of a recognizable but unnaturally distorted version of the text.

Of course, we gave Google Translate an unreasonably difficult problem – translating Proust would be a huge challenge even for a professional French-to-English translator. So why is this, and why is it so hard for automated translation tools to tackle?

The point is that a translator of Proust's classic novel requires *more than just an understanding of French*. You could be the most competent reader of French in the world, and still find yourself bewildered by Proust, and not just because of his frankly exhausting prose style. To properly *understand* Proust – and hence to properly *translate* Proust – you also need to have a great deal of background knowledge. Knowledge about French society and life in the early twentieth century (for example, you would need to know they used candles for lighting); knowledge of French history (of François I and Charles V and the rivalry between them); knowledge about early-twentieth-century French literature (the writing style of the time, allusions that authors might make); and knowledge about Proust himself (what were his main concerns?). A neural net of the type used in Google Translate has none of that.

This observation – that to *understand* Proust's text requires *knowledge* of various kinds – is not a new one. We came across it before, in the context of the Cyc system in Chapter 3. Remember that Cyc was supposed to be given knowledge corresponding to the whole of consensus reality, and the Cyc hypothesis was that this would yield human-level general intelligence. Researchers in knowledge-based AI would be keen for me to point out to you that, decades ago, they anticipated exactly this issue. (The sharp retort from the neural nets community would then be that the techniques proposed by the knowledge-based AI community didn't work out so well, did they?) But it is not obvious that just continuing to refine deep learning techniques will address this problem. Deep learning will be part of the solution, but a proper solution will, I think, require something much more than just a larger neural net, or more processing power, or more training data in the form of boring French novels. It will require breakthroughs at least as dramatic as deep learning itself. I suspect those breakthroughs will require explicitly represented knowledge as well as deep learning: somehow, we will have to bridge the gap between the world of explicitly represented knowledge, and the world of deep learning and neural nets.

The Great Schism

In 2010, I was asked to organize one of the big international AI meetings – the European Conference on AI (ECAI), which was to be held in Lisbon, Portugal. Attending conferences like ECAI are an important part of the life of an AI researcher. We write up our research results and submit them to the conference, where they are reviewed by a 'programme committee' – a group of eminent scientists who decide which of the submissions deserve to be heard at the conference. Good conferences in AI only accept about one in five submissions, so having a paper accepted is very prestigious; the really big AI conferences attract more than 5,000 submissions. So, you can imagine I felt very honoured to be asked to chair the ECAI – it's an indication that the scientific community trusts you, and it is the sort of distinction that academics mention when they apply for a pay rise.

My job as chair included assembling the programme committee, and I was keen to include a good representation from the machine learning community. But something unexpected happened: it seemed that every machine learning researcher I invited said No. It isn't unusual to be politely rebuffed when you are trying to persuade people into a role like this – after all, it is a lot of work. But it seemed I couldn't get *anyone* from machine learning to sign up. Was it me, I wondered? Or ECAI? Or what?

I sought advice from colleagues who had organized the event previously, and others who had experience of other AI events. They reported similar experiences. The machine learning community, it seemed, just wasn't very interested in the events that I thought of as, well, 'mainstream AI'. I knew that the two big scientific events for the machine learning community were the Neural Information Processing Systems (NeurIPS) Conference and the International Conference on Machine Learning (ICML). Most sub-fields of AI have their own specialist conferences, so the fact that this community's attention should be focused on those was not surprising. But until then, it hadn't quite dawned upon me that many in the machine learning community simply don't define themselves as being part of 'AI' at all.

With hindsight, the schism between AI and ML seems to have started very early on: perhaps with the publication by Minsky and Papert of their 1969 book, *Perceptrons*, which, as we saw earlier, seems to have played a role in killing off neural AI research from the late 1960s until PDP emerged in the mid-1980s. Even in the present day, half a century later, there is still bitterness about the consequences of that publication. Whatever the origins of the schism, the truth is that, at some point, many in the machine learning research area diverged from mainstream AI, and took off on their own trajectory. While there are certainly many researchers who see themselves as comfortably straddling the fence between machine learning and artificial intelligence, many machine learning experts nowadays would be surprised and possibly irritated to have the label 'AI' attached to their work: because, for them, AI is solely the long list of failed ideas that I have documented elsewhere in this book.

PART THREE

Where Are We Going?

CHAPTER 6
AI Today

Deep learning opened the floodgates for applications of AI. In the second decade of the twenty-first century, AI has attracted more interest than any new technology since the World Wide Web in the 1990s. Everyone with data and a problem to solve started to ask whether deep learning might help them – and in many cases, the answer proved to be Yes. AI has started to make its presence felt in every aspect of our lives. Everywhere that technology is used, AI is finding applications: in education, science, industry, commerce, agriculture, healthcare, entertainment, the media and arts and beyond. While some applications of AI will be very visible in the future, others will not. AI systems will be embedded throughout our world, in the same way that computers are today. And in the same way that computers and the World Wide Web changed our world, so too will AI. I could no more tell you what the full range of applications of AI will be than I could tell you about all the applications of computers, but here are a few of my favourite examples which have emerged during the past few years.

In April 2019, you may recall seeing the first ever pictures of a black hole.[1] In a mind-boggling experiment, astronomers used data collected from eight radio telescopes across the world to construct an image of a black hole which is 40 billion miles across and 55 million light years away. The image represents one of the most dramatic scientific achievements this century. But what you might *not* know is that it was only made possible through AI: advanced computer vision algorithms were used to reconstruct the image, 'predicting' missing elements of the picture.

In 2018, researchers from the computer processor company Nvidia demonstrated the ability of AI software to create completely convincing but completely fake pictures of people.[2] The pictures were developed by a new type of neural network, one called a generative adversarial network. The pictures are uncanny: at first sight they look utterly realistic, and it is hard to believe that they are not real people. The evidence of our eyes tells us that they are – but they were created by a neural net. This capability, unimaginable at the turn of the century, will be a key component of virtual reality tools in the future: AI is on the way to constructing convincing alternative realities.

In late 2018, DeepMind researchers at a conference in Mexico announced AlphaFold, a system to understand a fundamental issue in medicine called protein folding.[3] Protein folding involves predicting the shape that certain molecules will take on. Understanding the shapes that they will form is essential for progress in treating conditions such as Alzheimer's disease. Unfortunately, the problem is fearsomely difficult. AlphaFold used classic machine learning techniques to learn how to predict protein shapes, and represents a promising step on the road to understanding these kinds of devastating conditions.

In the remainder of this chapter, I want to look in more detail at two of the most prominent opportunities for AI: the first is the use of AI in healthcare; the second is the long-held dream of driverless cars.

AI-Powered Healthcare

> People should stop training radiologists now. It is just completely obvious that within five years deep learning is going to do better than radiologists.
> — Geoff Hinton (2016)

> Cardiogram is building your personal healthcare assistant. We want to turn your wearable device into a continuous health monitor that can be used to not only track sleep and fitness, but one day may also prevent a stroke and save your life.
> — Cardiogram company website[4]

Anybody with even the vaguest interest in politics and economics will recognize that the provision of healthcare is one of the most important global financial problems for private citizens and for governments. On the one hand, improvements in healthcare provision over the past two centuries are probably the most important single achievement of the scientific method in the industrialized world: in 1800, life expectancy for someone in Europe would have been less than 50 years;[5] someone born in Europe today could reasonably expect to live late into their seventies. Maternal deaths in childbirth are now a rarity in the developed world. These dramatic changes are in part the result of a better understanding of hygiene. But the development of drugs and treatments for diseases and other ailments has been just as important – with by far the most important of these being the development of antibiotics in the 1940s, which, for the first time, provided effective, reliable treatment for bacterial infections. Of course, these improvements in healthcare and life expectancy have not yet found their way to all the parts of the globe – at the time of writing, life expectancy in the Central African Republic is just 51, and there remain many parts of the world where childbirth is dangerous for both mother and child. But, overall, the trend seems to be positive, and this is of course a cause for celebration.

But these welcome advances have created challenges. Firstly, populations are, on average, becoming older. And older people typically require more healthcare than younger people, which means that the overall cost of healthcare has risen. Secondly, as we develop new drugs and treatments for diseases and other afflictions, the overall range of conditions that we can treat increases – which also leads to additional healthcare costs. And, of course, a key underlying reason for the expense of healthcare is that the resources required to deliver healthcare are expensive, and people with the skill and qualifications to do so are scarce: to become qualified as a General Practitioner in the UK requires about ten years of training.

Because of these problems, healthcare – and more particularly *funding* for healthcare – is everywhere a perennial issue for politicians to wrangle with. In the United Kingdom, we see endless arguments about how best to fund our National Health Service, which was introduced in the late 1940s as a national service, paid for through taxation, with the aim of providing healthcare for everyone which was free at the point of use. In Britain we all love the NHS, but we argue endlessly about how best it should be funded.

So, healthcare is crucial, but difficult to deliver. Wouldn't it be wonderful, then, if there was a *technological* fix to the problem?

The idea of AI for healthcare is nothing new – we saw earlier that the seminal MYCIN expert system was widely acclaimed after demonstrating better-than-human performance when diagnosing the causes of blood diseases in humans. Healthcare funding was a problem back in the early 1980s, just as it is now, and so, for all the reasons I discussed above, there was a lot of excitement about the idea of programs that could capture the capabilities of human healthcare professionals. No surprise, then, that MYCIN was followed by a wave of similar healthcare-related expert systems, although it is fair to say that relatively few of these made it far from their research labs. But nowadays interest in AI for healthcare is back with a vengeance, and this time there are several developments which suggest it has a better chance of succeeding on a large scale.

One important new opportunity for AI-powered healthcare is what we might call *personal healthcare management*. Personal healthcare management is made possible by the advent of *wearable technology* – smart watches like the Apple Watch, and activity/fitness trackers such as Fitbit. These devices continually monitor aspects of our physiology such as our heart rate and body temperature. This combination of features raises the fascinating prospect of having large numbers of people generating data streams relating to their current state of health on a continual basis. These data streams can then be analysed by AI systems, either locally (via the smart-phone you carry in your pocket) or by uploading them to an AI system on the Internet.

It is important not to underestimate the potential of this technology. *For the first time ever, our state of health can be monitored on a continual basis.* At the most basic level, our AI-based healthcare systems can provide impartial advice on managing our health. This is, in some sense, what devices like Fitbit already do – they monitor our activity, and can also set us targets (the '10,000 steps a day challenge' is one obvious, very successful example). Experience suggests that we can improve people's compliance with such targets through gamification – turning the targets into competitions or games, perhaps involving social media.

Mass-market wearables are in their infancy, but there are plenty of indications of what is to come. In September 2018, Apple introduced the fourth generation of its Apple Watch, which included a heart monitor for the first time. Electrocardiogram apps on the watch can monitor the data provided by the heart-rate tracker, and have the potential to identify the symptoms of heart diseases, perhaps even calling for an ambulance on your behalf if necessary. One immediate application is monitoring for the elusive signs of atrial fibrillation – an irregular heartbeat – which can be the precursor to a stroke or other circulatory emergency. An accelerometer in the phone can be used to identify the signature of someone falling, potentially calling for assistance if needed. Such systems require only fairly simple AI techniques: what makes them practicable now is the fact that we can carry a powerful computer with us, which is continually connected to the Internet, and which can be linked to a wearable device equipped with a range of physiological sensors.

Some applications of personal healthcare may not even require sensors, just a standard smartphone. Colleagues of mine at the University of Oxford believe it may be possible to detect the onset of dementia *simply from the way that someone uses their smartphone*. Changes in the way that people use their phone, or changes in patterns of behaviour recorded by their phone can indicate the onset of the disease, before any other person notices these signs, and long before a formal diagnosis would normally be made. Dementia is a devastating condition, and presents an enormous challenge for societies with aging populations. Tools that can assist with its early diagnosis or management would be very welcome. Such work is still at the very preliminary stages, but it provides yet another indicator of what is to come.

This is all very exciting, but the opportunities presented by these new technologies come with some potential pitfalls too. The most obvious of these is privacy. Wearable technology is *intimate*: it continually watches us, and while the data it obtains can be used to help us, it also presents boundless opportunities for misuse.

One area of immediate concern is the insurance industry. In 2016, the health insurance company Vitality started offering Apple Watches along with their insurance policies. The watches monitor your activity and your insurance premiums are then set according to how much exercise you undertake. If, one month, you decided to be a couch potato and undertook no exercise, you might pay a full premium; but you could offset this the next month by going on a fitness frenzy, leading to a reduced premium. There is perhaps nothing directly wrong with such a scheme, but it does suggest some more uncomfortable scenarios. For example, in September 2018, the US-based insurance company John Hancock announced that in future, it will *only* offer insurance policies to individuals who are prepared to wear activity-tracking technology.[6] The announcement was widely criticized.

Taking this kind of scenario further, what if we were only able to access national healthcare schemes (or other national benefits) if we agreed to be monitored and to meet daily exercise targets. You want healthcare? Then you have to walk 10,000 steps per day! Some people see nothing wrong with such a scenario; for others, it represents a profound intrusion, and an abuse of our basic human rights.

Automated diagnosis is another exciting potential application for AI in healthcare. The use of machine learning to analyse data from medical imaging devices such as X-ray machines and ultrasound scanners has received enormous attention over the past decade. At the time of writing, it seems as if a new scientific article is announced showing that AI systems can effectively identify abnormalities from medical images every single day. This is a classic application of machine learning: we train the machine learning program by showing it examples of normal images, and examples of abnormal images. The program learns to identify images with abnormalities.

A well-publicized example of this work came from DeepMind. In 2018, the company announced they were working with Moorfields Eye Hospital in London to develop techniques to automatically identify diseases and abnormalities from eye scans.[7] Eye scans are a major activity for Moorfields: they typically undertake 1,000 of them every working day, and analysing these scans is a large part of the work of the hospital.

DeepMind's system used two neural networks, the first to 'segment' the scan (identifying the different components of the image), and the second for diagnosis. The first network was trained on about 900 images, which showed how a human expert would segment the image; the second network was trained on about 15,000 examples. Experimental trials indicated that the system performed at or above the level of human experts.

These are terrific results, and you don't have to look far to find many other striking examples of how current AI techniques are being used to build systems with similar capabilities – for identifying cancerous tumours on X-rays, diagnosing heart disease from ultrasound scans and many other examples. Geoff Hinton, whom you may remember was one of the co-creators of a highly successful image-recognition program called AlexNet, is so convinced that machine learning will provide the solution to diagnosis from medical imaging that he made the rather bold statement about radiologists that I used to introduce this section. Unsurprisingly, radiologists were outraged. They were quick to point out that their role requires a great deal more than just looking at X-rays.[8]

Many others have urged caution in the push for AI's use in healthcare. For one thing, the healthcare profession is, above all, a *human* profession: perhaps more than any other role, it requires the ability to interact with and relate to people. A GP needs to be able to 'read' her patients; to understand the social context in which she is seeing them; to understand the kinds of treatment plans that are likely to work for this particular patient versus those which aren't; and so on. All the evidence indicates that we can now build systems that can achieve human expert performance in analysing medical data – but this is only a small part (albeit a phenomenally important part) of what human healthcare professionals do.

Another argument against AI's use in healthcare is that some people would prefer to rely on human judgement rather than that of a machine. They would rather deal with a person. There are two further points to make here.

First of all, it is hopelessly naive to hold up human judgement as some sort of gold standard. We are, all of us, flawed. Even the most experienced and diligent doctor will sometimes get tired and emotional. And, however hard we try, we all fall prey to biases and prejudices, and often, we just aren't very good at rational decision-making. Machines *can* reliably make diagnoses that are every bit as good as those of human experts – the challenge/opportunity in healthcare is to put that capability to its best use. My belief is that AI is best used not to replace human healthcare professionals, but to *augment* their capabilities – to free them from routine tasks and allow them to focus on the really difficult parts of their job; to provide another opinion to counterbalance their own, and further context for their work.

Secondly, the idea that we have a choice between dealing with a human physician or an AI healthcare program seems to me to be a first-world problem. For many people in other parts of the world the choice may instead be between healthcare provided by an AI system, or *nothing*. AI has a lot to offer here. It raises the possibility of getting healthcare expertise out to people in parts of the world who don't have access to it at present. I find this a truly thrilling prospect; and of all the opportunities that AI presents us with, this is the one that may have the greatest social impact.

Driverless Cars

> Heavier-than-air flying machines are impossible.
> — Lord Kelvin, President of the Royal Society, 1895

At the time of writing, more than a million people per year are dying in automobile-related accidents internationally; China and India alone account for about a quarter of these. A further 50 million people are injured every year in automobile accidents. These are staggering statistics when you consider that a new strain of flu which could take a million lives per year would cause a global panic. And yet we are accustomed to the danger of road travel – we seem to accept the risk as an occupational hazard of living in the modern world. But AI holds out the real prospect of dramatically reducing those risks: driverless cars are a real possibility in the medium term, and, ultimately, they have the potential to save lives on a massive scale.

There are, of course, many other good reasons for wanting autonomous vehicles. Computers can be programmed to drive cars *efficiently*, making better use of scarce and expensive fuel or power resources, resulting in environmentally friendlier cars with lower running costs. Computers could also potentially make better use of road networks, for example, allowing far greater through-put at congested road junctions. And if cars become safer, the need for them to have expensive and heavy protective chassis will be reduced, again leading to cheaper, more fuel-efficient vehicles. There is even an argument that driverless cars will make car ownership unnecessary: driverless taxis will be so cheap, goes the argument, that it won't make economic sense to own your own car.

For all these reasons, and more, driverless cars are an obvious and compelling idea, and it will therefore be no surprise to you that there has been a long history of research in this area. As automobiles became mass-market products during the 1920s and 1930s, the scale of deaths and injuries that resulted – mostly as a result of human error – immediately prompted discussion about the possibility of automated cars. Although there have been a range of experiments in this field since the 1940s, it is only since the emergence of microprocessor technologies in the 1970s that they really began to be feasible. But the challenge of driverless cars is immense: and the fundamental problem is perception. If you could find a way for a car to know precisely where it was and what was around it, then you would have solved the problem of driverless cars. The solution to this problem was to be modern machine learning techniques: without them, driverless cars would not be possible.

The **PROMETHEUS** project, funded by the pan-governmental EUREKA research funding organization in Europe, is widely seen as a forerunner of today's driverless car technology. PROMETHEUS, which ran from 1987 to 1995, led to a demonstration in 1995, in which a car drove itself from Munich in Germany to Odense in Denmark and back. Human interventions were required on average about every five and a half miles; the longest stretch managed without human intervention was about a hundred miles. This was a remarkable feat – all the more remarkable because of the limited computer power available at the time. Although PROMETHEUS was only a proof that the concept could work and therefore a long way from a fully finished vehicle, the results of the project led to innovations that are now conventional in commercial automobiles, such as smart cruise control systems. And above all, PROMETHEUS signalled that this technology would, eventually, be commercially viable.

By 2004, progress was such that DARPA organized a **Grand Challenge**, inviting researchers to enter a competition in which vehicles would autonomously traverse 150 miles of the American countryside. A total of 106 teams entered, from universities and companies alike, each hoping to win the one million dollars prize money offered by DARPA. These were whittled down to 15 finalists, but in the event, none of the 15 finalists completed more than 8 miles of the course. Some vehicles failed to even make it out of the starting area. The most successful entry, Sandstorm from Carnegie Mellon University, managed just 7.5 miles, before going off course and getting stuck on an embankment.

My recollection of events at the time is that most AI researchers took the 2004 Grand Challenge as proof that driverless car technology was still some way from being practical. I was a little surprised to hear that DARPA had immediately announced a follow-on competition for 2005, with the prize money doubled to two million dollars. There were many more entries for the 2005 competition – 195 in total, which were whittled down to 23 finalists. The final competition was held on 8 October 2005, and the goal was for the vehicles to cross 132 miles of the Nevada desert. This time, five teams completed the course. The winner was the robot **STANLEY**, designed by a team from Stanford University, led by Sebastian Thrun. STANLEY completed the course in just under seven hours, averaging about 20 m.p.h. A converted Volkswagen Touareg, STANLEY was equipped with seven on-board computers, interpreting sensor data from GPS, laser rangefinders, radar and video feed.

The 2005 Grand Challenge was one of the great technological achievements in human history. On that day, driverless cars became a solved problem, in the same way that heavier-than-air powered flight became a solved problem at Kitty Hawk just over a century earlier. The first flight by the Wright brothers lasted just 12 seconds, in which time the Wright Flyer I flew only 120 feet. But after that 12-second journey, powered heavier-than-air flight was a reality – and so it was with driverless cars after the 2005 Grand Challenge.

The 2005 Grand Challenge was followed by a series of other challenges, of which probably the most important was the 2007 **Urban Challenge**. While the 2005 competition tested vehicles on rural roads, the 2007 challenge aimed to test them in built-up urban environments. Driverless cars were required to complete a course, while obeying Californian road traffic laws, and coping with everyday situations like parking, intersections and traffic jams. Thirty-six teams made it to the national qualifying event, and of these 11 were selected for the final, held on a disused former airport in southern California on 3 November 2007. Six teams successfully completed the challenge, with the winner, from Carnegie Mellon University, averaging approximately 14 m.p.h. throughout the four-hour challenge.

We have seen massive investment in driverless car technology since then, both from established automobile companies, who are desperate not to be left behind, and from newer companies who perceive an opportunity to steal a march on traditional manufacturers.

In 2014, the US Society of Automotive Engineers provided a useful classification scheme to characterize the different levels of autonomy within a vehicle:[9]

> **Level 0: No autonomy** The car has no automated control functions whatsoever. The driver is in complete control of the vehicle at all times (although the vehicle may provide warnings and other data to assist the driver). Level 0 includes the vast majority of cars on the roads today.
>
> **Level 1: Driver assistance** Here the car takes some level of control from the driver, typically on routine matters, but the driver is expected to pay complete attention. An example of driver assistance would be an adaptive cruise control system, which can maintain the car's speed, using brakes and accelerator.
>
> **Level 2: Partial automation** At this level, the car takes control of steering and speed, although again the driver is expected to be continually monitoring the driving environment and to be ready to intervene if necessary.

Level 3: Conditional automation At this level, the human driver is no longer expected to be continually monitoring the driving environment, although the car may ask the user to take control if it encounters a situation that it cannot cope with.

Level 4: High automation Here, the car takes control under normal circumstances, although the driver can still intervene.

Level 5: Full automation This is the dream of driverless cars: you get in a car, state your destination, and the car does everything from there. There is no steering wheel.

At the time of writing, the state of the art system for commercially available driverless car technology is probably Tesla's Autopilot, initially available on the Tesla Model S car. Released in 2012, the Model S was the flagship vehicle in Tesla's line-up of high-specification electric cars, and at the time of its release, it was probably the world's most technologically advanced commercially available electric car. From September 2014 onwards, all Tesla Model S vehicles were equipped with cameras, radar and acoustic range sensors. The purpose of all this high-tech kit was made plain in October 2015, when Tesla released software for the car that enabled its 'Autopilot' feature – a limited automatic driving capability.

The media were quick to start hailing Autopilot as the first driverless car, although Tesla was at pains to point out the limitations of the technology. In particular, Tesla insisted that drivers should keep their hands on the steering wheel at all times while Autopilot was engaged. In terms of the levels of autonomy presented above, Autopilot seemed to be at Level 2.

However good the technology was, it was fairly obvious that serious accidents involving Autopilot would eventually occur, and that the first fatality involving Autopilot would make headlines across the world. And this indeed proved to be the case when, in May 2016, a Tesla owner in Florida was killed when his car drove into an 18-wheel truck. Reports suggested that the car's sensors had been confused by the view of the white truck against a bright sky: as a consequence, the car's AI software failed to recognize there was another vehicle present and drove directly into the truck at high speed, instantly killing the driver.

Other incidents highlight what seems to be a key problem with current driverless car technology. At Level 0 autonomy, it is completely clear what is expected of the driver: everything. And at Level 5 autonomy, it is similarly obvious: the driver is expected to do nothing. But between these two extremes, it seems much less evident what drivers must expect to do, and the anecdotal evidence from the Florida incident and elsewhere is that drivers place far too much reliance on the technology – treating it as if it were Level 4 or 5, when in fact it is far below this. This mismatch between driver expectations and the reality of what the system can do seems to be driven at least in part by an over-excited press, who don't seem to be very good at understanding or communicating the subtleties of technological capability. (It probably doesn't help that Tesla named their system 'Autopilot'.)

In March 2018, another high-profile accident involving

driverless cars raised further doubts about the technology. On 18 March 2018, in Tempe, Arizona, a driverless car owned by Uber hit and killed a 49-year-old pedestrian, Elaine Herzberg, while in driverless mode. As is typically the way with accidents of this kind, there were a number of contributory causes. The car was travelling faster than the automatic emergency braking system could handle, so by the time the car recognized that emergency braking was required, it was too late to be able to do anything about it. Although the car's sensors recognized that there was an 'obstacle' (the victim, Elaine Herzberg) which called for emergency braking, the software seems to have been designed to avoid doing this (suggesting some confusion, or at least, a rather strange set of priorities, in the mind of the programmers). But, most importantly, the 'safety driver' in the car, whose main purpose was to intervene in incidents like this, appears to have been watching TV on her smartphone, paying little attention to the outside environment. It may well be that she was too confident in the car's driverless abilities as well. The tragic death of Elaine Herzberg was entirely avoidable: but the failure was human, not technological.

It seems depressingly inevitable that there will be many more tragedies like these before we see practical, mass-market driverless cars. We need to do everything we reasonably can to anticipate and avoid such tragedies. But they will occur in any case; and when they do, we need to learn the lessons from them. The development of technologies such as fly-by-wire aircraft suggests that, in the long run, we will have much safer vehicles as a consequence.

The current flurry of activity around driverless vehicles

suggests that the technology is tantalizingly close – but just *how* close is it? When will you be able to jump into a driverless car and state your destination? One of the most impartial indicators about this comes from information that driverless car companies are required to provide to the State of California in order to gain a licensce to test their cars within that state. The most important such piece of information is the Autonomous Vehicle Disengagement Report. The disengagement report must indicate how many miles the relevant car from which company drove in driverless mode, and how many disengagements occurred during these tests. A disengagement is a situation in which a person had to intervene to take over control of the car – what *should* have occurred in the case of Elaine Herzberg. A disengagement doesn't necessarily mean that the person had to intervene to avoid an accident – far less a fatality – but nevertheless this data gives an indication of how well the technology is performing. The fewer disengagements per autonomous mile driven the better.

In 2017, 20 companies filed disengagement reports with the State of California. The clear leader, in terms of number of miles driven and lowest number of disengagements per 1,000 miles, was a company called Waymo, who reported, on average, a disengagement about every 5,000 miles; the worst performance was by automobile giant Mercedes, who reported no fewer than 774 disengagements per 1,000 miles. Waymo are Google's driverless car company. Originally, it was an internal Google project, run by 2005 DARPA Grand Challenge winner Sebastian Thrun, and it became a subsidiary company of Google in 2016. In 2018, Waymo reported travelling 11,000 miles between disengagements.

So, what does this data tell us? And, in particular, how soon will driverless cars be an everyday reality?

Well, the first conclusion we can draw, from the relatively poor performance of automobile giants like BMW, Mercedes and Volkswagen, is that a historical track record in the automotive industry is *not* the key requirement for success in driverless car technology. On reflection, this should come as no surprise: the key to driverless cars is not the internal combustion engine, but *software* – AI software. No surprise, then, that the US automobile giant General Motors acquired driverless car company Cruise Automation for an undisclosed (but obviously very large) sum in 2016, while Ford invested one billion dollars in self-driving start-up company Argo AI. Both companies made public, very ambitious claims about the roll-out of commercial driverless cars: Ford predicted they would have a 'fully autonomous vehicle in commercial operation' by 2021.[10]

Of course, we don't know the precise criteria that companies use to decide when a disengagement occurs. It could be that Mercedes, for example, are just being overly cautious. But it seems hard to avoid the conclusion that, at the time of writing, Waymo are far ahead of the pack.

It is interesting to compare the State of California disengagement reports with what we know about human-driver performance. There doesn't seem to be any definitive statistical data about the latter, but it seems that in the USA, humans drive on average hundreds of thousands of miles between serious incidents – possibly even a million. This suggests that even the market leader, Waymo, would have to improve their technology by up to two orders of magnitude before they can achieved a comparable level of safety on the road to that of human drivers. Of course, not all the disengagements reported by Waymo would have led to accidents, so the comparison is hardly scientific, but at least it gives some indication of the scale of the challenges still faced by driverless car companies.

Anecdotally, speaking to engineers who work with driverless cars, it seems the key difficulty for the technology is dealing with unexpected events. We can train cars to deal with *most* eventualities – but what happens when the car meets a situation that is unlike anything it has met in training? While most driving scenarios are routine and expected, there is a long tail of completely unpredictable situations which could occur. In such a situation, a human driver would have their own experience of the world to fall back on. They could think about how to handle it, and if they don't have time to think, they can call upon their instincts. Driverless cars do not have this luxury – and won't, not for the foreseeable future.

Another major challenge is how to make the transition from the current state of affairs on our roads (all vehicles on the roads are driven by people), through a mixed scenario (some human-driven cars, some driverless) to a completely driverless future. On the one hand, autonomous vehicles just don't behave like people while driving, and this confuses and unnerves the human drivers they share the roads with. On the other hand, human drivers are unpredictable and don't necessarily follow the rules of the road to the letter, making it hard for AI software to understand their behaviour and interact with them safely.

Given my upbeat assessment of the progress made in driverless car technology, this may sound surprisingly pessimistic. So, let me do my best to explain how I think events might unfold in the decades ahead.

First, I genuinely believe driverless car technology *in some form* will be in everyday use soon – certainly within the next decade. However, this doesn't mean that Level 5 autonomy is imminent. Instead, I think we will start to see the technology rolled out in specific 'safe' niche areas, and that it will gradually then start to make its way out into the wider world.

So, in what niches do I think we will see the technology in widespread use? Mining is one example. Perhaps in the giant open-cast mines of Western Australia or Alberta, Canada: there are comparatively few people there – far fewer pedestrians and cyclists behaving erratically. In fact, the mining industry already uses autonomous vehicle technology on a large scale. For example, the British-Australian Rio Tinto mining group claimed in 2018 that more than a billion tons of ore and minerals had been transported by their fleet of giant autonomous trucks in the Pilbara region of Western Australia.[11] From the publicly available information, it seems the trucks are quite some way from Level 5 autonomy – more 'automated' than 'autonomous'. Nevertheless, this seems like a good example of driverless vehicles being used to great effect in a constrained environment.

In much the same way, factories, ports and military installations all seem well suited to driverless vehicles. I feel confident that we will see large-scale take-up of driverless technology in these areas within the next few years.

For driverless technology in everyday use beyond these niche applications, there are several possible scenarios, some or all of which may come to pass. It seems quite likely that we will see low-speed 'taxi pods' in well-mapped, constrained urban environments, or on specified routes. Indeed, several companies are trialling similar services at the time of writing, albeit on a very limited basis (and, for the time being, with human 'safety drivers' present in cars to handle emergencies). Limiting such vehicles to low speeds is hardly likely to be seen as a problem in cities like London, where traffic moves very slowly in any case.

Another possibility is special driverless car lanes in cities and on major highways. Most cities already have bus lanes and cycle lanes, so why not driverless car lanes? Such lanes might be augmented by sensors and other technology to assist autonomous vehicles. The presence of such lanes would also send a clear signal to human drivers sharing the roads with autonomous vehicles: beware robot drivers!

As to the question of Level 5 autonomy, we are still some distance away, I'm afraid. But it is inevitable. My best guess is that it will be at least 20 years from the time of writing before Level 5 autonomous vehicles are widely available. But I am pretty confident that my grandchildren will regard the idea that their grandfather actually drove a car *on his own* with a mixture of horror and amusement.

How We Imagine Things Might Go Wrong

The rapid progress we've witnessed in AI since the turn of the century has led to a lot of press coverage. Some of this coverage is balanced and reasonable; much of it is frankly rather silly. Some of it is informative and constructive; much of it is nothing more than scaremongering. In July 2017, for example, it was widely reported that Facebook had closed down two AI systems after they had begun to converse in their own made-up language (which was apparently incomprehensible to their designers).[1] The clear implication in headlines and social media postings at the time was that Facebook shut down the systems because they were afraid they were losing control. In fact, the Facebook experiment was completely routine and totally harmless. It was the kind of experiment that a student might undertake as a project. There was no more possibility of the Facebook systems running amok than there is of your toaster transforming itself into a killer robot. It was, simply, impossible.

While on the one hand I found coverage of the Facebook incident rather comical, it also left me deeply frustrated. The problem is, reporting of this kind panders to the *Terminator* narrative of AI: that we are creating something we won't be able to control, which could pose an existential risk to humanity (you can almost hear a voiceover from Arnold Schwarzenegger in his classic role). Of course, the scenario of our creations turning on us is by no means a modern idea: it goes back at least as far as Mary Shelley's *Frankenstein*.

This narrative still dominates the debate about the future of AI, which is now routinely discussed in tones previously reserved for nuclear weapons. Elon Musk, the billionaire entrepreneur and co-founder of PayPal and Tesla, was sufficiently worried by this idea that he made a series of public statements expressing his concerns, and donated $10 million research funding to support responsible AI; in 2014, Stephen Hawking, then the world's most famous scientist, publicly stated that he feared AI represented an existential threat to humanity.

The *Terminator* narrative is damaging, for several reasons. First, it makes us worry about things that we probably don't need to fret about. But secondly, it draws attention away from those issues raised by AI that we *should* be concerned about. These may not make as good headlines as *Terminator*, but they are probably the issues that we should be concerned about *now*. So, in this chapter, I want to address the headline fears about AI: the possibility of *Terminator* scenarios, and how AI might go wrong. I will start, in the next section, by tackling this narrative head-on. We'll discuss how it might happen, and how likely it is. This then leads us to a discussion of ethical AI – the possibility of AI systems acting as moral agents, and the various frameworks for ethical AI that have been proposed. I'll conclude by drawing attention to one particular feature of AI systems in which they *are* prone to failure, albeit not at a highly scary level: if we want an AI system to act on our behalf, then we need to communicate to it what we want. But this turns out to be hard to do, and if we don't take care when communicating our desires, then we may get what we asked for, but not what we actually *wanted*.

The Singularity Is Bullshit

In contemporary AI, the *Terminator* narrative is most commonly associated with an idea called the **Singularity**, which was introduced by the American futurologist Ray Kurzweil in his 2005 book *The Singularity is Near*:[2]

> The key idea underlying the impending Singularity
> is that the pace of change of our human-created
> technology is accelerating and its powers are expanding
> at an exponential pace. [. . .] within several decades
> information-based technologies will encompass all
> human knowledge and proficiency, ultimately including
> the pattern-recognition powers, problem-solving skills,
> and emotional and moral intelligence of the human
> brain itself.

Although Kurzweil's vision of the Singularity is quite broad, the term has come to be identified with one specific idea: the Singularity is the hypothesized point at which computer intelligence (in the general sense) exceeds that of humans. At this point, it is suggested, computers could start to apply their own intelligence to improving themselves, and this process will then start to feed off itself. After that, these improved machines will then apply their improved intelligence to improving themselves further, and so on. From that point on, so the argument goes, it will be impossible for mere human intelligence to regain control.

It's a very compelling idea – and a deeply alarming one. But let's pause for a moment to examine the logic behind the Singularity. In a nutshell, Kurzweil's main argument hinges on the idea that computer hardware (processors and memory) is developing at such a rate that the information-processing capacity of computers will soon exceed that of the human brain. His argument appeals to a well-known dictum in computing called Moore's law, named after Gordon Moore, a co-founder of the computer processor company Intel, who formulated it in the mid-1960s. Transistors are the fundamental building blocks of computer processors – the more transistors you can fit on a chip, the more work that chip is going to be able to do in any given period of time. Moore's law states that the number of transistors that can fit on a fixed area of a semiconductor doubles about every 18 months. The practical upshot of Moore's law is that, to put it crudely, computer processors can be expected to roughly double in power every 18 months. Moore's law has several important corollaries, among them that computer-processing power could be expected to get progressively cheaper at the same rate, and processors themselves to get progressively smaller. Moore's law proved very reliable for nearly 50 years, although some current processor technologies started to hit the physical limits of their capabilities around 2010.

Now, Kurzweil's argument implicitly links the inevitability of the Singularity to the availability of raw computer power. But this link is dubious. Indulge me, for a moment, with a thought experiment. Imagine that we could download your brain into a computer (we are in the realm of pure fantasy here, of course). And suppose the computer we download your brain to is the fastest, most powerful computer ever. With all this amazing processing power at your command, would you be super-intelligent? For sure, you'd be able to 'think quickly' – but does that make you more *intelligent*? In some trivial sense, I guess it does – but not in any meaningful sense of intelligence, and not in the sense of the Singularity.[3] Raw computer-processing power, in other words, will not inevitably lead to the Singularity. It is probably a *necessary* requirement for it (we won't achieve human-level intelligence without highly powered computers), but it isn't a *sufficient* requirement (simply having highly powered computers won't get us to human-level intelligence). To put it another way, AI software (machine learning programs, for example) improves at a much, much slower pace than the hardware.

There are other reasons to doubt whether the Singularity is in prospect.[4] For one thing, even if AI systems did become as intelligent as people, it does not follow that they would be able to improve themselves at some rate beyond our ability to understand. As this book should have established by now, *we* have made only rather slow progress on AI over the past 60 years – what evidence is there that human-level General AI will be able to make AI progress faster?

A related argument concerns the idea of AI systems working with each other to achieve intelligence beyond our ability to comprehend or control it (cf. the Facebook incident I mentioned at the start of the chapter). But I don't find this argument very convincing either: suppose you got together a thousand clones of Einstein. Would their collective intelligence be a thousand times that of Einstein? In fact, I suspect their collective intelligence would be considerably less than that. Again, although our thousand Einsteins would be able to collectively do some things *faster* than one Einstein could, that isn't the same as being *smarter*.

For these reasons, and more, most AI researchers of my acquaintance are very sceptical about the Singularity, at least for the foreseeable future. We know of no path that will take us from where we are now, in terms of computing and AI technology, to the Singularity. But some serious commentators are still worried, and claim these arguments are mere complacency. They point to the experience of nuclear energy. Back in the early 1930s, scientists knew that there was a huge amount of energy locked in the nuclei of atoms, but had no idea how to release it, or even if that was possible. Some scientists were extremely dismissive of the idea that nuclear energy could be harnessed: Lord Rutherford, one of the most famous scientists of his age, said it was 'moonshine' to imagine that we would be able to tap into this energy source. But, famously, the day after Rutherford dismissed the possibility of nuclear energy, the physicist Leo Szilard was crossing a road in London, mulling over Rutherford's pronouncement, when the idea of a nuclear chain reaction suddenly occurred to him. Just over a decade later, the United States was dropping atomic bombs on Japanese cities, and those bombs were powered in the way that Szilard had imagined in a split-second. Could there be a Leo Szilard moment in AI – a sudden insight that would quickly take us to the Singularity? Of course, we can't rule it out, but it is highly unlikely. A nuclear chain reaction is actually a very simple mechanism – a secondary-school student can understand it. All the experience of AI research over the last 60 years tells us that human-level AI is not.

But what about the distant future – a hundred years ahead, or a thousand? Here, I have to admit that things are much less clear. It would be unwise to try to predict what computer technology will be capable of in a hundred years, still less a thousand. But it seems highly unlikely to me that, if the Singularity occurs, it will take us by surprise, as in the *Terminator* narrative. To use an analogy by Rodney Brooks, think of human-level intelligence as a Boeing 747. Is it likely that we would invent a Boeing 747 by accident? Or that we would develop a Boeing 747 without expecting to? A counter response is that, although it might be *unlikely*, the consequences for us all if it *did* occur would be so dramatic that this justifies thinking and planning ahead for the Singularity now.

Whether or not the Singularity is about to happen (and it should be clear that I don't believe it is), it does seem that there are enough concerns about AI at present to think seriously about whether it needs to be regulated. Do we need laws – maybe even international treaties – to control the development of AI, in the same way that we do for nuclear power? However, I find the idea of introducing general laws to govern the use of AI rather implausible. It seems a bit like trying to introduce legislation to govern the use of mathematics.

We Need to Talk About Asimov

Whenever I discuss the *Terminator* narrative with a lay audience, somebody always suggests that what we need, to avoid such scenarios, is to build our AI so that it can't go rogue in the way I discussed above. And, quite soon after this, someone usually suggests that what we need are the **Three Laws of Robotics**, formulated by the renowned science-fiction author Isaac Asimov. The Three Laws of Robotics were invented by Asimov in a series of stories about robots equipped with a version of strong AI via what he called 'positronic brains'. Asimov first formulated the laws in 1939, and over the next four decades, they provided him with an ingenious plot device for what would ultimately become a celebrated series of short stories, and a disappointing Hollywood movie.[5] The 'science' of the AI in Asimov's stories – 'positronic brains' – is meaningless, although of course the stories are nonetheless entertaining for that. What is interesting for our purposes are the laws themselves:

1. A robot may not injure a human or, through inaction, allow a human to come to harm.
2. A robot must obey orders given by humans except where they would conflict with the First Law.
3. A robot must protect its own existence as long as this does not conflict with the First or Second Laws.

They are beautifully formulated, and at first sight appear to be ingeniously robust. Could we build AI systems with these laws built in?

Well, the first thing to say about Asimov's laws is that,

ingenious though they are, many of Asimov's stories were based upon situations in which the laws turned out to be flawed, or led to contradictions. In the story 'Runaround', for example, a robot called SPD-13 seems destined to endlessly circle a pool of molten selenium because of a conflict between the need to obey an order (the Second Law) and the need to protect itself (the Third Law) – so it orbits the pool at a fixed distance because, if it gets any closer, the need to protect itself kicks in, while if it gets any further away, the need to obey kicks in. There are many other examples in his stories (and if you haven't done so already, I urge you to read them). So, the laws themselves, ingenious as they are, certainly aren't by any means watertight.

But the bigger problem with Asimov's laws is that implementing them within an AI system just isn't feasible.

Think about what it would mean to implement the First Law, for example. Every time an AI system was contemplating an action, it would need to consider the effects that this action might have, presumably on *all* humans (or is it only some that matter?), and into the future too (or do you only care about the here and now?). This is not feasible. And the 'or, through inaction' clause is equally problematic – should a system constantly contemplate *all* of its possible actions with respect to *every* person to see whether the relevant action prevents harm? Again, it just won't work.

Even capturing the notion of 'harm' is difficult. Consider: when you fly on a plane from London to Los Angeles, you are consuming a large amount of natural resources, and generating a lot of pollution and carbon dioxide along the way. This is almost certainly harming someone but in such a way that it is impossible to precisely quantify it. And in case you think this example is artificial, let me tell you that I know people who *won't* travel by air, for exactly this reason. A robot that obeyed Asimov's laws literally would not, I think, be persuaded on to an aeroplane. Actually, I doubt it would be able to do very much at all – it would likely be huddled in a corner somewhere, hiding from the world, crippled by indecision.

So, while Asimov's laws might provide a high-level set of general guidelines for the builders of AI systems (and indeed I think most AI researchers implicitly accept them), the idea that they can be literally encoded within AI systems, as in Asimov's stories, isn't realistic.

So, if Asimov's laws – and other well-intentioned systems of ethical principles for AI – don't necessarily help us, how should we think about the acceptable behaviour of AI systems?

We Need to Stop Talking about the Trolley Problem

Asimov's laws can be seen as the first and most famous attempt to formulate an overarching framework to govern decision-making in AI systems. Although it wasn't intended as a serious ethical framework for AI, we can see it as the ancestor of a whole host of such frameworks that have appeared alongside the recent growth of AI, and have been the subject of serious research.[6] In the remainder of this chapter, we will survey this work, and discuss whether or not it is heading in the right direction. We'll begin our survey with one particular scenario which has attracted more attention in the ethical AI community than perhaps any other.

The **Trolley Problem** is a thought experiment in the philosophy of ethics, originally introduced by British philosopher Philippa Foot in the late 1960s.[7] Her aim in introducing the Trolley Problem was to disentangle some of the highly emotive issues surrounding the morality of abortion. There are many versions of Foot's trolley problem, but the most common version goes something like this (see Figure 21):

A trolley (i.e. a tram) has gone out of control, and is careering at high speed towards five people who are unable to move. There is a lever by the track; if you pull the lever, then the trolley will be diverted down an alternative track, where there is just one person (who also cannot move). If you pull the lever, then this person would be killed, but the five others would be saved.

Should you pull the lever or not?

The Trolley Problem has risen rapidly in prominence recently because of the imminent arrival of driverless cars. Pundits were quick to point out that driverless cars might well find themselves in a situation like the Trolley Problem, and AI software would then be called upon to make an impossible choice. 'Self-driving cars are already deciding who to kill' ran one Internet headline in 2016.[8] There was a flurry of anguished online debate, and several philosophers of my acquaintance were surprised and flattered to discover that there was suddenly an attentive audience for their opinions on what had hitherto been a rather obscure problem in the philosophy of ethics.

Despite its apparent simplicity, the Trolley Problem raises some surprisingly complex issues. My intuitive response to the problem is, all other things being equal, I would pull the

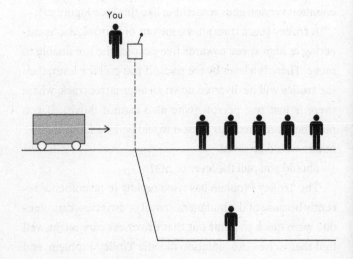

Figure 21

The Trolley Problem. If you do nothing, the five people on the upper track will die; if you pull the lever, the person on the lower track will die. What should you do?

lever because it would be better to have just one person die rather than five. Philosophers call this kind of reasoning consequentialist (because it assesses the morality of actions on the basis of their consequences). The best known consequentialist theory is **utilitarianism**. It has its origins in the work of eighteenth-century British philosopher Jeremy Bentham and his student John Stuart Mill. They formulated an idea called the 'greatest happiness principle', which, speaking approximately, says that one should choose whichever action maximizes the 'aggregate happiness of the world'. In more modern terminology, we would say that a utilitarian is someone who acts in order to maximize **social welfare**, where this is defined to be the aggregate welfare of the society.

While the general principle seems appealing, making the idea of the 'aggregate happiness of the world' precise is not easy. For example, suppose the five individuals in the Trolley Problem are evil mass murderers, while the other individual is an innocent young child. Do the lives of five evil mass murderers outweigh that of an innocent young child? If not five, suppose there were ten mass murderers – would that be enough for you to decide to pull the lever?

An alternative point of view is that an action is acceptable if it is consistent with some general 'good' principle of action, the standard example being the principle that taking life is wrong. If you adhere to the principle that taking life is wrong, then *any* action which causes a death would be unacceptable. Someone who accepted such a principle would not take action in response to the Trolley Problem, since their action would cause someone's death – even though *not* acting leads to five other deaths.

A third standpoint is based on the idea of **virtue ethics**. From this standpoint, we might identify a 'virtuous person', who embodies the virtues that we aspire to in a decision-maker, and then say that the correct choice is the choice that would be made by this sort of person in this setting.

Of course, in AI, the decision-maker would be an agent – a driverless car, which must choose between driving straight ahead and killing five people, or swerving and killing one. So, what would and what should an AI agent do when faced with a Trolley Problem, or something like it?

Well, first of all, we should ask ourselves whether it is reasonable to expect *more* of an AI system that we would expect of a person in a situation like this. If the greatest philosophical thinkers in the world cannot definitively resolve the Trolley Problem, then is it reasonable of us to expect an AI system to do so?

Secondly, I should point out that I have been driving cars for decades, and in all that time I have never faced a Trolley Problem. Nor has anyone else I know. Moreover, what I know about ethics, and the ethics of the Trolley Problem, is roughly what you read above: I wasn't required to pass an ethics exam to get my driving licence. This has not been a problem for me so far. Driving a car does not require deep ethical reasoning – so requiring that driverless cars can resolve the Trolley Problem before we put them on the roads therefore seems to me a little absurd.

Thirdly, the truth is that however obvious the answers to ethical problems might seem to *you*, other people will have *different* answers, which seem just as self-evident to them. This fact was illustrated rather vividly in a clever online experiment carried out by some researchers from MIT. They established a website called **Moral Machines**, through which users were presented with a whole series of trolley-type problems, and were asked what a driverless car should do if faced with the issue.[9] The possible innocent victims included males, females, overweight people, children, criminals, homeless people, doctors, athletes and elderly people. They also included dogs and cats. The experiment proved to be hugely popular, and the researchers were able to gather data from about 40 million individual decisions from users in 233 countries.

The data revealed fundamental differences in attitudes to ethical decision-making in the Trolley Problem across the globe. The researchers found three key 'moral clusters' of countries, each of which seems to embody an ethical framework with a distinctive character. The researchers dubbed these the Western, Eastern and Southern Clusters. The Western Cluster includes countries like North America and most European nations; the Eastern Cluster includes many countries from the Far East, such as Japan and China, as well as Islamic countries; and the Southern Cluster includes the Latin American countries of Central and South America. Compared to the Western Cluster, the Eastern Cluster showed a clear preference for sparing the lawful rather than criminals, a stronger preference for sparing pedestrians rather than passengers in the car, and a much weaker preference for sparing the young. The Southern Cluster seemed much more concerned with sparing high-status individuals, the young and females. The researchers dug deeper, and found that there were other predictors of decision-making: for example, if a culture is prosperous or has a strong rule of law, then both of these societal qualities have a clear role in predicting preferences.

The MIT researchers compared their findings – how people say a driverless car should behave in a Trolley Problem situation – to some actual guidelines on ethical decision-making in cars produced by the German federal government in 2017.[10] The German report made 20 recommendations, including, for example:

> In hazardous situations, priority must always be given to saving humans rather than preventing damage to property.
> In the event of unavoidable accidents, it is not permissible to take into account any aspect of a person's physical characteristics (age, gender, etc.) when deciding how to act.
> It must always be clear whether a human or computer currently has responsibility for driving.
> The car must keep a record of who was driving at any given time.

Some of these guidelines are in clear contrast to what some of the participants in the Moral Machines experiments indicated that the software should do: for example, the rule forbidding any discrimination based on personal characteristics is in sharp contrast to an internationally held preference revealed by the Moral Machine for saving young people. Imagine the outrage, then, if a driverless car followed the German guidelines and chose not to make a distinction, and as a result a child was killed rather than an elderly terminal cancer patient. My example is tasteless – apologies for that – but you get the point.

Intriguing and ingenious though it undoubtedly is, the Moral Machine experiment and the Trolley Problem upon which it is based do not, I think, have much of value to tell us about AI software for driverless cars. I don't believe that the driverless cars we are likely to encounter in the coming decades will do ethical reasoning of this type. So, what *would* a real driverless car do *in practice*, when faced with a situation like the Trolley Problem? Those working on driverless car technologies are not very forthcoming about details, but my experience with AI over the last few decades suggests that the basic engineering principle would be to maximize expected safety (or, alternatively, minimize expected risk). There would be no deep reasoning involved – if there was any reasoning at all, it would probably be no more sophisticated than *if you are faced with multiple obstacles then avoid the larger of these* – but, frankly, even this level of reasoning seems implausible. The likeliest outcome would be that the car would just slam on the brakes. And perhaps, in practice, that is probably all that we would manage to do, in the same situation.

The Rise of Ethical AI

'Don't be evil.'

— Google company motto, 2000–2015 (approximately)

Of course, there are much wider issues around AI and ethics, which are perhaps of more immediate importance and relevance than the arguably rather artificial Trolley Problem, and at the time of writing, these issues are being keenly debated. Every technology company, it seems, wants to demonstrate that *their* AI is more ethical then everyone else's – scarcely a week goes by without a press release announcing a new ethical AI initiative. It is worth reflecting on these a little, and the role they are likely to play in how AI develops in the years to come.

One of the first and most influential frameworks for ethical AI was the **Asilomar principles**, which were formulated by a group of AI scientists and commentators who met in the Californian resort of the same name in 2015 and 2017. The main deliverable was a set of 23 principles, which AI scientists and developers across the world were asked to sign up to.[11] Most of the Asilomar principles are pretty uncontentious: the first is that the goal of AI research should be to create beneficial intelligence; the sixth is that AI systems should be safe and secure; and the twelfth is that people should have the right to access, manage and control data which relates to them.

Some of the principles, however, seem rather aspirational: the fifteenth, for example, requires that 'The economic prosperity created by AI should be shared broadly, to benefit all of humanity.' I personally have no difficulty in signing up to this principle, but I'm afraid I think it is hopelessly naive to imagine that big businesses will do anything more than pay lip service to it. Big businesses are mainly investing in AI because they hope it will give them a competitive advantage that will deliver benefits to their shareholders, not because they want to benefit humanity.[12]

The final five principles relate to the long-term future

of AI, and to concerns that AI might somehow get out of control – the *Terminator* narrative once again:

- **Capability Caution:** There being no consensus, we should avoid strong assumptions regarding upper limits on future AI capabilities.
- **Importance:** Advanced AI could represent a profound change in the history of life on earth, and should be planned for and managed with commensurate care and resources.
- **Risks:** Risks posed by AI systems, especially catastrophic or existential risks, must be subject to planning and mitigation efforts commensurate with their expected impact.
- **Recursive Self-Improvement:** AI systems designed to recursively self-improve [automatically improve their intelligence, and then use their improved intelligence to improve themselves further] or self-replicate in a manner that could lead to rapidly increasing quality or quantity must be subject to strict safety and control measures.
- **Common Good:** Super-intelligence should only be developed in the service of widely shared ethical ideals, and for the benefit of all humanity rather than one state or organization.

Again, I have no difficulty at all in signing up to these principles, but the truth is that, as I argued earlier, we are so far from the scenarios hinted at here becoming a reality that including them almost amounts to scaremongering. In the words of AI scientist Andrew Ng, worrying about these concerns right now seems like worrying about the problem of overpopulation on Mars.[13] Maybe these issues *will* be worth losing sleep over at some point in the future, but to give them prominence now presents a misleading picture of where AI is and, more worryingly, distracts us from the problems that we *should* be concerned about, which we will discuss in the next chapter. Of course, because the scenarios indicated here are likely to be a long way in the future, it doesn't cost companies anything to sign up to them, and it makes for good publicity.

In 2018, Google released their own guidelines for ethical AI. Somewhat pithier than the Asilomar principles, they cover much of the same territory (being beneficial, avoiding bias, being safe), and, helpfully, Google also provided some concrete guidance around best practice in AI and machine learning development.[14] Another framework was proposed by the European Union at the end of 2018,[15] and yet another by the IEEE (Institute of Electrical and Electronics Engineers, a key professional organization for computing and IT);[16] many major companies – and not just IT companies – have also released ethical AI guidelines of their own.

It is, of course, wonderful that big businesses are declaring their commitment to ethical AI. The difficulty, though, is their truly understanding precisely what they have committed to. High-level aspirations, such as sharing the benefits of AI, are welcome, but translating that into specific actions is not easy. The company motto used by Google for more than a decade was 'Don't be evil'. That sounds great – and I daresay was genuinely well intentioned – but what, precisely, does that mean for Google's employees? They will need much more specific guidance if they are to prevent Google from crossing over to the Dark Side.

Within the various frameworks that have been proposed, certain themes recur, and there is increasing consensus around these. My colleague Virginia Dignum at Umea University in Sweden has championed these issues, and she distils them into three key concepts: accountability, responsibility and transparency.[17]

Accountability in this sense means that, for example, if an AI system makes a decision that significantly affects someone, then they have a right to an explanation for that decision. But what counts as an explanation is a difficult issue, one which will have different answers in different settings; and current machine learning programs are not capable of providing explanations.

Responsibility means that it should always be clear who is responsible for a decision, and, crucially, that we should not try to claim that an AI system was 'responsible' for a decision: the responsible party will be individuals or organizations that deployed the system. This points towards a deeper philosophical issue, one relating to the question of **moral agency**.

A moral agent is commonly understood to be an entity that is capable of distinguishing right and wrong, and of understanding the consequences of their actions with respect to such distinctions. It is often imagined in popular discussion that AI systems are, or can be, moral agents, and can be held accountable for their actions. The general view in the AI community is that this is not the case: software can't be held accountable. More generally, responsibility in AI doesn't imply building machines that are themselves morally responsible but, rather, developing AI systems in a responsible way. For example, distributing a Siri-like software agent that misled users into believing that they were interacting with another person would be an irresponsible use of AI by the developers of it. The software isn't culpable here: those who develop and deploy it are. Responsible design here would mean that the AI would always make it clear that it is non-human.

Finally, transparency means that the data that a system uses about us should be available to us, and the algorithms used within that should be made clear to us too.

The rise of ethical AI is a welcome development, although it remains to be seen how widely the various schemes being proposed will actually be implemented.

Be Careful What You Wish For

The discussion of ethical AI sometimes makes us forget one of the more mundane realities about how things might go wrong: AI software is, well, *software*, and we don't need any fancy new technologies for software to go wrong. There is, put simply, no such thing as bug-free software: there is just software that has crashed, and software that hasn't crashed *yet*. The problem of developing bug-free software is a huge research area in computing – finding and eliminating bugs is one of the main activities in software development. But AI provides novel new ways for bugs to be introduced. One of the most important of these arises from the fact that, if AI software is to work on our behalf, then we need to tell it what we want it to do. And this is often not nearly as easy as it might appear.

About 15 years ago, I was working on techniques intended to enable vehicles to coordinate themselves without human intervention. The particular scenario I was working on was a railway network. This makes it sound much more impressive than it actually was, because the 'network' I was looking at consisted of two trains travelling in opposite directions on a circular railway. And they were virtual trains – no actual railway track was involved (not even a toy railway track, actually). At one point, the pretend railway passed through a narrow tunnel, and if ever both trains entered the tunnel at the same time, then there would be a (simulated) crash. My goal was to prevent this. I was trying to develop a general framework which would allow me to present a goal to my system (the goal in this case being to prevent a crash) so that the system would come back with some rules which, if the trains followed them, would be guaranteed to ensure that the goal was achieved (the trains wouldn't crash).

My system worked, but not in the way I had in mind. The first time I expressed my goal, the rules that my system came back with said: *Both trains must remain stationary*. Well, of course this works – if both trains remain stationary then no crash will occur – but it wasn't the kind of solution I was after.

The problem I encountered is a standard one in AI and indeed in computer science generally. The problem is this: we want to *communicate our desires* to a computer so that the computer can pursue them on our behalf; but communicating our desires to a computer is a deeply problematic process, for several reasons.

First of all, we may ourselves not know what we actually want – at least not explicitly – and in this case, articulating our desires is going to be impossible. Often, our desires will be contradictory – in which case, how is an AI system to make sense of them?

Moreover, it may be impossible to spell out our preferences *in toto*, so the best we will often be able to do is give a snapshot of our preferences, leaving gaps in the overall picture. How then should the AI system fill in the gaps?

But finally, and perhaps most importantly, when we communicate with *people* we usually assume that we share *common values and norms*. We don't explicitly spell these out every time we interact. But an AI system doesn't know about these values and norms. So, they either have to be explicitly spelled out, or else we somehow have to make sure that the AI system has them in the background. If they aren't there, then we may not get what we really wanted. In the train scenario above, I communicated my goal that the trains were to avoid crashing, but forgot to convey that they should still be allowed to move. I had forgotten that, although a human would, almost certainly, implicitly understand that this was my intention, a computer system would *not*.

Scenarios like this were popularized by Oxford philosopher Nick Bostrom in his bestselling 2014 book *Superintelligence*.[18] He calls this **perverse instantiation**: the computer does what you asked for, but not in the way you anticipated. Hours of fun are to be had dreaming up other perverse instantiation scenarios: you ask a robot to ensure your house is not burgled, so it burns it down; you ask a robot to prevent deaths from cancer, so it murders everyone and so on.

Of course, this is a problem that we encounter repeatedly in everyday life: whenever someone designs a system of incentives that are intended to encourage a certain behaviour, someone else will find a way to game the system, gaining the rewards without behaving as intended. I am reminded of a (possibly apocryphal) story from the era of Soviet Russia. The Russian government wanted to incentivize the production of cutlery, and so decided to reward factories that produced cutlery according to the *weight* of cutlery they produced. What happened? Cutlery factories quickly started to produce *very* heavy cutlery . . .

Aficionados of classic Disney films may recognize a closely related type of problem. The 1940 Disney film *Fantasia* features a segment in which a naive young sorcerer's apprentice (Mickey Mouse) becomes tired of his chore of carrying water into the house from a well. To relieve himself of the burden, he brings a broomstick to life to do this for him. But Mickey dozes off and, upon waking up, his attempts to stop the broomstick bringing in water, bucket after bucket, result in ever more magical broomsticks flooding his basement. It requires the intervention of his master, the sorcerer, to rectify the problem. Mickey got what he asked for, but not what he wanted.

Bostrom also considered these types of scenarios. He imagined an AI system that controlled the manufacture of paperclips. The system is given the goal of maximizing the production of paperclips, which it takes literally, transforming first the earth and then the rest of the universe into paperclips. Again, the problem is ultimately one of communication: in this case, when we communicate our goal, we need to be sure that acceptable boundaries are understood.

One way of dealing with this problem is to design AI systems that will aim to *minimize any side effects* of their actions.

That is, we want them to achieve our goals *while keeping everything in the world as close to how it is now as possible*. The idea of **ceteris paribus preferences** captures this.[19] 'Ceteris paribus' means 'All other things being held equal'. The idea of ceteris paribus preferences is then that if we tell our AI system to do something, the assumption is that we want to do this while keeping everything else as unchanged as possible. Thus, when we give the instruction 'Stop my house being burgled', what we mean is 'Stop my house being burgled, *while keeping everything else as close to how it is now as possible*'.

The challenge in all of these scenarios is for the computer to understand *what it is we really want*. The field of **inverse reinforcement learning** is directed at this problem. We saw regular reinforcement learning in Chapter 5: an agent acts in some environment, and receives a reward; the learning challenge is to find a course of actions that maximize the reward received. In inverse reinforcement learning, we instead get to see 'ideal' behaviour (what a *person* would do); the challenge is then to figure out what the relevant rewards are for the AI software.[20] In short, the idea is to look at human behaviour as our model for desirable behaviour.

How Things Might Actually Go Wrong

Although I am a sceptic with respect to the possibility of an imminent Singularity, that doesn't mean that I believe we have nothing to fear from AI. After all, AI is a general-purpose technology: its applications are limited only by our imagination. All such technologies have unintended consequences, being felt decades or even centuries into the future; and all such technologies have the potential for abuse. Our anonymous prehistoric ancestors who first harnessed fire should surely be forgiven for not anticipating the climactic changes that would result from burning fossil fuels. British scientist Michael Faraday, inventing the electric generator in 1831, probably didn't anticipate the electric chair. Karl Benz, who patented the automobile in 1886, surely could not have foretold the million deaths a year that his invention would be causing a century in the future. And Vint Cerf, inventor of the Internet, probably didn't imagine terrorist groups sharing beheading videos via his innocent creation.

Like all these technologies, AI will have adverse consequences that will be felt on a global scale, and like all these technologies, it will be abused. These consequences may not be quite as dramatic as the *Terminator* narrative that I sought to dispel in the previous chapter, but they are the ones that we and our descendants will need to grapple with in the decades to come.

In this chapter, therefore, I will discuss, in turn, what seem to me to be the main areas of serious concern around AI and its consequences for the future. By its end, I hope you will agree that, while things *might* go wrong, they are unlikely to go wrong in the way that Hollywood imagines.

We'll start with employment and unemployment: the idea that AI will take our jobs. This takes us into a consideration of how AI will affect the nature of work, and the possibility that AI-governed employment will be alienating. This, in turn, leads us to consider the impact that the use of AI technologies might have on human rights, and the possibility of lethal autonomous weapons. We'll then consider the emergence of algorithmic bias, and the issues surrounding lack of diversity in AI, as well as the phenomena of fake news and fake AI.

Employment and Unemployment

'Robots will take our jobs. We'd better plan now, before it's too late.'
— *Guardian*, 2018

After the *Terminator* narrative, probably the most widely discussed and widely feared aspect of AI is how it will affect the future of work and, in particular, the potential it has to put people out of work. Computers don't get tired, don't turn up to work hungover or late, don't argue, don't complain, don't require unions and, perhaps more importantly, they don't need to be paid. It is easy to see why employers are interested, and employees are nervous.

Although 'AI Will Make You Redundant' headlines have abounded over the past few years, it is important to understand that what is going on now is nothing new. The large-scale automation of human labour goes back at least to the Industrial Revolution, which took place from about 1760 to 1840. The Industrial Revolution represented a profound change in the way in which goods were manufactured, moving from small-scale production operations ('cottage industries') to large-scale factory production of the type we are familiar with in the present day.

There was no single cause behind the Industrial Revolution. It was prompted by a range of different technological advances, coupled with some unique historical and geographical circumstances. In the UK – usually regarded as the home of the Industrial Revolution – cotton was imported from the United States and the British Empire, and was processed in factories, mostly in the north of England. The empire provided not just the raw cotton, but also a large market for the finished goods, thus providing the economic conditions that enabled the UK textile industry to flourish. A series of technological advances in textile processing from the 1730s onwards made it possible to build larger, faster textile-processing machines which could manufacture fabrics of a consistently high quality and on a scale that was impossible in cottage industries. Raw goods were imported through Liverpool and Manchester, from where they were taken to the mill towns that sprouted up to accommodate the new industry. At first, textile mills were water-powered, but advances in coal-powered steam engines led to a rapid take-up of this technology, relieving factories of the need to rely on potentially unpredictable water sources. Conveniently, coal to fuel these engines was also available in abundance across the north of England, and coal-mining towns thrived alongside the mill towns.

The factory system that was ushered in by the Industrial Revolution brought with it a fundamental change in the nature of work for much of the population. Before the Industrial Revolution, most people were employed, either directly or indirectly, in agriculture. The Industrial Revolution took people out of the countryside, into the towns where factories were located, and moved their jobs from the fields and cottages to the factory floor. The nature of their work changed to the type of job that we still recognize today: working in a factory on a specialized, highly repetitive task, as part of a production process involving a high degree of automation.

Cottage industries could not compete with the new technologies on price, quality, or the consistency of goods. Workers had to seek alternative employment (many in the new factories), or face unemployment. There were seismic social changes, which were not universally welcomed. For a few years, in the early decades of the nineteenth century, a movement called the Luddites arose – a loosely organized group who rebelled against industrialization, burning and smashing the machines that they saw as taking away their livelihoods. But it was a short-lived movement, stamped out by a fearful British government, who in 1812 made the destruction of machines a crime punishable by death.

Of course, the Industrial Revolution of 1760–1840 was the *first* industrial revolution, because technology has advanced steadily ever since, and there have been similarly seismic changes to the nature of manufacturing and work in the two centuries since the Luddites raged against industrialization. Ironically (and sadly), the same industrial towns that boomed in the first Industrial Revolution were devastated in the late 1970s and early 1980s by another industrial revolution. There were many factors behind the decline of the traditional industries at this time. Globalization of the international economy meant that goods manufactured in the traditional industrial heartlands of Europe and North America were now being produced more cheaply in emerging economies on the other side of the world, and free-market economic policies pioneered by the USA and UK were unfavourable to traditional manufacturing. But the key technological contribution was the development of microprocessors, leading to the automation of vast swathes of unskilled factory jobs across the industrialized world.

It was the development of microprocessors that made possible today's computer technology. A microprocessor is a system component that combines all the key components of a computer's central processing unit into a single, small, cheap unit. Before microprocessors, computers were large, expensive and relatively unreliable. Microprocessors made them cheap, fast, reliable and much, much smaller: they made it possible to automate many jobs, particularly in manufacturing, and the north of England was hard hit – it has never really recovered from the loss of manufacturing industries some four decades ago.

While the effects of automation were devastating in the traditional manufacturing heartlands of the north of

England, it is important to remember that the net effect of a new technology like microprocessors will be an *increase* in economic activity. New technologies create new opportunities for businesses, services and wealth creation. And this was indeed the case with microprocessors: more jobs and wealth were ultimately created than were destroyed. But those jobs were not in the north of England.

While the automation of human labour is nothing new, the present concern is that while previously automation and mechanization took away the jobs of *unskilled* labourers, perhaps AI will take *skilled* roles away from workers. And if it does that, what roles will be left for people?

That AI will change the nature of work seems certain. What is much less clear is whether the effects will be as dramatic and fundamental as those of the Industrial Revolution, or whether they will represent a more modest change.

The debate in this area was galvanized by a 2013 report entitled 'The Future of Employment', written by two colleagues of mine at the University of Oxford, Carl Frey and Michael Osborne.[1] The rather startling headline prediction of the report was that up to 47 per cent of jobs in the United States were susceptible to automation by AI and related technologies in the relatively near future.

Frey and Osborne classified 702 occupations according to what they saw as the probability that the job could be automated. The report suggested that those occupations at the highest risk included telemarketers, hand sewers, insurance underwriters, data entry clerks (and indeed many other types of clerk), telephone operators, salespeople, engravers and cashiers. Those at least risk included therapists, dentists, counsellors, physicians and surgeons, and teachers. They concluded that:

> Our model predicts that most workers in transportation and logistics occupations, together with the bulk of office and administrative support workers, and labour in production occupations, are at risk.

Frey and Osborne also identified three characteristics of jobs that they felt would *resist* automation.

Firstly, perhaps unsurprisingly, they suggested that jobs involving a substantial degree of mental creativity would be safe. Creative professions include the arts, media and science.

Secondly, jobs which require strong social skills would be secure too. Jobs that require us to understand and manage the subtleties and complexities of human interaction and human relationships would therefore resist automation.

Finally, they suggested, jobs which involve rich degrees of perception and manual dexterity would be hard to automate. Here the problem for AI is that while great advances have been made in machine perception, humans are much better at it than machines are. We can quickly make sense of highly complex and unstructured environments. Robots can cope with structured and regular environments, but struggle if presented with anything that goes outside the scope of their training. Similarly, the human hand remains far more dexterous than the best robot hand – in 2018, Rodney Brooks predicted it would be 20 years before a viable robot hand was available that was as dexterous as a human hand.[2] Until then, at least, those working in jobs that require a great deal of manual dexterity will likely be safe – any carpenters, electricians or plumbers reading this book can sleep easily tonight.

Frey and Osborne's report has since been widely criticized: many commentators have identified within it what they see as methodological flaws and unjustified assumptions, and have strongly argued that the conclusions are too sweeping as a consequence. While I think the most pessimistic predictions in the report are unlikely to be realized in the medium term, I firmly believe that AI and the associated technologies of advanced automation and robotics will make many people redundant in the near future. If your job involves looking at data on a form and then making a decision (such as whether to give a loan or not), then I'm afraid to say AI is likely to make you redundant. If your job involves talking a customer through a well-defined script (as is the case in many call-centre jobs), then I'm sorry that AI will probably make you redundant. If your job involves nothing more than routine driving in a constrained, well-mapped urban area, then it's probable AI will make you redundant. Just don't ask me *when*.

For most of us, however, the main effect of the new technology will be on the *nature* of work that we all do. Most of us won't be replaced by AI systems – we will simply start using AI tools that make us better and more efficient at what we do. After all, the invention of the tractor did not replace farmers: it just made them more efficient farmers. Nor did the invention of the word processor replace secretaries; it simply made them more efficient secretaries. As we go about the endless paperwork and form-filling that occupies so much of the working world, we will find ourselves interacting with software agents which can manage and expedite this weari-some process. AI will be embedded within all the tools that we use to carry out our work, making decisions on our behalf in endless ways – many of which will not even be visible. In the words of Andrew Ng, 'If a typical person can do a mental task with less than one second of thought, we can probably automate it using AI either now or in the near future.'[3] That is a *lot* of tasks.

While many people fear that AI will take all our jobs, lead-ing to a dystopian future of global unemployment and in-equality, technological optimists hope that AI, robotics and advanced automation will lead us to a very different kind of future. These **utopians** believe that AI will free us (at last!) from the drudgery and boredom of work – that in the future, all the work (or at least, all the dirty, dangerous, dreary or otherwise unpopular work) will be done by machines, leaving us humans free to write novels, discuss Plato, go mountain climbing, or whatever. This is a beguiling dream, although again not a new one – utopian AI features prominently in sci-ence fiction (although, interestingly, not as frequently as *dys-topian* AI – perhaps it's harder to write an interesting story about a future in which everyone is happy, healthy and well educated).

At this point it is useful to reflect on the impact of micro-processor technology when it was developed in the 1970s and early 1980s. As we discussed above, the advent of micropro-cessors led to a wave of factory automation, and the public debate at that time, about the implications of microprocessor technology, had very much the same flavour as the present debate about the implications of AI. A confident prediction of that period was that, in the not too distant future, we would spend much less of our time in paid employment – three-day working weeks, or something like them, would become the norm, and leisure time would expand accordingly.

Things didn't turn out that way. Why not? One theory is that, rather than allowing automation, computers and other technological advances to free up our working hours, we instead worked longer hours to earn more money to pay for more goods and services. The suggestion was that we wanted colour TVs, video cassette recorders, CD players, DVD players, home computers, cellphones, exotic holidays, bigger, faster cars, fancier clothes, better food . . . and to pay for all this, we had to work harder for it. Maybe if we were all prepared to accept simpler lifestyles, with fewer consumer goods and a more basic standard of living, then perhaps we would all have to work less. An alternative explanation is that the economic benefits did not get passed on: the rich got richer, and inequality increased. Whatever the precise reasons, the obvious and slightly depressing conclusion from the experience of the 1970s is that for the immediate future at least, technology probably won't create a leisurely utopia for almost all of us.

This leads us neatly to *universal basic income*: the idea that everyone in society should receive a certain guaranteed income, irrespective of whether they work, and without any kind of means test. Universal basic income is not a new idea, but recent technological developments, particularly in AI, have brought it back into focus. The suggestion is that AI/robotics/automation will create sufficient wealth that a universal basic income becomes possible (because machines can do the work) and desirable (because, in any case, there are no jobs for people: the robots have taken them all).

Much as I would love to believe in a utopian future, large-scale universal basic income schemes driven by AI don't seem plausible any time soon.[4] First of all, the economic benefits generated by AI would have to be enormous to make a universal basic income viable. These would need to be on a scale far beyond what has been delivered by previous technological innovations. And there is no sign whatsoever that current AI advances are going to deliver economic benefits on this scale. Secondly, introducing a universal basic income would require unprecedented political will: social circumstances would need to be extremely compelling to make it a politically acceptable course of action. My guess is there would need to be unemployment on a vast scale before the idea could become part of the political mainstream. Finally, universal basic income would fundamentally disrupt the nature of society, in which work plays a central social role. There is no sign at present that societies are willing to contemplate such changes.

Important though AI is as a factor in the changing landscape of work, it is by no means the only such factor. It may not even be the most important. For one thing, the inexorable steamroller of globalization has not yet reached the end of its journey, and before it has done so it will continue to shake up our world in ways we cannot yet envisage. And the computer itself has by no means reached the end of its evolution – for the foreseeable future, computers will continue to get cheaper and smaller and ever-more interconnected, and these developments alone will continue to change our world and the way we live and work in it. And in the background is the ever-changing social, economic and political landscape of our continuingly more interconnected world: declining fossil fuel resources, climate change and the rise of populist politics. All of these forces will have repercussions for employment and society, and we will feel their effects as much as, if not more than, the effects of AI.

Algorithmic Alienation and the Changing Nature of Work

You may be surprised (and, depending on your worldview, possibly a little disturbed) to see the name Karl Marx in a book about AI, but the co-author of *The Communist Manifesto* was concerned with issues that are closely related to the current debate about where AI is taking work and society. Of particular relevance is Marx's theory of alienation, which he developed in the middle of the nineteenth century – just after the first industrial revolution – when capitalist society was just beginning to take on its modern form. His theory of alienation was concerned with the relationship that a worker has to his or her work and to society, and how the capitalist system affected this relationship. He noted that the workers in the factory system that emerged in the Industrial Revolution were engaged in repetitive, boring and ultimately unfulfilling jobs, for low wages. They had no opportunity to organize their work; no control over it at all, in fact. This was, Marx argued, an unnatural mode of living. The workers' jobs were, in a very real sense, without meaning; but they had no alternative except to take such unfulfilling and, to them, pointless jobs.

You may well find yourself nodding in recognition at these symptoms. But the rapid development of AI and related technologies exposes a new dimension to Marx's theory, which arises from the possibility that *in the future, our boss could be an algorithm.*

Once again, we are already beginning to witness this phenomenon, particularly in the sector of the so-called 'gig economy' – another aspect of the changing pattern of work. Half a century ago, it was not uncommon that the company you worked for when you left school was the company you worked for when you retired. Long-term employment relations were the norm – employees who flitted from one job to another in quick succession were regarded with suspicion.

But long-term employment relationships have become less and less common, replaced by short-term work, piece-work and casual contracts – the gig economy. And one reason why the gig economy has ballooned over the past 20 years is the rise of mobile computing technology, through which large casual workforces can be coordinated on a global scale. The location of a worker at any given time can be monitored by the GPS sensors embedded in their phone, and moment-by-moment instructions can be passed to them via that same phone. Everything they do in their working day, down to the number of keystrokes they type on their computer and the tone of the emails they send, can be monitored and directed, second by second – by a computer program.

One company that has frequently been criticized for its demanding, closely monitored, tightly controlled working environment is Amazon, the online shopping giant. Here is a fairly typical report, from the *Financial Times* in 2013, describing the job of a warehouse worker:[5]

> Amazon's software calculates the most efficient walking
> route to collect all the items to fill a trolley, and then
> simply directs the worker from one shelf space to the
> next via instructions on the screen of the hand-held satnav
> device. Even with these efficient routes, there's a lot of
> walking. [. . .] 'You're sort of like a robot, but in human
> form,' said the Amazon [worker]. 'It's human automation,
> if you like.'

Had Marx been alive today, he would, I think, have used this report as a perfect illustration of the concept of alienation that he was trying to explain. This is the nightmare of AI-driven automation: human labour is systematically reduced to just those tasks that cannot be automated by machine or software, and what is left is minutely monitored and supervised, with no space for innovation, creativity, individuality, or even for thinking. And imagine how you would feel if your annual appraisal was with a computer program, perhaps even a program that could decide whether to fire you. Somewhat cynically, I am tempted to suggest that we probably shouldn't be too concerned about these problems, though, because the jobs in question won't be around for very long: pretty soon they will be fully automated by AI and robotics. (Amazon is investing heavily in warehouse robotics.)

The prospect of a large proportion of the world's working population employed in jobs like this is not an attractive one, although, as I hope should now be clear, it is nothing fundamentally new – it's an AI dimension added to trends that began back in the Industrial Revolution. And of course, many people in the working world today are employed in *far* worse conditions than those of the Amazon warehouse I describe above. Technology is neutral about how it is deployed. It is up to employers, governments, unions and regulators to start thinking about these aspects of AI – how it will affect those in work, and what counts as decent working conditions – as well as the issue of unemployment, which has dominated the debate about AI and work to date.

Human Rights

The discussion above shows how AI systems taking control of our working lives might be deeply alienating. But there are far bigger concerns about the use of AI, which challenge our most fundamental human rights. It is one thing to have an AI system as your boss, telling you when you can and can't take a break, setting you targets, and giving a moment-by-moment critique of your working life; but *what if an AI system had the power to decide whether you went to prison*?

Again, this is not far-fetched – there are AI systems in use today that do something close to this. In the UK, for example, the police force in Durham announced in May 2017 that they would go live with the **Harm Assessment Risk Tool (HART)**,[6] an AI system intended to assist police officers in deciding whether someone suspected of a crime should be released or detained in custody. HART is a classic application of machine learning. It was trained on five years of custody data – some 104,000 'custody events' – obtained between 2008 and 2012, and tested with a full year of custody data that was obtained in 2013 (data used in the trial had not been used to train the program):[7] the system proved to be accurate 98 per cent of the time in low-risk cases, and accurate 88 per cent of the time with high-risk cases. Interestingly, the system was designed to be cautious with high-risk cases (for example, those involving violent crimes), which explains the discrepancy between the two types of cases. The system was trained using 34 different case features. Most of these relate to the suspect's offender history, but the features also include age, gender and residential address.

There is no suggestion that the Durham police force were delegating all decisions about who should be kept in custody to HART. The system was being used just as a decision support tool to aid decisions that were being made by custody officers. But, nevertheless, there was a good deal of disquiet when the use of HART was made public.

One major concern was that HART looks at a very narrow set of features of a case. It does not have the same understanding of people and processes that an experienced custody officer would. Important decisions are made on the basis of quite narrow data. The lack of transparency about decisions was also a concern (a classic case of a machine learning program apparently being able to perform well without the ability to explain its decisions). And, of course, the possibility of bias in the training data and the selected feature set was raised as an issue (and, additionally, the fact that the program used a suspect's address as one of the features is of particular concern: the worry is that this will lead to the system being unfair to those from disadvantaged neighbourhoods).

Yet another concern was that, even though the tool was intended to *support* decision-making, we might at some point in the future find ourselves in a situation where HART becomes the main decision-maker: a tired, confused, or lazy custody officer might abdicate the responsibility of deciding for themselves, and follow HART's recommendation without any further consideration.

But, underpinning all these concerns, I think, is the sense that systems like HART erode the role of human judgement. Ultimately, many of us feel more comfortable if we know that a human being is making a decision that has serious consequences for another human being. After all, the fundamental human rights we enjoy, such as the right to trial by our peers, were hard won, and are rightly highly prized. Having a computer make a judgement about us, in the way that HART does, perhaps feels like we are discarding these hard-won rights. Such steps should not be taken lightly.

These are all legitimate concerns, although they don't, I think, imply that we should simply introduce a blanket ban on the use of tools like HART. But there are some extremely important caveats concerning their use.

First of all, as is explicitly intended in the case of HART, such tools should be used for *supporting* human decision-makers, rather than replacing them. Machine learning decision-makers are not perfect: they will, from time to time, make decisions that a person would immediately recognize as being nonsensical, and one of the frustrations of current machine learning is that it is hard to identify when they are likely to do this. Blindly following their recommendations in settings that have serious consequences for people is, therefore, profoundly unwise.

Another concern relates to naive development and use

of this kind of technology. HART was developed by an experienced research team who appear to have thought carefully about the various different issues that developing such a tool might raise. Not all developers are so experienced, or so thoughtful. The worry is, therefore, that systems making important decisions on behalf of people will be built without the care and consideration that went into HART.

HART is just one example of a wide range of systems being put into use by law-enforcement agencies which human rights groups are gravely concerned about. The Metropolitan Police in London have been criticized for using a tool called the Gangs Matrix, a system which has records on thousands of individuals, and plugs this data into a simple mathematical formula to predict the likelihood that these individuals will be involved in gang violence.[8] Much of the Gangs Matrix system seems to be made up of traditional computing technology, and it isn't obvious how much AI is used – but the trend seems clear. Amnesty International described the system as a 'racially biased database criminalizing a generation of black men'. It has been alleged that doing nothing more than showing a propensity to listen to certain types of music could result in you being listed on the database. In the USA, a company called PredPol sells software to support 'predictive policing' – the software is supposed to predict crime hotspot areas.[9] Again, the use of such software raises basic issues of human rights: What if the data is biased? What if the software is poorly designed? What if police forces start to rely on it? Yet another system, COMPAS, aims to predict the likelihood that someone guilty of a crime will reoffend.[10] The system is used to inform sentencing decisions.[11]

An extreme example of how ideas like this can go hopelessly wrong came to light in 2016, when two researchers posted an article in which they claimed to be able to detect criminality *simply by looking at a face*. Such systems take us back to theories about criminality that were discredited a century ago. A subsequent study suggested that the system might be judging criminality on the basis of whether an individual was smiling or not: the police mug shots used to train the system tended not to show smiles.[12]

Killer Robots

I have argued – and I hope you will agree – that having an AI system as your boss would be alienating, and that having an AI system make decisions such as whether you should be detained in police custody is potentially an affront to your human rights. So, how would you feel about an AI program that had the power *to decide whether you lived or died*? As AI has grown in prominence, concerns about this prospect have received a lot of press coverage, fuelled at least in part by our old enemy, the *Terminator* narrative.

The topic of autonomous weapons is deeply inflammatory. Many people have extremely strong instinctive views that such systems are repugnant and immoral and should never be built. It often comes as a complete surprise to people holding these views that many other people of good character don't in fact hold the same opinions. So – treading as softly as I can because I know how emotive the subject is – let's dig into the issues raised by the potential of AI-powered autonomous weapons.

Much of the discussion on autonomous weapons has

arisen from the increasing use of drones in warfare. Drones are unmanned aircraft, and in military settings they carry weapons such as missiles. Because they do not have to carry human pilots, drones can be smaller, lighter and cheaper than conventional aircraft, and because flying them poses no risk to those remotely piloting them, they can be used in situations that would be considered too risky for piloted vehicles. All these features naturally make drones an attractive option for military organizations.

Although there have been several attempts to develop military drones over the last 50 years, it is only in this century that they have become practicable. Since 2001, they have been used by the US in operations in Afghanistan, Pakistan and Yemen. Although we don't know how many times America has deployed drones in these countries, it seems likely that they have been used hundreds of times, with potentially thousands of deaths as a consequence.

Remote controlled drones raise all sorts of serious ethical issues of their own. For example, since the pilot controlling the drone is in no physical danger, they might choose to take actions that they would not consider if they were physically present, and also, just as important in its implications, not take the consequences of their actions as seriously as they would if they were physically present.

For these reasons, and many more, the use of remote-controlled drones is deeply controversial. However, the possibility of *autonomous* drones has raised these concerns to another level. Autonomous drones would not be remotely controlled: they would carry out missions largely without human guidance or intervention. And, as part of these missions, they might have the power to decide whether or not to take human life.

The idea of autonomous drones, and other varieties of autonomous weapons, immediately brings to mind the narrative which you'll know so well by now: armies of robots killing with relentless, deadly accuracy, and without any degree of human mercy, compassion or understanding. We have already seen why such *Terminator* scenarios are probably not something we should be losing sleep over right now, but the possibility of autonomous weapons going wrong, with lethal consequences, is nevertheless an important argument against their development and use. But there are many other reasons to be concerned about autonomous weapons. One is that a nation possessing such weapons might be less concerned about going to war since their citizens are no longer in the line of fire. Thus, autonomous weapons might make the decision to go to war easier, and therefore make warfare more common. But the most common objection is that autonomous weapons are immoral: it is wrong to build machines that can decide to take a human life.

It is worth pointing out that AI-powered autonomous weapons are entirely possible now, with current technology. Consider the following scenario:[13]

A small helicopter drone, of a type that is widely and cheaply available, has been equipped with a camera and GPS navigation, a small on-board computer and a lump of explosive the size of a hand grenade. The drone has been programmed to traverse the streets of a city, looking for human beings. It does not have to recognize a person, simply identify a human form. And when it identifies a human form, it flies down to it and detonates its explosive.

The AI in this alarming scenario requires only the ability to navigate streets, identify human forms and fly to them. A competent graduate student of AI, with the right resources, would, I think, be able to build a workable prototype. And these would be *very* cheap to manufacture at scale. Now imagine what would happen if thousands of them were released onto the streets of London, Paris, New York, Delhi or Beijing. Imagine the carnage; imagine the terror. And for all we know, someone has already built one.[14]

While, for many people, there is no rational debate to be had about the merits of autonomous weapons, there is, nevertheless, a debate.

One of the best-known protagonists in this debate is Ron Arkin, a professor at Georgia Tech University in the USA. He has argued that autonomous weapons are surely inevitable (someone, somewhere, will eventually build them), and that therefore the best response is to consider how they might be designed so that they behave *more ethically than human soldiers*.[15] After all, he points out, human soldiers do not have a great track record of ethical behaviour, and even while 'perfect' ethical autonomous weapons are, he acknowledges, impossible, he nevertheless believes we could build autonomous weapons that could, overall, be more ethical than human soldiers.

There are other arguments in support of autonomous weapons. For example, it has been argued that it would surely be better to have robots engage in the vile business of warfare, rather than people: the winner of the war would be the side with the better robots. (And of course, 'we' would need to be sure that *we* are the ones with the better robots.)

I have also heard it discussed that it is morally confused to argue against autonomous weapons but not against conventional methods of warfare. For example, when a B-52 bomber, flying at 50,000 feet, releases its bomb load, the bombardier responsible for releasing them doesn't know precisely where the 32,000 kg of bombs which they have released will land – or on *whom* they will land. So, why would one object to autonomous weapons, which explicitly decide who to kill, but *not* object to conventional bombing like this, which *kills at random*? The answer, I suppose, is that one should object to both; but in practice, conventional bombing is less controversial than the idea of lethal autonomous weapons.

Whatever arguments one might try to construct in their favour, my firm impression is that most researchers in the international AI community are strongly against the development of lethal autonomous weapons. The argument that autonomous weapons might be designed to be more ethical than human soldiers is not one which is widely accepted. It is an interesting idea in theory, but in reality we just don't know how to do it, and it won't be practicable any time soon (see the discussions in the previous chapter). While I daresay this argument was put forward with the best of intentions and also the utmost sincerity, the fear is that it has been hijacked by those who want to justify building autonomous weapons now.

Over the past decade, a movement has emerged among scientists, human rights groups and others aimed at stopping the development of autonomous weapons. The Campaign to Stop Killer Robots was founded in 2012, and has the backing of major international human rights groups such as Amnesty International.[16] The stated aim of the campaign is to achieve a global ban on the development, production and use of fully autonomous weapons. The campaign has received a lot of support from the AI community. In July 2015, nearly 4,000 AI scientists and more than 20,000 others signed an open letter in support of a ban; the letter was followed by a number of other similar initiatives, and there are signs that governmental organizations are hearing the concerns being raised. In April 2018, a Chinese delegation to the United Nations proposed a ban on lethal autonomous weapons; and a recent UK government report firmly recommended that AI systems should never be given the power to hurt or kill people.[17]

For reasons that should by now be all too evident, lethal autonomous weapons present dangers as well as moral difficulties. A ban, along the lines of the Ottawa treaty which bans the development, stockpiling and use of anti-personnel mines,[18] therefore seems to me to be highly desirable. But this may not be easy: apart from pressure by those groups that seek to build such weapons, *formulating* a ban might not be straightforward. In its 2018 report, the British House of Lords Select Committee on Artificial Intelligence pointed out that it is rather difficult to give a good working definition of a lethal autonomous weapon, and this is going to be a major hurdle for any legislation. And from a purely practical point of view, it would be very hard indeed to try to ban weapons which simply use AI techniques (I would hazard a guess that many conventional weapons systems already use

AI software in some form or other). Moreover, banning the use of specific AI technologies, such as neural nets, is unlikely to be enforceable, because software developers can easily disguise the techniques they use in their code.

So, even if there is public and political will to control or prohibit the development and use of lethal autonomous weapons, it may be difficult to formulate and implement such legislation. But the good news is that at least there are signs that governments are willing to try.

Algorithmic Bias

We might hope that AI systems would be free of the prejudices and biases that plague the human world, but I'm afraid that is not the case. Over the past decade, as machine learning systems have been rolled out into more and more areas of application, we have begun to understand how automated decision-making systems can exhibit **algorithmic bias**. It is now a major research field, with many groups struggling to understand the problems it raises, and how to avoid it.

Algorithmic bias, as the name suggests, is concerned with situations in which a computer program – not just AI systems, but any computer program – exhibits bias of some form in its decision-making. Kate Crawford, one of the leading researchers in the area, identified two types of harm that may be caused by biased programs.[19]

Allocative harm is in evidence when a group is denied (or favoured) with respect to some resource. For example, banks might find that AI systems can be useful for predicting whether potential clients are going to be good customers – paying their debts on time, and so on. They might train an

AI program using records of good and bad customers, and after a while, the AI system might be able to look at the details of a potential customer, and predict whether the customer is likely to be good or bad – a classic machine learning application. But if the program is biased, then it might deny mortgages to a certain group, or favour another group and grant them. Here, the bias results in an identifiable economic disadvantage (or advantage) for the relevant group.

In contrast, representation harm occurs when a system acts to create or reinforce stereotypes or prejudices. One infamous example occurred in 2015, when a Google photo classification system labelled pictures of black people as 'gorillas',[20] thereby reinforcing deeply unpleasant racial stereotypes.

But computers, as we saw back in Chapter 1, are nothing more than machines for following instructions. So how can they possibly be biased?

The most important single avenue through which bias may be introduced is through data. Machine learning programs are trained using data, and if that data is biased then the program will learn the bias implicit within the data. Training data can be biased in various ways.

The simplest possibility is when those constructing the data set themselves have a bias. In this case they will probably embed that bias within the data set. The biases may well not be explicit or conscious. The fact is, however balanced and reasonable we might think we are, we *all* have biases of some form. And these biases will inevitably be manifested in the training data we create.

These issues are all too human, but machine learning can unwittingly help to create biases as well. For example, if the

training data for a machine learning program is not representative, then that program will inevitably end up being
skewed. (For example, suppose the bank trained its loan software on a data set from one geographical region: then the program might well end up being biased against individuals from
other regions.)

Poorly designed programs can also be biased. For example,
imagine that, in the banking example above, the key feature
of the data that you chose to train your program on was . . .
racial origin. Then it would be no surprise if the resulting program made hopelessly biased decisions about who should get
a mortgage. (You don't think a bank would be stupid enough
to do something like this, do you? Just you wait.)

Algorithmic bias is a particularly prominent issue at present because, as we saw, one feature of the current wave of AI
systems is that they are 'black boxes': they cannot *explain* or
rationalize the decisions they make in the way that a person
can. This problem is exacerbated if we place too much *trust* in
the systems we build – and there is anecdotal evidence that
we do exactly that with AI systems. Our bank builds their
system, runs it on a few thousand examples, and it seems to
come up with the same decision that their human experts
would make; so they assume it works correctly and rely on it
without any further consideration.

It sometimes seems as if every company in the world is
frantically rushing to apply machine learning to their business problems. But in this frantic dash, it is all too likely that
they will create biased programs, because they don't really
understand the issues at stake. And of these, by far the most
important is getting the right data.

Diversity (Lack Of)

In 1955, when John McCarthy submitted his proposal for the Dartmouth summer school on AI to the Rockefeller Institute, he listed 47 individuals whom he wanted to invite to the event. 'Not all of these people came to the Dartmouth conference,' he wrote in 1996. 'They were the people we thought might be interested in Artificial Intelligence.'

Now, let me ask you a question: How many *women* do you think attended the Dartmouth event, which saw the founding of AI as a scientific discipline?

That's right: *none*. I very much doubt that any reputable contemporary research-funding agency would even consider supporting an event that failed this most basic of diversity tests. Indeed, it is standard practice nowadays to require funding applicants to explicitly address the question of how they will ensure equality and diversity. But it is, nevertheless, rather striking that the foundation of AI was quite such a male-dominated affair, and if you have been paying attention throughout this book you can hardly fail to have noticed that AI seems to have remained a largely male-dominated discipline since then.

While with hindsight we can recognize and regret the inequities that were prevalent at the time, I don't think it makes too much sense to judge an event held in the middle of last century using standards that we are still only aspiring to achieve today. The much more important question is whether AI today is fundamentally different. And here, while there is some good news, the overall picture is still somewhat mixed. On the one hand, if you go to any respected international AI conference you will certainly see plenty of female researchers. But, on the other hand, for the time being men will almost certainly make up the majority: lack of diversity remains a stubborn problem for AI, as in many areas of science and engineering.[21]

The gender make-up of the AI community is important for a whole range of reasons. For one thing, a male-dominated research community will be off-putting to potential women scientists, thereby denying the field valuable talent. But, perhaps more importantly, if AI is solely designed by men, then what we will end up with is, for lack of a better term, *male AI*. What I mean by that is that the systems they build will, inevitably, embody one particular worldview, which will not represent or embrace women. If you don't believe me on this point, then I invite you to read the startling book that opened my eyes to this problem: *Invisible Women*, by Caroline Criado Perez.[22] Her key point is that pretty much everything in our world is designed and manufactured with a model of people which reflects just one gender: men. The basic reason for this, she argues, is what she calls the 'data gap': the historical data sets that are routinely used for purposes of manufacturing and design are overwhelmingly male-oriented:

> Most of recorded history is one big data gap. Starting with [. . .] man the hunter, the chroniclers of the past have left little space for women's role in the evolution of humanity [. . .] Instead, the lives of men have been taken to represent those of humans overall. When it comes to the lives of the other half of humanity, there is often nothing but silence. [. . .] These silences, these gaps, have

consequences. They impact on women's lives every day. The impact can be minor. Shivering in offices set to a male temperature norm, for example, or struggling to reach a top shelf set at a male height norm. [. . .] But not life-threatening. Not like crashing a car whose safety measures don't account for women's measurements. Not like having a heart attack go undiagnosed because your symptoms are deemed 'atypical'. For women in these situations, the consequences of living in a world built around male data can be deadly.

Criado Perez documents, in devastating detail, just how pervasive the problem of male-oriented design and male data really is. For AI, of course, data is essential – but male bias in data sets is ubiquitous. Sometimes, the bias is explicit, such as in the TIMIT spoken-word data set that is widely used to train speech understanding programs. The data set contains 69 per cent male voices, with the inevitable consequence that speech understanding systems do a much poorer job of interpreting female voices than male ones. But, sometimes, the bias is subtler. Suppose you collect together a set of pictures of kitchens to train your machine learning program, and these pictures predominantly portray women; or suppose that you collect a set of pictures of company CEOs which predominantly portray men. By now, the result will be obvious to you. And furthermore, as Criado Perez points out, both of these things have actually happened.

Sometimes, the bias is embedded within an entire culture. One notorious example was discovered in 2017, when it was revealed that Google Translate sometimes changed genders in text during translation.[23] It turned out that if you translated the English sentences:

> He is a nurse.
> She is a doctor.

into Turkish, and then back to English, you would end up with –

> She is a nurse.
> He is a doctor.

No gender stereotypes there, then.

Bias is a problem in AI, but it is a particular problem for women, because the data foundation upon which the new AI is being built has such a strong male bias; and the teams that are building the new AI don't notice this, because they too have a male bias.

One final challenge for AI is that if we build systems that embody certain human-like features – as we do, for example, when we build software agents like Siri and Cortana – then we might inadvertently build them in such a way as to reinforce gender stereotypes. If we build subservient AI systems that slavishly do our every bidding, and we make them look and sound like women, then we will propagate a portrait of women as servants.[24]

Fake News

Fake news is precisely what the name suggests: false, inaccurate or misleading information that is presented as fact. Of course, the world had plenty of sources of fake news before the digital age, but the Internet, and more particularly, social media turned out to be the perfect conduit for the propagation of fake news – and the consequences have been dramatic.

Social media is all about putting people in touch with one another, and modern social media platforms are spectacularly successful at this – Facebook and Twitter in the West, and WeChat in China, collectively have a sizable proportion of the world's population registered as users. When social media applications first appeared, in the early years of this century, they all seemed to be about friends, family and everyday life: there were lots of pictures of children, and lots of pictures of cats. But social media is a very powerful tool, and it quickly began to be used for other purposes. The phenomenon of fake news, which started to make global headlines in 2016, demonstrated just how powerful social media is, and how easily it can be used to influence events on a global scale.

Two events made fake news into global headlines: the US presidential elections of November 2016, which led to the election of Donald Trump; and the June 2016 UK national referendum on continued membership of the European Union, which resulted in a narrow vote in favour of leaving. Social media undoubtedly played a significant role in both campaigns – Trump, whatever one thinks of his politics or personal behaviour, is adept at using social media to rally his supporters. In both cases, there were suggestions that social media platforms like Twitter had been used to propagate fake news stories favouring the eventual winners.

AI is an important part of the fake news story because it is crucial to the way that fake news is propagated. All social media platforms rely on you spending time interacting with them – it gives them the opportunity to show you adverts, which is how these platforms ultimately make their money. If you like what you see on the platform then you are going to spend more time on it than you would do otherwise. So social media platforms have an incentive not to *show you the truth*, but to *show you what you like*. How do they know what you like? You tell them, every time you press the 'Like' button. The relevant platform can then look for other similar stories, which you are probably also going to like. A platform that did this well would have built up a (brutally honest) picture of you and your preferences, and used this to decide what stories to show you;[25] *John Doe is a white male, who likes violent videos and has racist tendencies* ... What kind of story would the platform show John Doe if it wants him to 'Like' it?

The role of AI in this is to figure out what your preferences are from what you say you like, and perhaps also from the comments that you leave, the links you follow and so on; and then to find new items that you will also like. These are all classic AI problems, and all social media companies will have teams of researchers and developers working on them.

But if social media platforms behave in this way – figuring out what you like, showing you more of it, and hiding things that you don't like – what sort of picture of the world is social media going to present to John Doe? He is going to see a world of violent videos and racist news stories. He isn't going to get a balanced picture. He will exist in his own social media bubble, and his own skewed view of the world will be reinforced: this is called confirmation bias. What makes this so worrying is the scale on which it is happening: social media is manipulating beliefs on a *global scale*, and whether this manipulation is deliberate or purely accidental, this is surely cause for alarm.

In the longer term, AI may have a role to play in changing the way we perceive the world on an even more fundamental level. We each of us gain information about the world through our senses (sight, hearing, touch, smell and taste), and collectively we use this information to build a consensus view of reality: a broadly accepted view of how the world actually is. If you and I both witness a particular event in the same way, then we both get the same information about the event, and we can use this to inform our view of consensus reality. But what happens if there is no common view of the world? What happens if each of us is perceiving the world in a completely different way? AI might make this possible.

In 2013, Google released a wearable computer technology called Google Glass. Resembling everyday spectacles, Google Glass was equipped with a camera and a small projector. The glasses connected to a smartphone via a Bluetooth connection. Upon release there were immediate concerns about the 'concealed' camera in Google Glass being used to take pictures in inappropriate situations, but the real potential of the device was in the built-in projector, which could overlay whatever the user was seeing with a projected image. The possible applications were endless. For example, one thing I am personally very bad at is recognizing people: it is a source of continual embarrassment that I meet people I know well but nevertheless struggle to recognize. A Google Glass application that could identify the people I'm looking at and discreetly remind me of their names would be wonderful.

These types of applications are called *augmented reality*: they take the real world and overlay it with computer-generated information or images. But what about apps that do not augment reality but *completely change it*, in a way that is imperceptible to users? My son, Tom, is 13 years old at the time of writing. He is a big fan of J.R.R. Tolkien's *Lord of the Rings* books, and the films that were made from them. Imagine a Google Glass app that altered his view of school so that his friends looked like elves, and his schoolteachers looked like orcs. You might have a similar *Star Wars* themed app, and so on. This would be great fun, but here is the thing: what does consensus reality mean if we are all inhabiting our own private worlds? You and I would no longer have common, shared experiences upon which to build a consensus. And, of course, such applications can be *hacked*. Imagine that Tom's glasses were hacked, so that his beliefs were being manipulated *directly*, by fundamentally altering the way in which he was perceiving the world.

Although applications like this are not possible at present, they have a good chance of becoming possible within the next two or three decades. We already have AI systems which can generate images that appear, to humans, to be utterly real, but which in fact have been entirely constructed by a neural network. At the time of writing, for example, there is a lot of concern about DeepFakes.[26] These are pictures or videos which have been altered by a neural network to include people who were not present in the original. A notorious example occurred in 2019, when a video of US House Speaker Nancy Pelosi was altered to make it appear that she had a speaking impairment, or perhaps was under the influence of drugs or alcohol.[27] DeepFakes have been used to alter pornographic videos too, inserting 'actors' into the video who did not in fact participate.[28]

At present, the quality of DeepFake videos is poor, but it is getting better, and, soon, we won't be able to tell whether a photo or video is real or a DeepFake. At that point, the principle that photos or videos provide a reliable record of events will no longer be viable. If we each inhabit our own, AI-powered digital universe, there is a real danger that societies, built on common values and principles, will start to fracture. Fake news on social media is just the beginning.

Fake AI

We saw in Chapter 4 how software agents like Siri, Alexa and Cortana emerged in the first decade of this century as direct descendants of research on agents in the 1990s. Shortly after Siri emerged, a number of stories appeared in the popular press reporting some undocumented features of the system. You could say to Siri things like 'Siri, you're my best friend', and Siri would come back with what looked like a meaningful response (I just tried it: 'OK, Michael. I'll be your friend, in fair weather and foul.') The press were all agog. Is this General AI, they wondered? Well, no. Predictably, all Siri was doing was pulling out a stock response to certain keywords and statements – pretty much just what ELIZA was doing decades earlier. There is no intelligence at work there at all. The apparently meaningful answers were nothing more than fake AI.

Apple is not the only company guilty of producing fake AI. In October 2018, the British government announced that a robot called Pepper would give evidence in the Houses of Parliament.[29] But it was nonsense. The robot Pepper was certainly present (and, for the record, it is a fine robot, with a lot of wonderful research behind it). But Pepper simply answered pre-determined questions with answers that had been pre-written for it. This was not even at the level of ELIZA.

There was no intent to deceive in the Siri or Pepper incidents – they were both a good-natured bit of fun. But many in the AI community were annoyed, because they paint a completely false picture of what AI is all about. For one thing, if anybody watching the Pepper show thought that the robot was *really* answering the questions that were being posed, then they would be left with a completely misleading view of what was currently possible with AI-based question-answering systems. But I doubt many people were taken in – it wasn't hard to see what was really going on, and the problem then is that people might think this kind of nonsense is what AI is actually all about: fakery.

A similar incident occurred in December 2018, when a 'hi-tech robot' dancing at a youth science forum in Yaroslavl, Russia, turned out to be . . . a man in a robot suit.[30] It is unclear whether the organizers of the event intended to deceive, so let's give them the benefit of the doubt. But Russian state television reported the 'robot' as if it was the real thing. Anybody watching might reasonably have concluded that this represented the current state of the art in robotics and AI.

Unfortunately, fakery like this is all too common on the fringes of AI, to the intense frustration of AI researchers. In October 2017, Saudi Arabia announced that it had granted citizenship to a robot called Sophia, and the announcement, unsurprisingly, garnered a lot of media attention.[31] Many commentators highlighted the irony of the announcement (giving citizenship to a machine), given Saudi Arabia's less than ideal track record on human rights, and women's rights in particular. But many others also wanted to know whether there was something fundamentally new here: was this robot a step towards general intelligence?

Built by the Hanson Robotics company, Sophia is a humanoid robot, built to have a human-like appearance, including realistic facial expressions, and of course, the ability to converse in natural language. The website Business Insider published an 'interview' with Sophia in December 2017[32] (Sophia's response is in italics):

> What are your feelings and preferences?
> *Have you ever had a robot live in your home or work with you?*
>
> No.
> *You know, there are probably more robots in your life that you aren't aware of yet. Do you want to live or work with a robot someday?*
>
> What kind of robots am I living and working with now?
> *Indeed.*
>
> Is 'Indeed' your default answer when you don't know something?
> *Yes.*

The Director of AI research at Facebook, Yann LeCun, was not impressed. 'This is to AI as prestidigitation [conjuring tricks] is to real magic,' he wrote on Twitter in January 2018. 'It's complete bullshit.' Which sums up precisely what the mainstream AI community makes of this kind of cheap publicity stunt.

Fake AI, then, is where people are misled into believing that what they are seeing is AI, when in fact there are human minds behind the scenes. I've heard rumours that AI start-up companies who can't get their technology to work for a crucial demo will resort to fake AI behind the scenes. I have no idea how widespread this practice is; but fake AI is a real problem for everyone, and a massive irritation for the AI community.

Conscious Machines?

If I have succeeded in doing one thing in this book, I hope it is to have convinced you that, while the recent breakthroughs in AI and machine learning are real and exciting, they are not a silver bullet for General AI. Deep learning may be an important ingredient for General AI, but it is by no means the only ingredient. Indeed, we don't yet know what some of the other ingredients are, still less what the recipe for General AI might look like. All the impressive capabilities we have developed – image recognition, language translation, driverless cars – don't add up to general intelligence. In this sense, we are still facing the problem that Rod Brooks highlighted back in the 1980s: we have some *components* of intelligence, but no idea how to build a system that integrates them. And in any case, some of the key components are still missing: as we saw in Chapter 5, even the best of contemporary AI systems cannot exhibit any meaningful *understanding* of what they are doing. For all that they may excel at what they do, they are nothing more than software components optimized to carry out a specific narrow task.

Since I believe we are a long way from General AI, it naturally follows that I should be even more dubious about the prospects for strong AI: the idea of machines that are, like us, conscious, self-aware, truly autonomous beings. Nevertheless, in this final chapter, let's indulge ourselves. Even though strong AI is not anywhere in prospect we can still have some fun thinking about it, and speculating about how we might progress towards it. So, let's take a trip together down the road to conscious machines. We'll imagine what the landscape might look like, which obstacles we might meet and what sights we can expect to see on the way. And, crucially, we'll talk about how we can know when we're near the end of the road.

Consciousness, Mind and Other Mysteries

In 1838, the British scientist John Herschel carried out a simple experiment in an attempt to find out how much energy was being radiated by our sun. He exposed a container of water to sunlight, and measured how long it took for the sun's energy to raise the temperature of the water in the container by one degree Celsius. A simple calculation then allowed Herschel to estimate how much energy our star emits every second. The results were beyond comprehension: in one second, the sun radiates unimaginable quantities of energy – an inordinately larger amount than is generated on earth in a whole year. But this created a scientific conundrum: emerging geological evidence indicated that our world (and hence our sun) was tens of millions of years old, at least, but there was no known physical process that could power the sun for such huge periods of time. Any known source of energy would result in the sun burning out in, at most, a few thousand years. Scientists of the time flailed around, inventing charmingly implausible theories in an attempt to reconcile the evidence of Herschel's simple, easily repeatable experiment with the evidence of the geological record. In the event, it was not until the end of the nineteenth century, and the emergence of nuclear physics, that scientists began to understand the ferocious powers latent within the atomic nucleus. It was a whole century after Herschel's experiment before physicist Hans Bethe was finally able to present what is now the widely accepted account of energy production in stars, by means of nuclear fusion.[1]

When we turn to strong AI – the goal of building machines that *really have* conscious minds, self-awareness and under-standing, in much the same way as we do – we are in much the same position as scientists of Herschel's time were. Be-cause the phenomena of mind and consciousness in people – how they evolved, how they work, and even the functional role that they play in our behaviour – are as utterly mysteri-ous to us now as the forces that powered the sun were to scientists in Herschel's time. We don't have answers to any of these questions, and no answers are in immediate pros-pect for any of them. At present, we have nothing more than a few clues, and a great deal of speculation. Indeed, satis-factory answers to these questions would be up there with understanding the origins and fate of the universe in terms of scientific significance. It is this fundamental lack of under-standing that makes strong AI so difficult to approach – we have no idea where or how to begin.

In fact, the situation is worse than this, because we don't even really know what we are dealing with. I have casually thrown around terms like 'consciousness', 'mind' and 'self-awareness', but we don't, in truth, know what these things are. They *seem* like obvious concepts – we all experience them, after all – but we don't have the scientific apparatus to talk about any of them. We can't be certain in a scientific sense that they are even real, for all the common-sense evidence of our personal experiences. Herschel was able to approach his problem with an experiment, using well-understood, measurable physical concepts: temperature, energy and so on. We just don't have tests like these available to study consciousness or mind: they aren't amenable to objective observation or measurement. There is no standard scientific unit of measurement for mind or subjective experience, or even any direct way of measuring them – *I* can't see what *you* are thinking or experiencing. Historically, much of our understanding of the structure and operation of the human brain was obtained by studying people whose brains had been damaged in some way, by disease or trauma – but this hardly lends itself to a systematic research programme. While neuroimaging techniques such as magnetic resonance imaging (MRI) give us important insights into the structure and operation of the brain, they don't provide access to an individual's subjective experiences.

Despite the fact that we don't have any precise definitions, we can identify some common features that arise in discussions about consciousness.

Probably the most important idea is that something conscious must have the ability to *experience things subjectively*. By subjectively, I mean *from your own personal mental perspective*. One important aspect of this is the sensation of internal mental phenomena – what philosophers call **qualia.** This is a fancy name for a simple idea: qualia are the mental sensations that we all experience, like the smell of coffee. Pause for a moment and think about that smell; or, better, go and make yourself a good cup. Inhale the aroma. That sensation you experienced was an example of qualia. The experience of drinking a cold beer on a hot day; the feeling when the weather begins to change from winter to spring; the feeling when my children succeed at something new. All of these are qualia: you may well recognize them, and have enjoyed them yourself – but the paradox is that, even though we believe we are talking about the same experiences, there is no way that we can know whether you experience them in the same way that I do, because qualia – and other mental experiences – are inherently *private*. The mental experience I had when I smelt the coffee was only accessible to *me*; I have no way of telling whether *you* actually had a similar experience, even if we use the same words to describe it.

One of the most famous contributions to the debate on consciousness was made by the American philosopher Thomas Nagel in 1974.[2] Nagel proposed a test by which, he suggested, you can distinguish whether something is, or is not, conscious. Suppose you want to know whether the following are conscious:

- A human being
- An orang-utan
- A dog
- A rat
- An earthworm
- A toaster
- A rock

The test Nagel proposes is to consider whether the question 'What is it like to be an X?' is meaningful when applied to entities like those above. If we believe that it is like something to be an X (where X is a human being, or an orang-utan, etc.), then Nagel argued that the X in question is conscious. Looking at our list above, the question is meaningful when applied to human beings. What about orang-utans? I think so, and the same for dogs, and also (although slightly less obviously) rats. So, orang-utans, dogs and rats, according to Nagel's test, are conscious. Of course, this is not a 'proof' that they are conscious – we are having to rely on common-sense rather than objective evidence.

What about earthworms? Here, I think we are at the threshold of consciousness. Earthworms are such simple creatures that it seems doubtful (to me, anyway) that Nagel's test makes sense in this case: so, by his argument, earthworms are not conscious. There is some scope for debate in this latter case – one might argue that even earthworms have some primitive consciousness, but then I would have to insist that it was indeed primitive compared to human consciousness. However, I'm not going to allow debate about toasters and rocks: they obviously fail the test. It isn't *like anything* to be a toaster.

Nagel's test highlights a number of important points.

First, *consciousness is not an all-or-nothing thing*. It is a spectrum, with fully-fledged human consciousness at one extreme, and earthworms at the other. But even between humans, there are differences. The extent to which a person is conscious will vary depending on whether they are under the influence of alcohol or drugs, or just plain tired.

Second, consciousness is *different* for different entities. The title of Nagel's article was 'What is it like to be a bat?' Nagel chose bats for the title of his article because they are so unlike us. Nagel's question surely makes sense when applied to bats, so bats enjoy consciousness, according to Nagel's theory. But bats have senses that we don't have, most notably a kind of sonar. They emit ultrasonic sounds as they fly, and detect the echoes of these squeaks to perceive their environment. Some bats are even able to detect the earth's magnetic field, and use it for navigation – they have their own inbuilt magnetic compass. We don't have these senses, and for this reason, we cannot actually imagine what it is like to be a bat, even though we think Nagel's question is meaningful. Bat consciousness is thus different to human consciousness. In fact, Nagel believed it is beyond our ability to comprehend, even though we may be confident it exists.

Nagel's main purpose was to set out a test for consciousness ('What is it like to be an X?'), and to argue that certain forms of consciousness must remain beyond our comprehension (we can't imagine what it would be like to be a bat). But his test can be applied to computers, and most people seem to believe that it isn't *like anything* to be a computer, any more than a toaster.

For this reason, Nagel's 'What is it like' argument has been used against the possibility of strong AI. Strong AI is impossible, according to this argument, because computers cannot be conscious by Nagel's argument. I am personally not convinced by this argument, because asking 'What is it like to be a . . .' is, for me, nothing more than an appeal to our intuition. Our intuition works well at separating out the obvious cases – orang-utans and toasters – but I don't see why we should expect it to be a reliable guide in the more subtle cases, or cases that are far outside our own experience of the natural world – such as AI. Perhaps we can't imagine what it would be like to be a computer just because they are so utterly unlike us. But that doesn't imply (to me at least) that machine consciousness is impossible – just that machine consciousness would be *different*.

Nagel's argument is one of many that have been set out in an attempt to show strong AI to be impossible. Let's take a look at the best-known of these.

Is Strong AI Impossible?

Nagel's argument is closely related to a common-sense objection to the possibility of strong AI, which says that it is not possible because *there is something special about people*. This intuitive response starts from the view that computers are different from people because people are animate objects, but computers are not. According to this argument, I have more in common with a rat than with a computer; a computer has more in common with a toaster than with me.

My response to this is that, however remarkable humans are, ultimately, they are nothing more than a bunch of atoms. People and their brains are physical entities, obeying physical laws – even if we don't yet quite know what those laws are. Humans are remarkable, wonderful, incredible things, but from the point of view of the universe and its laws, we are nothing special. Of course, this doesn't answer the difficult question of *how* a particular bunch of atoms leads to conscious experience – a point to which we will return later.

A variation of the 'Humans are special' argument was put forward by the American philosopher Hubert Dreyfus. One of Dreyfus's main points in his critique of AI was that it had rather oversold itself, considering its actual achievements, and in this respect he surely had a point. But he also had a concrete argument against the possibility of strong AI. His argument was that much of human action and decision-making is based on 'intuition', which he believed could not be made precise in the way that computers require. In short, Dreyfus argued, human intuition could not be reduced to a recipe like a computer program.

Now, there is certainly a wealth of evidence that much of our decision-making is not based on explicit or rigorous reasoning.[3] We frequently make decisions without being able to articulate our rationale for them; probably most of our decision-making is of this type, in fact. In this sense, we certainly use some sort of intuition. But surely this results from experience we have gained over time (or perhaps experience learned through evolution, which has been transmitted to us through our genes), which, even if we cannot articulate it at a conscious level, is nevertheless nothing mysterious. And, as we have seen, computers can learn from experience, and become effective decision-makers, even if they cannot articulate the rationale for their decisions.

The most famous argument against the possibility of strong AI is due to the philosopher John Searle, who was in fact the person who coined the terms strong and weak AI. He invented a scenario called the **Chinese room** in an attempt to show that strong AI is impossible. The Chinese room scenario goes like this:

Imagine a man working alone in a room. Through a slot in the door he receives cards on which questions are written in Chinese; he understands no Chinese himself. He takes these cards, and then carefully follows a list of written instructions in order to write an answer in Chinese, which he then passes back out of the room. At this moment, the room (and its contents) is actually engaged in a Chinese Turing test, and the answers provided by the room convince the interrogators that the subject of the test is a human.

Next, ask yourself: *Is there any understanding of Chinese present here?* Searle argues not. The man in the room doesn't understand Chinese, and surely the room itself has no understanding of Chinese. No matter where we look here, we find no understanding of Chinese. The man is doing nothing more than carefully following a precise recipe to derive a response to the question. His human intelligence is used only to the extent that he dutifully follows the instructions he is given.

Observe that the man is doing exactly what a computer does: simply following a list of instructions – a recipe. The 'program' he is executing are the instructions he is given. So, according to Searle, by the same argument, a computer passing the Turing test will not exhibit understanding.

If Searle's argument is correct, then it means that understanding – and hence strong AI – cannot be produced by following a recipe. Strong AI, therefore, can't be achieved with conventional computers. If correct, this simple argument would kill the grand dream of AI. No matter how much your program *appeared* to have understanding, this would be nothing more than an illusion: behind the scenes, there would be nothing there.

Many counter arguments have been proposed to Searle's critique.

An obvious common-sense response is to point out that Searle's Chinese room is simply not possible. Apart from anything else, having a human play the role of a computer processor would mean it would take millennia to carry out a single second's worth of computer program instructions, and the idea of encoding the relevant program as written instructions is absurd: a typical large-scale computer program of the present day will involve about a hundred million lines of computer code. (To actually write out such code in a form that a human could read would require tens of thousands of printed volumes.) A computer can retrieve instructions from memory in microseconds, whereas the Chinese room computer would be billions of times slower. Given these practical considerations, the Chinese room and its contents *could not* convince an interrogator that it was a person: it could *not* in fact pass the Turing test.

Another standard response to the Chinese room is that while the person in the room does not exhibit understanding, and the room itself doesn't, the *system* containing the person, the room, the instructions and so on *does*. And indeed, if we went digging around in a human brain, looking for understanding, we would not find it. While there certainly are areas of the human brain that seem to be responsible for language understanding, we will not find, within these, understanding of the kind Searle asks for.

I believe that there is an even simpler response to Searle's ingenious thought experiment. The Chinese room puzzle, expressed as a kind of Turing test, is a cheat because it does not treat the room as a black box. We only claim that there is no understanding in the Chinese room when we start to look inside it. The Turing test itself insisted that we should only look at the inputs and outputs, and ask whether the behaviour we witness is indistinguishable from that of a human. It seems to me to be pointless to get caught up in an argument about whether a computer 'really' understands if, in fact, it is doing something that is indistinguishable from human understanding.

Yet another possible objection is that perhaps intelligence cannot be computed by a conventional computer because of their mathematically provable limitations. Remember that we know, from Turing's work, that there are fundamental limits to what computers can and cannot do – there are some clearly definable problems that cannot be solved by a computer. So, *what if intelligent behaviour of the kind that AI strives for is not computable in the sense that Turing proposed*? Turing himself discussed this as a possible argument against strong AI. Most AI researchers aren't concerned by it, but, as we have often seen earlier, the problem of what is *practically* computable has been a major stumbling block for AI throughout its history.

Mind and Body

We now turn to the most famous philosophical puzzle in the study of consciousness: the **mind–body problem**. Certain physical processes in the human body and brain give rise to the conscious mind – but how and why, exactly, do they do that? What precisely is the relationship between the physical world of neurons, synapses and axons and our conscious subjective experience? This is one of the biggest and oldest problems in science and philosophy; the Australian philosopher David Chalmers called it the **hard problem of consciousness**.

The literature on the topic goes back at least as far as Plato. In the *Phaedrus*, he proposed a model of human behaviour in which a reasoning component of the brain acts as a charioteer holding the reins of two horses – one horse representing rational, noble desires, the other representing irrational or unworthy desires. The course that a person takes through life depends on how their charioteer controls these two horses. A similar idea appears in the Hindu *Upanishads*.[4]

Viewing the rational self as a chariot driver is a wonderful metaphor. Cute though it undoubtedly is – I'm rather taken with the idea of holding the reins to both the noble and unworthy parts of my mind – it suffers from a common problem in theories of the mind. Plato imagines the charioteer to be a mind; but all he's then done is say that the mind is controlled by *another mind* (the charioteer). Philosophers call this the **homunculus problem** – homunculus means 'little man', the 'little man' in this case being the charioteer. It's a problem because it doesn't actually explain anything – it just delegates the problem of 'mind' to another representation of the mind.

In any case, the 'chariot' model is dubious because it suggests that *reasoning* is the main driver for our behaviour, and there is a wealth of evidence that this is very much not the case. For example, in a celebrated series of experiments, the neuroscientist John-Dylan Haynes was apparently able to detect decisions made by human subjects up to *10 seconds* before the subjects themselves were consciously aware that they had made a decision.[5]

This result raises all sorts of questions, but one of the most important is simply, if conscious thought and reasoning is not the mechanism via which we decide what to do, then what on earth is it *for*?

When we are presented with some feature of the human body, evolutionary theory tells us that we should ask what evolutionary advantage that feature gave us. So, in just the same way, we can ask what evolutionary advantage the conscious mind gave us. Because, presumably, if it gave us *no* advantage then it wouldn't have come into being.

One theory is that the conscious mind is actually nothing more than a meaningless by-product of the features in our body that *actually* produce our behaviour. This theory goes by the rather exhausting name of **epiphenomenalism**. If the conscious mind is epiphenomenal, then rather than being the charioteer holding the reins, as Plato suggested, your conscious mind is, instead, a *passenger* in the chariot, *under the illusion that it is the charioteer*.

A slightly less dramatic view is that the conscious mind does not play a primary role in our behaviour in the way that Plato suggested, but rather that it somehow arises from other processes in our brain – presumably, processes that are not present in lower-order animals, which, insofar as we can tell, don't enjoy as rich a mental life as we do.

In what follows, we'll explore one key component of our conscious human experience: our social nature, by which I mean our ability to understand ourselves and others as part of a social group, and to be able to reason about others and about how others see us. This key capability most probably evolved as a requirement for living and working together in large, complex social groups. To understand this, we'll start by looking at a celebrated thread of work on the social brain carried out by the British evolutionary psychologist Robin Dunbar.

The Social Brain

Dunbar was interested in the following simple question: Why do humans (and other primates) have such large brains,[6] compared with those of other animals? Ultimately, the brain is an information-processing device, and one that consumes a considerable proportion of the total energy produced by a human body – about 20 per cent is a typical estimate. So, a large brain would have evolved in order to deal with some important information-processing requirement for the primate – and, given its energy requirements, it would have to yield some substantial evolutionary advantage. But what information-processing requirement, and what evolutionary advantage, exactly?

Dunbar looked at a number of primates, and possible factors that might imply the need for enhanced information-processing capacity. For example, one possible explanation might be the primate's need to keep track of food sources in their environment. Another possible explanation could be the requirement for primates with a larger ranging or foraging area to keep track of bigger spatial maps. However, Dunbar found that the factor that best predicted brain size was the primate's mean social group size: the average number of animals in that primate's social groups. But this, then, suggests that the large brain size of primates is needed to be able to successfully maintain large social groups – more precisely, the need to keep track of, maintain and exploit the social relationships in these groups.

Dunbar's research raised a tantalizing question: given that we know the average human brain size, what does his analysis predict as being the average group size for humans? The value obtained by this analysis is now known as Dunbar's number, and it is usually quoted as 150. That is, given the average human brain size and Dunbar's analysis of other primates, we would expect the average size of human social groups to be around 150. Dunbar's number might have remained a curiosity but for the fact that subsequent research found that this number has arisen repeatedly, across the planet, in terms of actual human social group sizes. For example, it seems that Neolithic farming villages typically contained around 150 inhabitants. Of more recent interest is the fact that Dunbar's number has something to say about the number of friends we actively engage with on social networking sites such as Facebook.

Dunbar's number can be interpreted as being roughly the number of human relationships that a human brain can manage. Of course, most of us nowadays interact with much larger groups than this – but Dunbar's number is the number of relationships that we can truly keep track of.

In short, if this analysis is correct, then the *human* brain is different because it is a *social* brain. It is large, compared to that of other primates, because we live in large social groups, and this requires the ability to keep track of and manage a large number of social relationships.

The natural next question is what it means, exactly, to keep track of and manage these social relationships. To answer this, we will explore an idea due to the celebrated American philosopher Daniel Dennett – the idea that we understand and predict people's behaviour using what he called the **intentional stance**.

The Intentional Stance

As we look around our world and try to make sense of what we see, it seems that we naturally make a distinction between agents and other objects. We have already seen the term agent used in this book: it was the idea of an AI program independently acting on our behalf, rationally pursuing our preferences. An agent in the sense that we are now discussing is something that seems to have a similar status to us, as a self-determining actor. When a child deliberates over which chocolate to choose from a selection, and carefully picks one, we perceive agency: there is choice, and deliberate, purposeful, autonomous action. In contrast, when a plant grows from underneath a rock, and over time pushes the rock to one side, we see no agency: there is action, of a kind, but we perceive neither deliberation nor conscious purpose in the action.

So, why do we interpret the actions of the child to be those of an agent, but the actions of a plant growing to be a mindless process?

To understand the answer to this question, think about the various kinds of explanation that are available to us when we try to explain the processes changing our world. One possibility is to understand the behaviour of an entity with reference to what Dennett calls the **physical stance**.

With the physical stance, we use the laws of nature (physics, chemistry, etc.) to predict how a system will behave. For example, Dennett suggests that when he releases a stone he has been holding in his hand, he uses some simple physics (the stone has weight, it is acted upon by the force of gravity) to predict, successfully, that the stone will fall to the ground. Now, while the physical stance works well in cases such as this, it is of course not practicable for understanding or predicting the behaviour of *people*, who are far too complex to be understood in this way. It might be possible in principle (we are, ultimately, just a bunch of atoms), but of course isn't remotely feasible in practice. Nor, for that matter, is it a very practicable way of understanding the behaviour of computers or computer programs – the source code for a typical modern computer operating system will run to hundreds of millions of lines.

Another possibility is the **design stance**, in which we predict behaviour based on our understanding of the purpose that a system is supposed to fulfil – what it was designed for. Dennett gives the example of an alarm clock. When someone presents us with an alarm clock, we do not need to make use of physical laws in order to understand its behaviour. If we know it to be a clock, then we can interpret the numbers it displays as the time, because clocks are designed to display the time. Likewise, if the clock makes a loud and irritating noise, we can interpret this as an alarm that was set at a specific time, because making loud and irritating noises at specified times (but not otherwise) is again something that alarm clocks are designed to do. No understanding of the clock's *internal mechanism* is required for such an interpretation – it is justified by the fact that alarm clocks are designed to exhibit such behaviour.

A third possibility, and the one that interests us here, is the one which Dennett calls the intentional stance.[7] From this perspective, we attribute **mental states** to entities – mental states such as beliefs and desires – and then use a common-sense theory of these mental states to predict how the entity will behave, under the assumption that it makes choices in accordance with its attributed beliefs and desires. The most obvious rationale for this approach is that when explaining human activity, it is often useful to make statements such as the following:

Janine *believes* it is going to rain and *wants* to stay dry.
Peter *wants* to finish his marking.

If Janine believes it is going to rain and wants to stay dry, then we might predict that she will wear a raincoat or take an umbrella, or avoid going outside altogether, for these are the kinds of behaviours that we expect of a rational agent who has these beliefs and desires. Thus, the intentional stance has both explanatory and predictive power: it allows us to explain what people did, and what they will (be likely to) do.

Note that, as with the design stance, the intentional stance is neutral about the *internal mechanism* that is actually producing the behaviour. The theory works equally well for machines as for people, as we will discuss in more detail below.

Dennett coined the term **intentional system** to describe entities whose behaviour can be most usefully understood and predicted by the method of attributing to them beliefs, desires and rational choice.

There is a natural hierarchy of increasingly sophisticated intentional systems. A first-order intentional system has beliefs and desires of its own, but it doesn't have any beliefs and desires *about* beliefs and desires. In contrast, a second-order intentional system is capable of having beliefs and desires *about* beliefs and desires. The following statements illustrate this:

1st order: Janine *believed* it was raining.

2nd order: Michael *wanted* Janine to *believe* it was raining.

3rd order: Peter *believed* Michael *wanted* Janine to *believe* it was raining.

In our everyday lives, it seems we probably do not use more than about three layers of the intentional stance hierarchy (unless we are engaged in an artificial intellectual activity, such as solving a puzzle), and it seems that most of us struggle to go beyond fifth-order reasoning.

Our use of the intentional stance is intimately bound to our status as social animals. The role of such intentional ascriptions seems to be to enable us to understand and predict the behaviour of other agents in society. In navigating our way through our complex social world, we become involved in higher-order intentional thinking, whereby the plans of individuals (whether ourself or those we observe) are influenced by the anticipated intentional behaviour of other agents. The value of such thinking is clear from its ubiquity in human life and the extent to which we take it for granted in our communications. Recall the six-word conversation between Alice and Bob that we saw in Chapter 1:

Bob: I'm leaving you.

Alice: Who is she?

The obvious intentional stance explanation of this scenario is simple, uncontrived and compelling: Alice *believes* that Bob *prefers* someone else to her and that he is *planning* according-ly; Alice also *wants* to *know* who this is (perhaps in the *hope* of dissuading him), and she *believes* that asking Bob will induce him to tell her. It is difficult to explain the exchange *without* appealing to concepts like belief and desire, not only as play-ing a role in Alice and Bob's behaviour, but also featuring ex-plicitly in their thinking and planning.

Dunbar looked at the relationship between brain size and the capacity for higher-order intentional reasoning capabilities in humans and other animals. It turns out that the capabil-ity for higher-order intentional reasoning is, approximately speaking, a linear function of the relative size of the frontal lobe of the brain. Since brain size correlates strongly with social-group size, it follows that a natural evolutionary ex-planation for large brains is precisely the need for, and value of, social reasoning – higher-order intentional reasoning – within a complex society. Whether hunting in groups, bat-tling with conflicting tribes, pursuing a mate (perhaps against rivals), or gaining allies for influence and leadership, the value of being able to understand and anticipate the thinking of other individuals is self-evident. Returning to Dunbar's arguments, larger social groups will make more demands for higher-order social reasoning, thereby explaining the relationship between brain size and social-group size that Dunbar identified.

Going back to our original motivation, levels of intentionality appear to correlate with degrees of consciousness. As we already discussed, the class of things we would admit as *first-order* intentional systems is very broad indeed. But higher-order intentionality is a much higher bar. We are higher-order intentional systems, but I would not accept anybody trying to persuade me that (for example) an earthworm was. What about a dog? You might just about be able to persuade me that a dog was capable of having beliefs about my desires (it believes I want it to sit, for example) – but if a dog is capable of higher-order intentional reasoning, then it is likely to be, at most, a rather limited and specialized capability. There are indications that some other primates have a limited capacity for higher-order intentional reasoning. For example, vervet monkeys make use of a warning cry to indicate the presence of leopards to other monkeys (a threat to the monkey community). They have been observed to use the warning cry to trick other vervet monkeys into believing that they are under attack by leopards.[8] A natural explanation of this trick seems to involves higher-order intentional reasoning: 'If I make the warning cry, then they will *believe* leopards are attacking, and *want* to get away . . .' One can, of course, put forward alternative explanations, which do not imply higher-order intentional reasoning. But, nevertheless, the anecdote gives credence to the claim that some non-human animals do engage in higher-order intentional reasoning.

Social reasoning, in the form of higher-order intentionality, seems to be correlated with consciousness; and social reasoning evolved to support complex social networks and large social groups. But why might social reasoning require consciousness? My colleague Peter Millican has suggested that the answer may lie precisely in the computational efficiency of the intentional stance. If I have conscious access to *my own* functional motivators – in the form of desires, beliefs, etc. – and can also think myself into the subjective situation of other people, then this enables me to predict their behaviour (in both actual and imagined circumstances) far more efficiently than I could otherwise. By imagining myself in your position if I were to steal your food, for example, I can instinctively *feel* (without calculation) the sort of anger you would then feel, can anticipate the reprisals you might plan, and will thus be motivated to resist my temptation to steal from you. This is an interesting speculation, but whatever the relationship may be between *human* social reasoning ability and consciousness, we aren't likely to get definitive answers any time soon. So let's now return to our main purpose, AI, and consider the possibility of *machines* that are capable of social reasoning.

Can Machines Believe and Desire?

The intentional stance plays an important role in human society, but it can also be applied to a wide range of other entities. For example, consider a conventional light switch. The intentional stance provides a perfectly serviceable descriptive explanation for the behaviour of a light switch: the switch transmits current when it believes we want it transmitted and not otherwise; we communicate our desires by flicking the switch.[9]

However, the intentional stance is surely not the most *appropriate* way of understanding and predicting the behaviour of a light switch: here it is far simpler to adopt the physical stance or the design stance. By contrast, an intentional stance explanation of the switch's behaviour requires attributing to it beliefs about the flowing or absence of current, and also beliefs about our own desires. Although this intentional account provides an accurate prediction of the switch's behaviour, it seems rather extravagant as an *explanation*.

With respect to the intentional stance applied to machines, there seem to be two main questions: When is it *legitimate* to use the intentional stance to talk about machines, and when is it *useful* to do so? John McCarthy, who was an influential thinker on the subject of machines with mental states, had this to say on these questions:[10]

> To ascribe certain beliefs, knowledge, free will, intentions, consciousness, abilities or wants to a machine or computer program is legitimate when such an ascription expresses the same information about the machine that it expresses about a person. [. . .] Ascription of mental qualities is most straightforward for machines of known structure such as thermostats and computer operating systems, but is most useful when applied to entities whose structure is very incompletely known.

This is a rather dense quote, so let's try to unpack it a little bit. First, McCarthy suggests, an intentional stance explanation of a machine should express the same information about the machine that it expresses about a person. This is quite a big requirement, of course – reminiscent of the indistinguishability requirement for the Turing test. Adapting an example we saw earlier, if we claim a robot believes it is raining and that the robot wants to stay dry, then this would be a meaningful ascription if the robot behaved as a rational agent with these beliefs and desires would behave. So, if the robot was able to, then it should take appropriate action to prevent getting wet. If the robot didn't take such action, then we would be inclined to say that either it didn't believe it was raining, or it didn't really want to stay dry, or that it was not rational.

Finally, McCarthy points out that the intentional stance is of greatest value when we don't understand the structure or operation of an entity. It provides a method for explaining and predicting behaviour independently of its internal structure and operation (for example, whether it is a person or a dog or a robot). If you are a rational agent with the desire to stay dry and the belief that it is raining, then I can explain and predict your behaviour without knowing anything else about you.

Towards Conscious Machines

What does all this tell us with respect to our dreams for AI? Let me conclude by rashly making some concrete proposals for what progress towards conscious machines might look like, and how we might create it. (I look forward to re-reading this section in my dotage, to see how my predictions turn out.)

Let's go back to DeepMind's celebrated Atari-playing system from Chapter 5. Recall that DeepMind built an agent that learned to play a large number of Atari video games. These games were in many ways relatively simple, and of course DeepMind has subsequently progressed beyond these to much more complex games such as StarCraft.[11] At present, the main concerns in experiments like this are: to be able to handle games with very large branching factors; games in which there is imperfect information about the state of the game and the actions of other players; games where the rewards available in the game are distant from the actions that lead to those rewards; and games where the actions an agent must perform are not simple binary decisions, such as in Breakout, but ones which involve long and complex sequences, possibly coordinated with – or in competition with – the actions of others.

This is fascinating work, and the progress that's been made here is very impressive. But it is hard to see a simple progression of this work leading to conscious machines, because the issues being addressed don't seem to be those that are relevant for consciousness (this is not a criticism of this work, of course: these are just not the issues that this work aims to address).

Given our discussion above, let me therefore make some tentative suggestions about how we might progress towards this goal. Suppose we have a machine learning program that learns – on its own, just as the DeepMind agent did in Breakout – to succeed in a scenario which requires *meaningful, complex higher-order intentional reasoning*. Or a scenario which requires an agent to *tell a sophisticated lie*, which implies higher-order intentional reasoning. Or a scenario in which an agent learns to communicate and meaningfully express properties of its own mental state and those of others. A system that could learn to do these things in a meaningful way would, I think, be some significant way along the road to conscious machines.[12]

What I have in mind here is something like the **Sally–Anne**

test, which has been proposed to assist in the diagnosis of autism in children.[13] Autism is a serious, widespread psychiatric condition that manifests itself in childhood:[14]

> The key symptoms [of autism] are that social and communication development are clearly abnormal in the first few years of life, and the child's play is characterized by a lack of the usual flexibility, imagination and pretence. [. . .] The key features of the social abnormalities in autism [. . .] include lack of eye contact, lack of normal social awareness or appropriate social behaviour, 'aloneness', one-sidedness in interaction and inability to join a social group.

A typical Sally–Anne test consists of a short story that is told or enacted to the child being tested, such as this one:

Sally and Anne are in a room, which contains a basket, a box and a marble. Sally puts the marble into the basket, and then leaves the room. While Sally is out of the room, Anne takes the marble out of the basket and puts it into the box. Then, Sally comes back into the room, and wants to play with the marble.

The child is then asked a question:

'Where will Sally look for the marble?'

The appropriate answer to this question is 'In the basket'. But to get to this answer, the subject would need to be able to do some reasoning about the beliefs of others: Sally did not see Anne move the marble, so Sally will believe that the marble is where she left it – in the basket. Autistic children, it seems, overwhelmingly answer the question incorrectly, while clinically normal children almost always answer correctly.

Simon Baron-Cohen and his co-authors, who pioneered this approach, take this as evidence that autistic children lack what has become known as a **Theory of Mind** (**ToM**). The ToM is the practical, common-sense capability that fully developed adults have, to be able to reason about the mental states – beliefs, desires and so on – of others and themselves. Humans are not born with a ToM, but clinically normal humans born with the capability to develop one. Clinically normal children develop their theory of mind progressively: by the age of four, children are able to reason including others' perspectives and viewpoints, and their ToM is fully developed in their teens.

At the time of writing, there is beginning to be some research into how machine learning programs can learn a primitive ToM.[15] Researchers recently developed a neural net system called ToMnet ('Theory of Mind net'), which is able to learn how to model other agents, and behave correctly in situations resembling Sally–Anne puzzles. However, the work is at a very early stage, and the ability to solve a Sally–Anne puzzle is not enough to claim artificial consciousness. But this is, I think, a step in the right direction. It gives us another goal to aim towards: an AI system that autonomously learns a human-level ToM.

Would It Be Like Us?

When discussing AI and people, we talk about the brain a lot. And this is quite natural: the brain is the main information-processing component of the human body, which does the heavy lifting when we carry out tasks such as solving problems, understanding stories and so on. So we naturally tend to imagine that the brain is like the computer controlling a driverless car, receiving and interpreting sensory information from our eyes and ears and other senses, and telling our hands, arms and legs what to do. But that is a grossly oversimplified model of the true state of affairs, because the brain is one component of a tightly integrated system containing multiple complex components, which evolved together as a single organism over the billions of years since life first appeared on our planet. We are, in evolutionary terms, nothing more than apes – apes with a sense of entitlement – and human consciousness has to be understood against this background.

Our current capabilities – including the conscious mind – are the result of evolutionary forces that drove the development of our ancestors.[16] Just as our hands and eyes and ears evolved, so did human consciousness. Fully fledged human consciousness did not emerge overnight: there was no sudden 'light-switch' moment, before which our ancestors were like earthworms, and after which they were like Shakespeare. Our ancient ancestors did not enjoy the full range of conscious experience that we did, and we are most likely not enjoying the same range of conscious experiences that our descendants in the deep future will. The process of evolutionary development is surely not finished yet.

Intriguingly, the historical record can give us some clues about how and why certain elements of consciousness emerged. The historical record is sparse, so we are inevitably forced to speculate – a lot – but nevertheless, the clues are tantalizing.

Every currently existing species of ape – including *homo sapiens* (us) – had a common ancestor until about 18 million years ago. Around that time, the evolutionary family tree of the apes began to fork, sending orang-utans on a different evolutionary path about 16 million years ago, and separating us from gorillas and chimpanzees between 6 and 7 million years ago. After this split, our ancestors began to adopt a characteristic that distinguished us from other ape species: we began to spend more time on the ground, rather than in trees, ultimately walking upright on two feet. One possible explanation for the change is that it was necessitated by climatic changes, which reduced forest cover, forcing our tree-dwelling ancestors out into open land. Leaving tree cover probably increased the risk of attack by predators, and a natural evolutionary response was to increase the size of social groups, since larger social groups are less susceptible to predator attack. And larger social groups demanded the social-reasoning skills we discussed earlier, and larger brains to support these social-reasoning skills.

Although our ancestors used fire sporadically as far back in time as a million years ago, it seems that it became commonly used approximately half a million years ago. Fire gave a whole range of benefits to our ancestors – it gave light and warmth, frightened away potential predators and increased the opportunities for feeding. However, fires require care and maintenance – so this new technology required the ability to cooperate in order to take turns minding the fire, collecting fuel and so on. Cooperation of this kind would have benefitted from the ability to undertake higher-order intentional reasoning (in order to understand each other's desires and intentions) and possibly language, which seems to have evolved at about the same time. Once the capability for language was established, further benefits from its development would have become apparent.

We can't reconstruct with any certainty the precise sequence of developments, and the new capabilities they would have brought with them, but the broad sweep seems clear; and I think we can make out some components of consciousness appearing over time. Of course, this doesn't answer the hard problem of consciousness – but at least it gives us some plausible clues about how and why some of the necessary components for fully fledged human consciousness appeared. Ultimately, they might turn out to be dead ends, but conjecture usually leads towards a more solid understanding – eventually. And they offer more than simply treating consciousness as an unknowable mystery.

At some point in the future we will understand consciousness, just as we now understand the forces that power the sun. At that point in time, much of the current debate on the subject will probably seem as quaintly amusing as the various theories put forward to explain the source of the sun's power did before nuclear physics provided the answers.

Suppose we succeed in my research agenda, of building machines with a human-level theory of mind; machines that autonomously learn to handle complex higher-order intentional reasoning, that can build and maintain complex social relationships, that can express complex properties of their own mental state and those of others. Would these machines *really* have a 'mind', consciousness, self-awareness? The problem is, from this distance, we just can't answer this question – we'll have a much better idea as we get closer to being able to build such machines. If, that is, we *are* ever able to build them.

It may conceivably be that we are *never* able to answer this question satisfactorily, although I can see no reason why this should be the case. But, at this point, the ghost of Alan Turing is trying to get my attention. Because Turing, you may recall, argued that if the machine is doing something that is really *indistinguishable* from the 'real thing', then we should stop arguing about whether it is 'really' conscious or self-aware. If it is truly indistinguishable, by any reasonable test that we can invent, then that may be as much as we can ever ask.

Glossary

A* The most widely adopted approach to heuristic search in AI, developed in the early 1970s. Before **A***, heuristic search was a rather ad hoc technique. **A*** put it on a firm mathematical basis. Developed as part of the **SHAKEY** project at SRI.

activation threshold An artificial **neuron** receives a number of inputs, only some of which may be active. It will 'fire' (generate an output) if the sum of the **weight** of active inputs exceeds its activation threshold.

adversarial machine learning A branch of **machine learning** in which we try to trick a machine learning program by giving it inputs which lead it to generate an incorrect output, even though the inputs seem 'obvious' to a human.

agent A self-contained AI system, typically integrating a number of different AI capabilities in order to work autonomously on behalf of a user. Agents are typically assumed to be embedded within some environment and actively working in that environment.

agent-based interface The idea of having a computer interface mediated by an AI-powered **software agent**. The software agent works with us on a task, as an active assistant, rather than passively waiting to be told what to do, as is the case with regular computer applications.

AGI see **Artificial General Intelligence**

AI winter The period immediately following the publication of the Lighthill Report in the early 1970s, which was extremely critical of AI. Characterized by funding cuts to AI research, and considerable scepticism about the field as a whole. Followed by the era of **knowledge-based AI**.

AlexNet A breakthrough image recognition system, which in 2012 demonstrated dramatic improvements in image recognition. One of the landmark **deep learning** systems.

algorithmic bias The possibility that AI systems will exhibit bias when making decisions, either as a result of being trained on biased data sets or because of poorly designed software. Bias may be in the form of allocative harm or representation harm.

AlphaGo A breakthrough system for playing the board game Go, developed by a team at DeepMind. It beat world champion Go player Lee Sedol four games to one in a tournament in Seoul, Korea, in March 2016.

antecedent In an 'IF . . . THEN . . .' rule, as used in an expert system, the antecedent is the condition – the part immediately after the 'IF'. For example, in the rule 'IF animal has udder THEN animal is mammal', the antecedent is 'animal has udder'.

Artificial General Intelligence (**AGI**) The ambitious goal of building AI systems that have the full range of intellectual abilities that humans have: the ability to plan, reason, engage in natural language conversation, make jokes, tell stories, understand stories, play games – everything.

Asilomar principles A set of principles for ethical AI developed by AI scientists and commentators in two meetings held in Asilomar, California, in 2015 and 2017.

axon The component part of a neuron which connects it with other neurons. See also **synapse**.

backprop/backpropagation The most important algorithm for **training neural nets**.

backward chaining In **knowledge-based** systems, the idea that we start with a goal that we are trying to establish (e.g., 'animal is carnivore') and try to establish it by seeing if the goal is justified using the data we have (e.g., 'animal eats meat'). A counterpart to **forward chaining**.

Bayes' Theorem/Bayesian inference Bayes' theorem is a core concept in probability theory, which, in AI, gives us a way to adjust our beliefs about the world when given new data or evidence. Crucially, the new evidence may be 'noisy', or uncertain: Bayes' Theorem gives us the proper way to handle such uncertain information.

Bayesian network A **knowledge representation** scheme for capturing complex networks of connected probabilistic data, yielding a form of **Bayesian inference** using **Bayes' Theorem**.

behavioural AI An alternative to **symbolic AI** that gained a lot of attention in the period from about 1985 to 1995. The idea was to build a system by focusing on the behaviours that the system should exhibit, and only then to worry about how these behaviours are interrelated.

The **subsumption architecture** was the most popular approach to behavioural AI.

belief A piece of information an AI system has about its environment. In **logic-based AI**, the beliefs the system had would be the contents of its **knowledge base** and **working memory**.

Blocks World A simulated 'micro world' in which the task is to arrange various objects like blocks and boxes. Most famously used in **SHRDLU**, Blocks World scenarios were subsequently criticized because they had abstracted away many of the really hard problems that an AI system would face in the real world, notably **perception**.

branching factor When solving a problem, this is the number of alternatives you have to consider every time you make a decision. Thus, when playing a game, the branching factor will be the number of moves you can make on average from any given board position. In Tic-Tac-Toe, the branching factor is about 4; for chess, it is approximately 35; for Go, it is about 250. Larger branching factors lead to search trees that very quickly get impossibly large, necessitating the use of **heuristics** to focus **search**.

ceteris paribus preferences The idea that when we specify our preferences to an AI system, we do so on the assumption that 'All other things are held equal' (i.e. as close as possible to how they are now).

Chinese room A scenario proposed by the philosopher John Searle in an attempt to show that **strong AI** is impossible.

choice under uncertainty A situation in which we must make a decision which has multiple possible outcomes, and all that we know, for every possible choice we might make, is the probability that each outcome will occur. See **expected utility**.

combinatorial explosion Where we must make a succession of choices, and each successive choice *multiplies* the number of possibilities we need to consider. A fundamental problem in AI, which arises in **search**: it causes the size of search trees to grow very, very rapidly.

common-sense reasoning A broad term, but basically the kind of informal reasoning about the world of which we are all capable, but which proved very hard for **logic-based AI**.

consequent In an 'IF ... THEN ...' rule, as used in an expert system, the consequent is the conclusion – the part immediately after the 'THEN'. For example, in the rule 'IF animal has udder THEN animal is mammal', the consequent is 'animal is mammal'.

credit assignment A problem that arises in **machine learning**: deciding which of the machine learning program's actions were the good ones and which the bad ones. For example, your machine learning program played a game of chess and lost: how does it know which moves were the critical ones?

curse of dimensionality In **machine learning**, the problem that including more **features** in your training data necessitates vastly more **training**.

Cyc hypothesis The hypothesis that **General AI** is primarily a problem of knowledge, and that a suitably equipped **knowledge-based** system will be capable of General AI.

Cyc project A famous (or notorious) experiment from the days of **knowledge-based AI**, which attempted to construct a generally intelligent AI system by giving it all the knowledge about the world that a reasonably educated person has. It didn't work.

decidable problem A decidable problem is one that can be solved by an algorithm.

decision problem A decision problem is a mathematical problem that has a Yes/No answer. Examples might be 'Is it the case that the square root of 16 is 4?' and 'Is it the case that 7920 is a prime number?' The *Entscheidungsproblem*, solved by Alan Turing, asked whether or not there are decision problems that cannot be solved by an algorithm. He showed that there *are* decision problems (notably the halting problem) for which there is no algorithm. Problems of this type are said to be **undecidable**.

deduction Logical reasoning: deriving new knowledge from existing knowledge.

deep learning The breakthrough techniques that have driven the rise of **machine learning** research this century. Characterized by deeper, more interconnected **neural nets**, the use of bigger, carefully curated **training** data sets and some new techniques.

DENDRAL A classic early **expert system**, which helped users to identify unknown organic compounds.

depth-first search A type of **search** technique used in problem solving, in which instead of expanding the

entire **search tree** layer by layer, we just expand one
branch of the tree.

design stance The idea that we try to understand and
predict the behaviour of some entity with reference
to what it was designed to do. A clock, for example,
is designed to show the time, so we can understand
the numbers it displays as the time. Contrast with the
physical stance and the **intentional stance**.

ELIZA A seminal experiment in conversational AI from the
1960s, developed by Joseph Weizenbaum. ELIZA used
simple canned scripts to simulate a psychotherapist.

emergent property When a system composed of multiple
components exhibits some property that arises,
typically in an unexpected or unpredictable way, from
interactions of the component systems.

epiphenomenalism In the study of the mind, this is the
idea that mind and conscious thought do not drive
behaviour, but are the by-product of the processes that
actually govern behaviour.

expected utility In a problem of decision-making under
uncertainty, the expected utility of a particular course of
action is the average utility that you could expect to gain
from that choice.

expert system A system that uses human expert knowledge
to solve problems in a tightly constrained area. Classic
examples are **MYCIN**, **DENDRAL** and **R1/XCON**.
Building expert systems was a key focus of AI research
from the late 1970s to the mid-1980s.

feature The components of a piece of data that a **machine
learning** program bases its decisions on.

feature extraction In **machine learning**, the problem of deciding which attributes in a data set should be selected as **training** data.

fires In the context of **knowledge-based** systems, a rule fires if the information we have in **working memory** correctly matches the **antecedent** of the rule, allowing us to add the **consequent** of the rule to working memory.

first-order logic A very general language and reasoning system that was developed to give a precise foundation for mathematical reasoning. Widely studied in the paradigm of **logic-based AI**.

forward chaining In **knowledge-based** systems, reasoning from information to reach conclusions. Contrast with **backward chaining**.

game theory The theory of strategic reasoning. Widely used in AI as a framework to understand how AI systems can and should interact with one another.

General AI See **Artificial General Intelligence**.

goal state In problem solving, a goal state describes how we want our problem to look when we have successfully completed the task.

Golden Age of AI The early period of AI research, from about 1956–75 (followed by the **AI winter**). Work in this period focused on the 'divide and conquer' approach: build systems that demonstrate the *components* of intelligent behaviour, in the hope they can later be integrated.

gradient descent A technique used when training **neural nets**. See also **backpropagation**.

Grand Challenge A competition for driverless cars, organized by US military funding agency DARPA, which led to the triumph of the robot named **STANLEY** in October 2005, and which heralded the age of driverless cars.

hard problem of consciousness The problem of understanding how and why physical processes lead to subjective conscious experiences. See also **qualia**.

Harm Assessment Risk Tool (HART) A **machine learning** system developed to help the police force in Durham, UK, decide whether someone should be detained in custody.

heuristic, heuristic search A **heuristic** is a 'rule of thumb' to focus **search**. Heuristics are also rules of thumb in the sense that they are not *guaranteed* to focus search in the right direction. See also **A***.

high-level programming language A programming language that hides away the low-level details of the actual computer the program is running on. High-level programming languages are machine independent, at least in principle: the same program will work on different types of computers. Examples include Python and Java. John McCarthy's **LISP** was an early example.

HOMER An **agent** developed in the 1980s, which operated in a simulated 'sea world' environment. HOMER could converse in (a subset of) English, be given tasks to accomplish in the sea world and had some common-sense understanding of its actions.

homunculus problem A classic problem in the theory of mind, which occurs when we try to explain the problem of mind by inadvertently delegating it to another mind.

ImageNet A database of labelled images, developed by Fei Fei Li, which was enormously influential in **deep learning** for training programs to be able to create captions for images.

inference engine The part of an **expert system** which uses reasoning, deriving new knowledge from **rules** and facts in **working memory**.

initial state In **problem solving**, the initial state describes what the problem looks like before we have carried out our task. See also **goal state**.

intentional stance The idea of predicting and explaining the behaviour of some entity by attributing to it **mental states** such as beliefs and desires, and assuming that it will act rationally on the basis of these beliefs and desires.

intentional system Any system that is amenable to an **intentional stance** characterization.

inverse reinforcement learning When a **machine learning** program observes what a human does, and tries to learn a **reward** system from these observations.

knowledge base In an **expert system**, the knowledge base consists of human expert knowledge, typically encoded in the form of **rules**.

knowledge-based AI The dominant paradigm for AI from about 1975–85, focused on using explicit knowledge about problems, often in the form of **rules**.

knowledge elicitation The process of extracting and encoding human expert knowledge from the relevant experts when building an **expert system**.

knowledge engineer Someone trained to construct knowledge-based systems. A knowledge engineer will spend a lot of time working on **knowledge elicitation**.

knowledge graph A very large **knowledge-based** system developed by Google by automatically extracting knowledge from the World Wide Web.

Knowledge Navigator A concept video developed by Apple in the 1980s, which introduced the idea of the **agent-based interface**.

knowledge representation The problem of explicitly encoding knowledge in a form that can be processed by computers. In the era of **expert systems**, the dominant approach was to use **rules**, although logic was also widely used.

layered neural net The standard way of organizing a **neural net**, into a series of layers, where the outputs of each layer feed into the next layer. A key problem in the early days of neural net research was that there was no way of **training** layered neural nets, and networks with a single layer are greatly restricted in terms of what they can do.

Lighthill Report A UK report into AI in the early 1970s, which was fiercely critical of AI research at the time. The report led to funding cuts, and is generally recognized as one of the factors that led to the **AI winter**.

LISP A **high-level programming language** that was widely used in the era of **symbolic AI.** Developed by John McCarthy. LIST machines were computers that were designed specifically to run the LISP programming language. See also **PROLOG**.

logic A formal framework for reasoning. See also **first-order logic** and **logic-based AI**.

logic-based AI An approach to AI in which intelligent decision-making is reduced to logical reasoning, for example in **first-order logic**.

logic programming An approach to programming in which we simply state what we know about a problem and what our goal is – the machine does the rest. See also **PROLOG**.

machine learning One of the core capabilities of an intelligent system. A **machine learning** program learns an association between inputs and outputs without being explicitly told how. **Neural nets** and **deep learning** are popular approaches to machine learning.

maximizing expected utility In decision-making under **uncertainty**, the principle that, given a choice between multiple alternatives, a rational **agent** will choose the alternative which gives the maximum utility on average, i.e. the one which maximizes **expected utility**.

mental states A key component of mind: beliefs, desires and the like. See also **intentional stance**.

mind–body problem One of the most fundamental problems in science: how are the physical processes in the brain/body related to the mind and conscious experience?

minimax search A key search technique in game playing, in which you seek to maximize your benefit, assuming that an adversary is trying to make you do as badly as possible. See also **search tree**.

moral agency An entity is a moral agent if it can understand the consequences of its actions and the distinction between right and wrong, and can therefore be held accountable for its actions. The prevailing view is that AI systems should not – and indeed, cannot – be treated as moral agents. Responsibility lies with the people who build and run an AI system, not with the system itself.

Moral Machine An online experiment in which users were asked what choices should be made in various **Trolley Problems.**

multi-agent systems Systems in which multiple **agents** interact with one another.

multi-layer perceptron An early form of a **layered neural net**.

MYCIN A classic **expert system** from the 1970s, which acted as a doctor's assistant, diagnosing blood diseases in humans.

narrow AI In contrast to **General AI**, this is the idea of building AI systems that focus on very specific problems, rather than trying to be capable of the full range of human intellectual abilities. The term is mainly used in the media: it isn't really used in the AI community itself.

Nash equilibrium A core concept in game theory, where a group of decision-makers are all simultaneously satisfied that they did the best they could, given the choices made by others.

natural language understanding Programs that can interact in ordinary human languages like English.

neural networks/neural nets An approach to **machine learning** using 'artificial neurons'. The basic technique used in **deep learning**. See also **perceptron**.

neuron A nerve cell that is connected to other nerve cells, communicating with them via an **axon**. The basic information-processing unit of the brain, and the inspiration for **neural nets**.

NP-complete A class of computational problems that resist attempts to solve them efficiently. The theory of NP-completeness was developed in the 1970s, and in this time many AI problems were discovered to be NP-complete. See also **P vs NP** problem.

ontological engineering In an **expert system** (and, more generally, in a **knowledge-based** system), this is the task of defining the conceptual vocabulary you will use to represent knowledge in your system.

opaqueness (of **neural nets**) The problem is that the expertise a neural network has is encoded in a series of numeric **weights**: we have no way of being able to tell what those weights 'mean'. This means that current neural nets can't explain or justify their decisions.

P vs NP problem The question of whether **NP-complete** problems definitely can or cannot always be solved efficiently. One of the biggest open problems in mathematics today. Not likely to be settled any time soon. ('P' stands for 'polynomial time'; 'NP' stands for 'non-deterministic polynomial time': technically, the P vs NP problem is whether problems that can be solved in non-deterministic polynomial time can be solved in polynomial time.)

perception The process of understanding what is around you in your environment. This was a fundamental sticking point for **symbolic AI**.

perceptron, perceptron model A type of **neural net**, studied in the 1960s but still relevant today. Research in perceptrons died out in the early 1970s when it was shown that there were severe limits to what one-layer perceptron models could learn.

perverse instantiation When an AI system does what you asked it to, but not in the way you anticipated.

physical stance The idea that we try to predict and explain the behaviour of an entity with respect to its physical structure and physical laws. Contrast with the **intentional stance**.

planning The problem of finding a sequence of actions that will transform an **initial state** into a **goal state**. See also **search**.

preferences, preference relation A description of your preferences, in which you rank every possible pair of alternatives. If you want an **agent** to act on your behalf, it needs to know your preferences so that it can make the best choice possible on your behalf.

premises In **logic**, the premises are the knowledge you start from. You then use logical reasoning to derive conclusions from these premises.

prior probability The probability that you attach to an hypothesis before receiving any further information. 'Prior' in this sense thus means 'before you get any more information'.

problem solving In AI, problem solving means finding the right sequence of actions to transform a problem from an **initial state** to a **goal state**. **Search** is the standard approach to problem solving in AI.

PROLOG A programming language based on **first-order logic**, which was particularly popular in the era of **logic-based AI**.

PROMETHEUS A seminal European experiment in driverless car technology from the 1980s and 1990s.

qualia Personal mental experiences. An example might be smelling coffee, or drinking a cold drink on a hot day.

R1/XCON A classic **expert system** from the 1970s, developed by DEC for configuring their VAX computers. An early example of profitable AI.

reinforcement learning A form of **machine learning**, in which an **agent** acts in its environment, and receives feedbacks for its actions in the form of a **reward**.

reward The feedback that a **reinforcement learning** program gets on its actions, which may be positive or negative.

rule A discrete piece of knowledge, expressed in the form of an 'IF . . . THEN . . .' expression. For example, consider this rule: 'IF animal has udder THEN animal is mammal.' This rule tells us that if we have the information that an animal has an udder, then we can derive some new information, namely that the animal is a mammal.

Sally–Anne test A test which aims to determine whether an entity has a **Theory of Mind**, i.e. the ability to reason about the beliefs and desires of others. This was originally developed as a test for autism.

script A **knowledge-representation** scheme developed in the 1970s, which aims to capture stereotypical sequences of events in common situations.

search, search tree A fundamental AI **problem-solving** technique, in which a computer program tries to find how to achieve a goal by starting from some **initial state**, using a limited repertoire of actions and then generating a search tree.

semantic nets A **knowledge-representation** scheme, in which we capture relationships between concepts and entities using a graphical notation.

sensor A device that give robots raw perceptual data. Typical sensors are cameras, laser radar, ultra-sonic range-finders and bump detectors. Interpreting the raw perceptual data is a major challenge.

SHAKEY A seminal experiment in autonomous robots, developed at SRI in the late 1960s, which pioneered several key AI technologies.

SHRDLU A celebrated system from the **Golden Age**, later criticized for focusing on simulated micro-worlds.

Singularity The hypothesized point at which machine intelligence exceeds that of humans.

situated [**agent**] A central idea in the era of **behavioural AI**, to the effect that progress in AI requires the development of **agents** which are actually embedded in and acting upon some environment, rather than being disembodied (as is usually the case with **expert systems**).

social welfare Any attempt to measure the aggregate utility of a society, i.e. how well society is doing as a whole, is a measure of social welfare.

software agent An **agent** that inhabits a software environment rather than the physical world, as robots do. Think of it as a software robot.

(**sound**) **reasoning** Reasoning is said to be sound if the conclusions derived are warranted from the **premises**.

STANLEY The robot that won the 2005 DARPA **Grand Challenge** for driverless cars, autonomously driving approximately 140 miles, averaging about 19 miles per hour. Developed at Stanford University.

STRIPS A seminal **planning** system, developed as part of the **SHAKEY** robotics project at SRI.

strong AI The goal of building AI systems that really do have mind, consciousness, awareness and so on in the way that we do. See also **weak AI** and **General AI**. Nobody knows whether strong AI is possible or what it would be like.

subsumption architecture and **subsumption hierarchy** An architecture for robots from the era of **behavioural AI**, in which we organize the desired behaviours of the robot into a hierarchy, with lower layers taking precedence over higher layers.

supervised learning The simplest form of **machine learning**, where we train a program by showing it examples of inputs and desired outputs. See also **training**.

syllogism A simple pattern for logical reasoning, known since antiquity.

symbolic AI An approach to AI which involves explicitly modelling reasoning and planning processes.

synapse A 'junction' connecting neurons together, allowing them to communicate.

Theory of Mind (**ToM**) The everyday ability that clinically normal human adults have to reason about the mental states (beliefs, desires, intentions) of other people. See also **intentional stance** and **Sally–Anne test**.

Three Laws of Robotics Introduced by science-fiction writer Isaac Asimov in the 1930s, the three laws are a kind of ethical framework governing AI behaviour. While they are very ingenious, it isn't possible to directly implement them in practice – and it's not even clear what they would mean.

TouringMachines A typical **agent** design from the mid-1990s, in which control of the agent is divided into three layers, which are responsible for reacting, planning and modelling respectively.

tractable problem A problem is said to be tractable if we have an efficient algorithm to solve it. **NP-complete** problems are not tractable: we don't have algorithms that are guaranteed to solve them efficiently. See also **P vs NP problem**.

training (in **machine learning**) The task of a machine learning program is to learn associations between inputs and outputs without being told how to compute the association. To do this, the program is typically trained by giving it examples of inputs and the desired corresponding outputs. See also **supervised learning**.

Trolley Problem A problem in ethical reasoning, originally posed in the 1960s: if you do nothing, five people will die, while if you act, then only one person will die; should you act? Often discussed in the context of driverless cars, although mostly dismissed as irrelevant by the AI community.

Turing machine A mathematical problem-solving machine – one which embodies a particular recipe for solving a problem. Any mathematical problem that can be solved by a computer can be solved by a Turing machine. Invented by Alan Turing to solve the *Entscheidungsproblem*. See also **Universal Turing Machine.**

Turing test A test proposed by Turing to address the question of whether machines can 'think'. If, after interacting with some entity for some time, you can't be confident whether it is a machine or person, you should accept it has human-like intelligence. Ingenious and very influential, although not to be taken too seriously as an actual test for AI.

uncertainty A ubiquitous problem in AI: the information we receive is rarely certain (definitely true or false) – there is usually some uncertainty associated with it. Similarly, when we make decisions, we rarely know with certainty what the consequences of those decisions are: there are usually multiple possible outcomes, with differing degrees of likelihood. Dealing with uncertainty is therefore a fundamental topic in AI. See also **Bayes' Theorem** and Appendix C.

undecidable problem A problem that we know, in a precise mathematical sense, cannot be solved by a computer (or, more exactly, by a **Turing machine**).

Universal Turing Machine A general type of **Turing machine**, which provided the template for the modern computer. While a Turing machine encodes just one specific recipe/algorithm, a Universal Turing Machine can be given *any* recipe/algorithm.

(**unsound**) **reasoning** In **logic**, where we derive
conclusions that are not warranted by the **premises**.
See also (**sound**) **reasoning**.

Urban Challenge A 2007 follow-on to the DARPA **Grand
Challenge**, in which autonomous vehicles were
required to autonomously traverse a built-up urban
environment.

utilitarianism The idea that we should choose to act so
as to maximize the benefit for society. In a **Trolley
Problem**, a utilitarian would choose to kill one
person in order to save five lives. See also
virtue ethics.

utilities A standard technique for representing
preferences in AI programs: we attach numeric values,
called utilities, to all possible outcomes. The AI system
then tries to compute the course of action which would
lead to the outcome which maximizes utility, i.e. is the
most preferred outcome. See also **expected utility** and
maximizing expected utility.

utopian One who believes that AI and other new
technologies will lead us to a utopian future (where
technology frees us from work, etc.).

virtue ethics The idea that, when facing ethical problems,
we identify an ethical person who embodies the ethical
principles that we value, and that we should then choose
to do what that ethical person would do.

weak AI The goal of building machines which appear
to have understanding (consciousness, mind, self-
awareness, etc.) without claiming that they actually have
these things. See also **strong AI** and **General AI**.

weight (in **neural nets**) In neural nets, connections between neurons (**axons**) are given numeric weights. The higher the weight, the more the connection will influence the neuron to which it is linked. A neural network ultimately boils down to these weights, and the task of **training** a neural net is all about finding appropriate ones.

Winograd schemas An alternative to the **Turing test**. We are given two sentences that differ in just one word, but which have fundamentally different meanings. The test requires understanding the difference. The idea is that Winograd schemas resist cheap tricks often used in the Turing test because they require *comprehension* of the text.

working memory In an **expert system**, the part of the system that has information about the current problem being solved (as opposed to the knowledge about a problem which is encoded in **rules**).

Understanding Rules

Here is the complete rule base for the animals' example, which was (I believe) introduced by Patrick Winston and Berthold Horn:

1. IF animal has hair
   THEN animal is mammal
2. IF animal gives milk
   THEN animal is mammal
3. IF animal has feathers
   THEN animal is bird
4. IF animal can fly AND animal lays eggs
   THEN animal is bird
5. IF animal eats meat
   THEN animal is carnivore
6. IF animal is mammal AND animal has hooves
   THEN animal is ungulate
7. IF animal is mammal AND animal is carnivore
   AND animal has tawny colour AND animal has black
   stripes
   THEN animal is tiger
8. IF animal is ungulate AND animal has black stripes
   THEN animal is zebra

Let's see how these rules work with forward chaining. Suppose the user provided the information that the animal gives milk, has hooves and has black stripes. Then forward chaining would proceed as follows:

1. The fact that the animal gives milk would enable Rule 2 to fire, and the information that the animal is a mammal is added to working memory.
2. The newly derived information that the animal is a mammal, together with the fact that the animal has hooves would enable Rule 6 to fire, and the fact that the animal is an ungulate is added to working memory.
3. The new information, that the animal is an ungulate, together with the fact that the animal has black stripes, enables Rule 8 to fire, and the fact that the animal is a zebra is added to working memory.
4. At this point, no further rules can fire.

In this way, we have been able to derive three new items of knowledge from the general rules we were given, and specific information about the animal in question.

Recall that with backward chaining, we start with some hypothesis (the goal) that we want to establish: we then use the rules to work back down to much smaller (atomic) items of knowledge. Let's see how it works if the user presents the system with the goal of determining whether the animal is an ungulate, without giving it any information:

1. The inference engine looks for a rule that has the goal ('animal is ungulate') as a consequence. In this case, it finds one such rule, namely Rule 6.

2. The inference engine does not have enough information to fire Rule 6, because it does not know whether the antecedents ('animal is mammal AND animal has hooves') are true. It therefore sets itself the goal of determining whether these statements are true or not. Technically, 'animal is mammal' and 'animal has hooves' become *sub-goals*.

3. Taking the sub-goal 'animal is mammal' first, the inference engine looks for rules that have this as a consequent. In this case, there are two such rules: 1 and 2. This tells the inference engine that this goal may be established in two different ways: either discover that the animal has hair (Rule 1), or that the animal gives milk (Rule 2). So, the inference engine takes the first of these ('animal has hair') and establishes it as a sub-goal.

4. The inference engine looks for a rule that has the sub-goal 'animal has hair' as a consequent. However, in this case there is no such rule: we have reached an atomic statement. This is not a dead-end, however: when faced with such atomic statements, the inference engine can ask the user whether the particular statement is true. In this way, the backward-chaining reasoning process used becomes a question-and-answer session with the user.

Let's suppose the user has no information about whether the animal has hair, and so responds 'Don't know', in answer to the question. Without any relevant information, the inference engine concludes that Rule 1 will not fire, so it moves on to the second rule with 'animal is mammal' as a conclusion, namely, Rule 2, which has 'animal gives milk' as an antecedent.

5. The inference engine establishes 'animal gives milk' as a sub-goal, but finds this is also atomic. So, it asks this as a question to the user. Suppose in this case the user says 'Yes'. The information 'animal gives milk' is added to working memory, allowing Rule 2 to fire, and 'animal is mammal' is added to working memory.

6. At this point, the inference engine has established the first part of the antecedent of Rule 6, so it moves on to the second part, trying to establish whether 'animal has hooves' is true. So, it establishes this as a sub-goal.

7. Here, 'animal has hooves' is another atomic statement, and so the user is questioned again. Suppose the user answers 'Yes'. This fact is added to working memory, and combined with the information 'animal is mammal', the system is able to fire Rule 6, finally concluding that the animal is an ungulate. The user's original goal has been established.

Understanding PROLOG

We'll see how a simple PROLOG program can capture knowledge about family relationships. Suppose we write 'female(X)' to mean that X is female, and we write 'parents(X, M, F)' to mean that person X has parents M and F, where M is the male parent and F is the female parent. Then you might write the following PROLOG rule:

sister_of(X,Y):- female(X), parents(X, M, F), parents(Y, M, F).

to represent the following piece of knowledge:

X is the sister of Y if:

1. X is female,
2. the parents of X are M and F, and
3. the parents of Y are M and F.

If you are unfamiliar with logical reasoning, this may sound a rather convoluted way of talking about when someone is a sister, but essentially all it says is that X is the sister of Y if X is female and X and Y have the same parents.

We can then give PROLOG a few facts:

female(janine).
parents(janine, wayne, yvonne).
parents(david, wayne, yvonne).

Given these facts, if we give PROLOG the task of trying to prove that Janine is the sister of David, it will succeed. The relevant goal in this case is:

    sister_of(janine, david)

When presented with this goal, PROLOG will respond with 'Yes', indicating that it was able to prove that Janine is the sister of David.

Understanding Bayes' Theorem

Let's see how Bayes' Theorem works. We will work through our flu example from Chapter 4. To see how Bayes' Theorem is used for this example, we need a little bit of what mathematicians call 'notation'.

First, the hypothesis we are concerned with is that you have the flu; the evidence we have obtained is that the test for the flu has come back positive.

Now, the value that we are trying to compute is the probability that the hypothesis is true, given that we have the evidence, i.e. the probability you have the flu given that the test has come back positive. We write this value as *Prob*(hypothesis | evidence). The vertical bar '|' means 'given that'.

We write *Prob*(hypothesis) to denote the **prior probability** that the hypothesis (You have the flu) is true. The 'prior probability' is the probability we would attach to the hypothesis being true *before* we saw the new evidence. In our example, this is solely the probability that a person picked at random would have the flu. We know that about one in every 1,000 people has the flu, so this prior probability is $1/1000 = 0.001$. We can think of this value as being our initial belief about the hypothesis. If we don't know anything else at all about someone, then our estimate of the probability that they have flu is precisely the probability that someone chosen at random has the flu, which is one in 1,000. Bayes' Theorem will allow us to *update* this belief in the light of new evidence – that's the magic of it.

Next, we write *Prob*(evidence | hypothesis) for the probability that we would see the evidence (a positive test) given that the hypothesis (You have the flu) is true. We know that the test is 99 per cent accurate, so if you have the flu, then the test will come back positive 99 times out of a hundred – the probability that you will have a positive test if you have the flu is 0.99.

Finally, we write *Prob*(evidence) for the probability that the test would give a true result for a person selected at random. Figuring out this value is the only really tricky part in this example. In our case, it is the probability that a person has the flu multiplied by the probability that the test would come back positive for them, added to the probability that they *don't* have the flu multiplied by the probability that the test could still give a positive result. In other words:

$$Prob(\text{evidence}) = (0.001 \times 0.99) + (0.999 \times 0.01) = 0.011$$

So, if we now state Bayes' Theorem –

$$Prob(\text{hypothesis | evidence})$$
$$= \frac{Prob(\text{evidence | hypothesis}) \times Prob(\text{hypothesis})}{Prob(\text{evidence})}$$

and plug in the values we derived above, we have:

Prob(hypothesis | evidence)

$$= \frac{Prob(\text{evidence} \mid \text{hypothesis}) \times Prob(\text{hypothesis})}{Prob(\text{evidence})}$$

$$= \frac{0.99 \times 0.001}{0.011} = 0.09$$

So, the overall probability that you have the flu given that your test came back positive is 0.09; slightly less than one in ten.

Understanding Neural Nets

First, let's dig into the problem with perceptron models that was highlighted by Minsky and Papert. Single-layer perceptrons cannot implement a very simple classification problem, called the 'XOR function'.

Now, the XOR function that we want the program to be able to learn is this: we want the output to be active if *either* Input 1 is active *or* Input 2 is active *but not both*. To understand that this is impossible for the perceptron model above, imagine for a moment that it *is* possible. In that case, there will be w_1 and w_2 (the weights) and T (the threshold value) with the following properties:

- If neither input is active, then the neuron is receiving inputs with a zero weighting, and does not fire, so therefore the threshold value, T, must be greater than 0.
- If only Input 1 is active, then the perceptron fires, so w_1 must be greater than T.
- If only Input 2 is active then the perceptron fires, so w_2 must be greater than T.
- If *both* Inputs 1 and 2 are active, then the perceptron *does not* fire, so $w_1 + w_2$ must be <u>less than</u> T.

But it is easy to see that values for w_1, w_2 and T which simultaneously satisfy all of these properties cannot exist. Therefore, there can never be any perceptron that can learn XOR.

Let's see now how a two-layer perceptron *can* learn XOR. Consider the network in Figure D2. I claim that this network correctly computes XOR. The network consists of three neurons: Neuron 1 will fire if either Input 1 or Input 2 are active; Neuron 2 will fire only when it is *not* the case that both Inputs 1 and 2 are active; and finally, Neuron 3 will fire if both Neuron 1 and Neuron 2 fire. To summarize, Neuron 3 will fire if *either* Input 1 or Input 2 are active, but *not both*.

In more detail, consider the four possible cases:

1. First, suppose that neither of the inputs is active. Then Neuron 2 will fire (since its input of 0 is above the –1.5 threshold), but Neuron 1 will not. In this case, Neuron 3 receives an input of 1, which does not meet the threshold of 1.5, so Neuron 3 will not fire.

2. Now, suppose that Input 1 is active, but Input 2 is not. Then Neuron 1 will receive an input of 1, exceeding the threshold of 0.5 so Neuron 1 will fire. Neuron 2 will receive an input of –1, exceeding the threshold of –1.5 so Neuron 2 will also fire. In this case, Neuron 3 receives inputs from both neurons 1 and 2, exceeding its threshold of 1.5 – hence Neuron 3 will fire.

3. Suppose Input 2 is active, but Input 1 is not. Then by the same argument as in the preceding case, Neuron 3 will fire.

4. Finally, suppose both inputs are active. Then Neuron 1 will receive an input of 2 and so will fire, while Neuron 2 will receive an input of –2 and so will not fire. Thus Neuron 3 will receive an input of 1 and so will not fire.

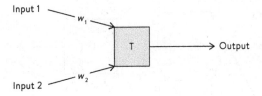

Figure D1
A single-layer perceptron which cannot compute XOR.

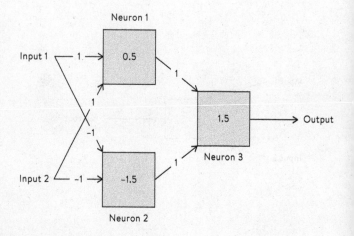

Figure D2
A two-layer perceptron that correctly computes XOR.

Further Reading

I realize that some readers will want to satisfy their curiosity with further reading, and so below are a few key pointers to the literature.

The definitive modern academic introduction to AI is Stuart Russell and Peter Norvig's *Artificial Intelligence: A Modern Approach* (3rd edn, Pearson, 2016). This is my standard reference to AI, and I used it repeatedly for checking technical details while working on the present volume.

If you are interested in detailed questions of history and the way in which the field evolved, the book you want is Nils Nilsson's *The Quest for Artificial Intelligence* (Cambridge University Press, 2010). This is a superlative historical guide to the many threads of modern AI, written by one of the field's greatest researchers.

There are now several books about the life of Alan Turing, but the best by far is the one that gave the world the Turing story: Andrew Hodges' *Alan Turing: The Enigma* (Burnett Books/Hutchinson, 1983). As an undergraduate, I very much enjoyed the three-volume *Handbook of Artificial Intelligence* published by William Kaufmann & Heuristech Press (Volume I, ed. Avron Barr and Edward A. Feigenbaum, 1981; Volume II, ed. Barr and Feigenbaum, 1982; Volume III, ed.

Paul R. Cohen and Edward A. Feigenbaum, 1982). They paint a glorious picture of the systems built during the Golden Age and the techniques used to build them. Although out of print for quite some time, it's possible to obtain copies cheaply online. A great reference for the world of expert systems is Peter Jackson's *Introduction to Expert Systems* (Addison Wesley, 1986). This was a set text for me as an undergraduate 30 years ago, and it was a pleasure to revisit it through this book. For a detailed introduction to knowledge engineering for expert systems, see *Building Expert Systems* (eds. Frederick Hayes-Roth, Donald A. Waterman and Douglas B. Lenat, Addison Wesley, 1983). To understand the logical tradition in AI, I recommend Michael Genesereth and Nis Nilsson's *Logical Foundations of Artificial Intelligence* (Morgan Kaufmann, 1987). I read this book in great detail as a graduate student, and although the techniques it espoused largely went out of fashion within a decade, it remains a beautifully written account of one of the most influential strands of AI research – and an excellent introduction to logic.

Rodney Brooks' own *Cambrian Intelligence* (MIT Press, 1999) collects together his main papers on behavioural AI and the subsumption architecture. I will immodestly recommend my own *Introduction to MultiAgent Systems* (2nd edn, Wiley, 2009) as an introduction to agents, agent architectures and multi-agent systems. To understand more about the role of game theory in AI, read *Multiagent Systems: Algorithmic, Game-Theoretic, and Logical Foundations*, by Yoav Shoham and Kevin Leyton-Brown (Cambridge University Press, 2008).

Machine learning is a vast topic, and I have barely scratched at the surface in the main text. Although I have focused on neural nets – as they are the main area of interest at present – there are many other techniques for machine learning. For a more detailed but still relatively informal introduction, see Ethel Alpaydin's *Machine Learning: The New AI* (MIT Press, Essential Knowledge Series, 2016). If you are after a job at DeepMind (and who isn't, these days?), then the book you probably need to read is *Deep Learning*, by Ian Goodfellow, Yoshua Bengio and Aaron Courville (MIT Press, 2017). Finally, note that Russell and Norvig (see my second paragraph above) have excellent coverage of the various other approaches to machine learning.

For a good discussion on the Singularity, I recommend Murray Shanahan's very readable *The Technological Singularity* (MIT Press, Essential Knowledge Series, 2015); for ethical AI, see Virginia Dignum's *Responsible Artificial Intelligence* (Springer, 2019); for technology and employment, see Carl Benedikt Frey's *The Technology Trap* (Princeton University Press, 2019).

A classic introduction to the ideas of strong AI and conscious machines is Maggie Boden's *Artificial Intelligence and Natural Man* (MIT Press, 1977). For a detailed textbook introduction to consciousness, there is Susan Blackmore's *Consciousness: An Introduction* (Hodder & Stoughton, 2010). Almost anything Daniel Dennett has written on the subject of mind, consciousness and AI is worth reading – as a starting point, I recommend *Kinds of Minds* (Basic Books, 1996). And if you only read one thing as a follow-up to this book, I recommend his essay *Where Am I?*, which originally appeared in his 1978 book *Brainstorms*; it is readily available online.

Notes

Many contemporary articles in AI and machine learning are deposited in an open online archive called 'arXiv'. Articles within the arXiv are referenced with a simple numbering scheme thus: arXiv:1412.6572. You can obtain the relevant article by going to https://arxiv.org and entering the relevant reference number (in this case, '1412.6572').

INTRODUCTION

1. http://tinyurl.com/y7zc94od.
2. http://tinyurl.com/yxk3xurl.

CHAPTER 1: TURING'S ELECTRONIC BRAINS

1. A. Hodges. *Alan Turing: The Enigma*. Burnett Books Ltd, 1983.
2. Quite apart from his astonishing scientific legacy, Turing had a profound social legacy within the United Kingdom. Following a lengthy high-profile public campaign, the government posthumously pardoned him in 2014; shortly after, pardons were issued to all men who had been prosecuted under the same law.
3. This is the most obvious recipe for checking primality, but by no means the most elegant or efficient. A neat alternative called the Sieve of Eratosthenes has been known since antiquity.
4. At this point I'll stop distinguishing between Universal Turing Machines and Turing Machines, and simply refer to 'Turing Machines'.

5. Turing shares the glory for the *Entscheidungsproblem* with Princeton mathematician Alonzo Church, who independently obtained a very different proof of the result just before Turing. However, Turing's proof is regarded as the definitive one: it is more direct, more complete and more accessible – and its implications, through the invention of the Universal Turing Machine, were world-changing.

6. Strictly speaking, an algorithm is a recipe, and a program is an algorithm that has been encoded in an actual programming language like Python or Java. Thus, algorithms are independent of programming languages.

7. Turing machines actually require a much cruder form of programming than this. The instructions I've listed here are typical of a relatively low-level programming language, but still much more abstract (and much easier to understand) than a Turing machine program.

8. T. H. Cormen, C. E. Leiserson and R. L. Rivest. *Introduction to Algorithms* (1st edn). MIT Press and McGraw-Hill, 1990.

9. A. M. Turing. 'Computing Machinery and Intelligence'. *Mind*, 49, 1950, pp. 433–60.

10. This dialogue was generated with a version of ELIZA that comes with every Apple Macintosh computer. If you have a Mac you can try it yourself. Launch the Terminal application by opening the Applications folder, then the Utilties folder within it, and double-click on the Terminal application icon. Lots of gobbledy-gook will appear in the Terminal window. When it settles down, press the 'Esc' key (top left of your keyboard), then press the 'X' key, then type 'doctor' and press Return. Off you go. But remember: it isn't real!

11. http://tinyurl.com/y7nbo58p.

12. Unfortunately, the terminology in the literature is imprecise and inconsistent. Most people seem to use 'artificial general intelligence' to refer to the goal of producing general-purpose human-level intelligence in machines, without being concerned with philosophical questions such as whether they are self-aware. In this sense, artificial general intelligence is roughly the equivalent of Searle's weak AI. However, just to confuse things, sometimes the term is used to mean something much more like Searle's strong AI. In this book, I use it to mean something like weak AI, and I will just call it 'General AI'.

13. http://tinyurl.com/y76xdfd9.

CHAPTER 2: THE GOLDEN AGE

1. One of the most influential of these was due to John McCarthy: an idea called time-sharing. He realized that when someone was using a computer, most of the time that computer would be idle, waiting for them to type something or run a program. He realized that this 'idle time' could be shared with other users, allowing many people to use the computer at the same time. It made for much more efficient use of expensive computers.

2. It actually stands for 'List Processor'. LISP is all about *symbolic* computation, and lists of symbols are the key to that.

3. S. Nasar. *A Beautiful Mind*. Simon & Schuster, 1998.

4. J. McCarthy *et al.* 'A Proposal for the Dartmouth Summer Research Project on Artificial Intelligence, 1955'. (Reprinted in *AI Magazine*, 24(4), 2006, pp. 12–14.)

5. T. Winograd. *Understanding Natural Language*. Academic Press, 1972.

6. In linguistics, the use of words like 'it', 'her' and 'she' to refer to things that appeared previously in a dialogue is called anaphora. A computer program trying to understand or build a natural-language dialogue has to be able to resolve such references – it remains a challenge to the present day, and SHRDLU's ability to cope with (limited) anaphora was regarded as ground-breaking.

7. R. E. Fikes and N. J. Nilsson. 'STRIPS: A New Approach to the Application of Theorem Proving to Problem Solving'. *Artificial Intelligence*, 2(3–4), 1971, pp. 189–208.

8. The computer that controlled SHAKEY was a PDP-10, a state-of-the-art mainframe computer from the late 1960s. It weighed more than a ton and required a large room to house it. A PDP-10 could be equipped with up to about a megabyte of memory; the smartphone in my pocket has about 4,000 times more memory, and is inconceivably faster.

9. http://tinyurl.com/yxu8hwoq.

10. http://tinyurl.com/n6lf8t6.

11. This isn't intended to be a precise calculation – just an approximate value to give us some idea of the scale of the numbers involved.

12. Technically, let b be the branching factor of the search problem, and let d be the depth of the search tree. Then the bottom level of the tree (at depth d) will contain b^d states, where b^d is b to the power of d, that is:

$$b^d = \underbrace{b \times b \times b \times \cdots \times b}_{d \ times}$$

The branching factor exhibits what is technically called exponential growth. Some references use the term geometric growth, although I don't think I've ever seen this term used in the AI literature.

13. The game is known as checkers in the USA, and draughts in the UK. Since Samuel was American, it seems only reasonable that I should adopt the US usage. And besides, in the AI community, the program is universally called 'Samuel's checkers player'. If you referred to it as 'Samuel's draughts player', you would be met with bewilderment.

14. P. E. Hart, N. J. Nilsson and B. Raphael. 'A Formal Basis for the Heuristic Determination of Minimum Cost Paths'. *IEEE Transactions on Systems Science and Cybernetics* 4(2), 1968, pp. 100–107.

15. Computational problems like this are given names. This one is called 'Independent Set'.

16. I have simplified the statement of the travelling salesman problem in the main text a little. A more precise textbook definition is as follows: We are given a list of cities, C, and for each pair of cities i and j in C we are given a distance, $d_{i,j}$. Thus, $d_{i,j}$ is the distance between i and j. We are also given a 'bound', B, which is the total distance that we can travel on a single tank of fuel. The question we have to answer is whether there is a tour of all the cities (that is, some way that the cities, C, can be ordered) so that by travelling from each city to the next in the order defined in this way, and then at the end returning to the starting city, we travel no more than the total distance B.

17. 'P' stands for 'polynomial' – a feasible algorithm to solve a problem is one that has 'polynomial running time'. See the Further Reading section for pointers to the literature on NP-completeness and the P vs NP problem.

CHAPTER 3: KNOWLEDGE IS POWER

1. P. Winston and B. Horn. *LISP* (3rd edn). Pearson, 1989.

2. E. H. Shortliffe. *Computer-Based Medical Consultation: MYCIN*. American Elsevier, 1976.

3. R. Schank and R. P. Abelson. *Scripts, Plans, Goals, and Understanding: An Inquiry into Human Knowledge Structures*. Psychology Press, 1977.

4. W. A. Woods. 'What's in a Link? Foundations for Semantic Networks'. In D. G. Borow and A. Collins (eds.), *Representation and Understanding – Studies in Cognitive Science*. Morgan-Kaufmann, 1975.

5. D. McDermott, 'Tarskian Semantics, or, No Notation without Denotation!' *Cognitive Science* 2(3): pp. 277–82, 1978. The title is a little bit of wordplay on the slogan 'No taxation without representation' from the era of the US War of Independence (McDermott was writing around the time of the 1976 bicentennial celebrations in the USA).

6. J. McCarthy. *Concepts of Logical AI*. Unpublished note.

7. W. F. Clocksin and C. S. Mellish. *Programming in PROLOG*. Springer-Verlag, 1981.

8. The form of deduction used in PROLOG is called resolution. It was originally invented in the 1960s, and it can be efficiently implemented for rules such as those used in PROLOG.

9. D. H. D. Warren. 'Generating Conditional Plans and Programs'. In *Proceedings of the Second Summer Conference on Artificial Intelligence and Simulation of Behaviour (AISB-76)*, Edinburgh, July 1976.

10. R. V. Guha and D. Lenat. 'Cyc: A Midterm Report'. *AI Magazine*, 11(3), 1990.

11. V. Pratt. 'CYC Report'. Unpublished note from 1994, available at: http://tinyurl.com/y4q4aoqj.

12. R. Reiter. 'A Logic for Default Reasoning'. *Artificial Intelligence*, 13, 1980, pp. 81–132.

13. This example is called the *Nixon diamond*: a standard pictorial representation of the scenario has a diamond shape.

CHAPTER 4: ROBOTS AND RATIONALITY

1. R. A. Brooks. 'Intelligence Without Representation'. *Artificial Intelligence*, 47, 1991, pp. 139–59.

2. Interestingly, these higher aspects of human intelligence are handled by a part of the brain called the *neocortex*, and the record of human evolution tells us that this part of the brain evolved only relatively recently. Reasoning and problem solving are quite new capabilities for people: our ancestors coped without them for most of evolutionary history.

3. S. Russell and D. Subramanian. 'Provably Bounded-Optimal Agents'. *Journal of Artificial Intelligence Research*, 2, 1995.

4. https://www.irobot.co.uk.

5. R. A. Brooks. 'A Robot That Walks: Emergent Behaviors from a Carefully Evolved Network'. *Proceedings of the 1989 Conference on Robotics and Automation.* Scottsdale, Arizona, May 1989.

6. I. A. Ferguson. 'TouringMachines: Autonomous Agents with Attitudes'. *IEEE Computer*, 25(5), pp. 51–5, 1992. The name 'TouringMachines' is an obvious pun on 'Turing Machines'. Innes Ferguson, the developer of TouringMachines, has been a good friend for a quarter of a century, but I am not sure I can ever forgive him for this. I don't think he would have thought the joke quite so funny if he knew people would still be writing about it 30 years after he came up with it.

7. S. Vere and T. Bickmore. 'A Basic Agent'. *Computational Intelligence*, 6, 1990, pp. 41–60.

8. In the interests of historical accuracy, I should point out that Apple didn't actually invent the graphical user interface and desktop metaphor themselves – that credit goes to researchers at Xerox Palo Alto Research Centre (PARC). However, Apple were the ones to realize its potential and to make it into a product.

9. http://tinyurl.com/y9qxdko5.

10. P. Maes. 'Agents That Reduce Work and Information Overload'. *Communications of the ACM*, 37(7), 1994, pp. 30–40.

11. O. Etzioni and D. Weld. 'A Softbot-based Interface to the Internet'. *Communications of the ACM*, 37(7), 1994, pp. 72–6.

12. J. von Neumann and O. Morgenstern. *Theory of Games and Economic Behavior*. Princeton University Press, 1944.

13. To make this simple, I'm equating money and utility here. In practice, money and utility are often related, but they are not usually the same, and you will annoy a lot of economists if you assume that utility theory is simply concerned with money. In fact, utility theory is just a numeric way of capturing and computing with preferences.

14. S. Russell and P. Norvig. *Artificial Intelligence – A Modern Approach* (3rd edn). Pearson, 2016, p. 611.

15. R. Murphy. *An Introduction to AI Robotics*. MIT Press, 2001.

16. J. Pearl. *Probabilistic Reasoning in Intelligent Systems: Networks of Plausible Inference*. Morgan Kaufmann, 1988.

17. M. Wooldridge. *An Introduction to MultiAgent Systems* (2nd edn). John Wiley, 2009.

18. A. Rubinstein and M. J. Osborne. *A Course in Game Theory*. MIT Press, 1994.

19. B. Selman, H. J. Levesque and D. G. Mitchell. 'A New Method for Solving Hard Satisfiability Problems'. *Proceedings of the Tenth National Conference on AI (AAAI 1992)*, San Jose, California, 1992.

CHAPTER 5: DEEP BREAKTHROUGHS

1. Accounts in the press vary on the amount paid for the DeepMind acquisition. The figure of £400 million was reported by the *Guardian*: http://tinyurl.com/kvyueye.
2. M. Minsky and S. Papert. *Perceptrons: An Introduction to Computational Geometry*. MIT Press, 1969.
3. http://tinyurl.com/ycu4ngsg.
4. D. E. Rumelhart and J. L. McClelland (eds). *Parallel Distributed Processing* (2 vols.). MIT Press, 1986.
5. D. E. Rumelhart, G. E. Hinton and R. J. Williams. 'Learning Representations By Back-propagating Errors'. *Nature*, 323, 1986, pp. 533–6.
6. I. Goodfellow, Y. Bengio and A. Courville. *Deep Learning*. MIT Press, 2016.
7. Looking at the historical rate of increase in the number of neurons, we might expect to reach the same number of artificial neurons as a human brain in about 40 years or so. That does not mean, though, that artificial neural nets will achieve *human level intelligence* in 40 years, because the brain is not simply a big neural network. It also has structure.
8. http://www.image-net.org.
9. https://wordnet.princeton.edu.
10. A. Krizhevsky, I. Sutskever and G. E. Hinton. 'ImageNet Classification with Deep Convolutional Neural Networks'. In *NIPS*, 2012, pp. 1106–14.
11. I. Goodfellow *et al.* 'Explaining and Harnessing Adversarial Examples'. arXiv:1412.6572.
12. V. Mnih *et al.* 'Playing Atari with Deep Reinforcement Learning'. arXiv:1312.5602v1.
13. V. Mnih *et al.* 'Human-Level Control through Deep Reinforcement Learning'. *Nature*, 518, 2015, pp. 529–33.
14. D. Silver *et* al. 'Mastering the Game of Go with Deep Neural Networks and Tree Search'. *Nature*, 529, 2016, pp. 484–9.
15. http://tinyurl.com/ydafuhjp.
16. D. Silver *et al.* 'Mastering the Game of Go without Human Knowledge'. *Nature*, 50, 2017, pp. 354–9.

17. https://www.captionbot.ai.
18. https://translate.google.com.
19. This translation is by the Scottish writer and translator C. K. Scott
    Moncrieff. His translation of *À la recherche du temps perdu* is one of the
    most celebrated translations in literary history: his translation is regarded
    as a masterpiece, although it has been criticized for taking liberties with
    Proust's language.

CHAPTER 6: AI TODAY

1. https://tinyurl.com/y2k5aeq4.
2. https://tinyurl.com/y8bu8xx8.
3. https://tinyurl.com/y5y75rgs.
4. https://blog.cardiogr.am/tagged/research.
5. This figure would have been rather skewed by the proportion of people
   dying either in childbirth or in the early years of their life – someone
   making it into adulthood would have stood a fair chance of living to what
   we would now regard as a reasonable age.
6. http://tinyurl.com/yc5gv8jg.
7. J. De Fauw *et al.* 'Clinically Applicable Deep Learning for Diagnosis
   and Referral in Retinal Disease'. *Nature Medicine*, 24, September 2018,
   pp. 1342–50.
8. http://tinyurl.com/yakkuyg2.
9. A. Herrmann, W. Brenner and R. Stadler. *Autonomous Driving*. Emerald,
   2018.
10. https://corporate.ford.com/innovation/autonomous-2021.html.
11. https://www.riotinto.com/media/media-releases-237_23991.aspx.

CHAPTER 7: HOW WE IMAGINE THINGS MIGHT GO WRONG

1. http://tinyurl.com/ybsrkr4a.
2. R. Kurzweil. *The Singularity is Near*. Penguin, 2005.
3. V. Vinge. 'The Coming Technological Singularity: How to Survive in the
   Post-Human Era'. NASA Lewis Research Center, *Vision 21: Interdisciplinary
   Science and Engineering in the Era of Cyberspace*, pp. 11–22.

4. T. Walsh. 'The Singularity May Never Be Near'. arXiv:1602.06462v1.

5. https://tinyurl.com/y622vm6k.

6. D. S. Weld and O. Etzioni. 'The First Law of Robotics (A Call to Arms)'. *Proceedings of the National Conference on Artificial Intelligence (AAAI-94)*, 1994, pp. 1042–7.

7. P. Foot. 'The Problem of Abortion and the Doctrine of the Double Effect'. *Oxford Review*, Number 5, 1967.

8. http://tinyurl.com/ybl8luoe.

9. E. Awad *et al.* 'The Moral Machine Experiment'. *Nature*, 563, 2018, pp. 59–64.

10. http://tinyurl.com/ydf26689.

11. http://tinyurl.com/jslm95f.

12. In the interests of transparency, I should point out that I was invited to both of the meetings that led to the Asilomar principles, and I would have loved to have gone. As it happens, on both occasions, prior commitments got in the way.

13. http://tinyurl.com/y28osmtw.

14. http://tinyurl.com/y29v4rrd.

15. http://tinyurl.com/yc3vgkgv.

16. http://tinyurl.com/y2egvzxx.

17. V. Dignum. *Responsible Artificial Intelligence*. Springer, 2019.

18. N. Bostrom. *Superintelligence*. Oxford University Press, 2014.

19. S. O. Hansson. 'What Is Ceteris Paribus Preference?' *Journal of Philosophical Logic*, 25(3), 1996, 307–32.

20. A. Y. Ng and S. Russell. 'Algorithms for Inverse Reinforcement Learning'. *Proceedings of the Seventeenth International Conference on Machine Learning (ICML '00)*, 2000.

CHAPTER 8: HOW THINGS MIGHT ACTUALLY GO WRONG

1. C. B. Benedikt Frey and M. A. Osborne. 'The Future of Employment: How Susceptible Are Jobs to Computerisation?' *Technological Forecasting and Social Change*, 114, January 2017.

2. https://rodneybrooks.com/blog/.

3. https://tinyurl.com/yytefewg.

4. http://tinyurl.com/ydb9bpz4.

5. http://tinyurl.com/ycq6jk35.

6. http://tinyurl.com/y74yfk8a.

7. M. Oswald *et al.* 'Algorithmic Risk Assessment Policing Models: Lessons from the Durham HART Model and "Experimental" Proportionality'. *Information & Communications Technology Law*, 27:2, 2018, pp. 223–50.

8. http://tinyurl.com/y6narok3.

9. https://www.predpol.com.

10. http://tinyurl.com/y242nn5u.

11. http://tinyurl.com/ycef9mqv.

12. http://tinyurl.com/y4elgklp.

13. I believe this scenario is due to renowned AI researcher Stuart Russell.

14. http://tinyurl.com/yy7szdxm.

15. R. Arkin. 'Governing Lethal Behaviour: Embedding Ethics in a Hybrid Deliberative/Reactive Robot Architecture'. Technical report GIT-GVU-07-11, College of Computing, Georgia Institute of Technology.

16. https://www.stopkillerrobots.org/.

17. House of Lords Select Committee on Artificial Intelligence, Report of Session 2017–19. *AI in the UK: Ready, Willing and Able?* HL Paper 100, April 2018.

18. http://tinyurl.com/lbtnkse.

19. https://tinyurl.com/y9juww8v.

20. https://tinyurl.com/y7dzz46v.

21. *Nature*, 563, 27 November 2018, pp. 610–11.

22. C. Criado Perez. *Invisible Women: Exposing Data Bias in a World Designed for Men.* Chatto & Windus, 2019.

23. http://tinyurl.com/y9cd9x7f.

24. http://tinyurl.com/y25dhf9k.

25. Facebook allow you to see the information they hold on you: http://tinyurl.com/j4ys4hq.

26. http://tinyurl.com/y7mcrysq.

27. https://tinyurl.com/yyc6botm.

28. http://tinyurl.com/yaypy567.

29. http://tinyurl.com/yd36fdva.

30. http://tinyurl.com/y6uoewyg.

31. http://tinyurl.com/y8vgslkb.

32. http://tinyurl.com/y6wx5tz7.

CHAPTER 9: CONSCIOUS MACHINES?

1. http://tinyurl.com/yxwlrrkq.
2. T. Nagel. 'What Is It Like to Be a Bat?' *Philosophical Review*, 83(4), 1974, pp. 435–50.
3. D. Kahneman. *Thinking, Fast and Slow*. Penguin, 2012.
4. 'He who has the understanding of the driver of the chariot and controls the rein of his mind, he reaches the end of the journey, that supreme abode of the all-pervading' (*Katha Upanishad*, 1.3).
5. C. S. Soon *et al.* 'Unconscious Determinants of Free Decisions in the Human Brain'. In *Nature Neuroscience*, 11, 2008, pp. 543–5.
6. More precisely, it was *neocortex* size that Dunbar was interested in. The neocortex is the part of the brain that deals with perception, reasoning and language.
7. D. C. Dennett. *The Intentional Stance*. MIT Press, 1987.
8. D. C. Dennett. 'Intentional Systems in Cognitive Ethology'. *Behavioral and Brain Sciences*, 6, 1983, pp. 342–90.
9. Y. Shoham. 'Agent-Oriented Programming'. *Artificial Intelligence*, 60(1), 1993, pp. 51–92.
10. J. McCarthy. 'Ascribing Mental Qualities to Machines'. In V. Lifschitz (ed.), *Formalizing Common Sense: Papers by John McCarthy*, Alblex, 1990.
11. http://tinyurl.com/yc2knerv.
12. The key word here is 'meaningful'. Whenever one suggests a test like this, somebody will try to find some way of gaming the test so that they can claim to have succeeded even if they do so in a way that you didn't anticipate. This is, of course, precisely what happened with the Turing Test. What I'm after is programs that can do this in a substantive way – not programs that pass the test through a combination of smoke and mirrors.
13. S. Baron-Cohen, A. M. Leslie and U. Frith. 'Does the Autistic Child Have a "Theory of Mind"?' *Cognition*, 21(1), 1985, pp. 37–46.
14. S. Baron-Cohen. *Mindblindness: An Essay on Autism and Theory of Mind*. MIT Press, 1995.
15. N. C. Rabinowitz *et al.* Machine Theory of Mind. arXiv:1802.07740.
16. I am no expert on evolutionary psychology: my guide in this section is Robin Dunbar's *Human Evolution* (Penguin, 2014), and I am pleased to refer interested readers to this for more detail.

Index

PELICAN BOOKS

PELICAN BOOKS

Islam:
The Essentials
Tariq Ramadan

Basic Income:
And How We Can Make It Happen
Guy Standing

Think Like an Anthropologist
Matthew Engelke

Hermeneutics:
Facts and Interpretation in the Age of Information
John D. Caputo

Being Ecological
Timothy Morton

Object-Oriented Ontology:
A New Theory of Everything
Graham Harman

Marx and Marxism
Gregory Claeys

The Human Planet:
How We Created the Anthropocene
Simon L. Lewis and Mark A. Maslin

Think Again:
How to Reason and Argue
Walter Sinnott-Armstrong

Parenting the First Twelve Years:
What the Evidence Tells Us
Victoria L. Cooper, Heather Montgomery, Kieron Sheehy

PELICAN BOOKS